Test Bank

Human Resource Management
Tenth Edition

Robert L. Mathis
University of Nebraska at Omaha

John H. Jackson
University of Wyoming

Prepared by

Roger A. Dean
Washington and Lee University

THOMSON

SOUTH-WESTERN

Australia · Canada · Mexico · Singapore · Spain · United Kingdom · United States

THOMSON

SOUTH-WESTERN

Test Bank for Human Resource Management 10e

Robert L. Mathis and John H. Jackson

Publisher:
Melissa Acuña

Sr. Acquisitions Editor:
Charles E. McCormick, Jr.

Developmental Editor:
Mardell Toomey

Marketing Manager:
Larry Qualls

Sr. Production Editor:
Deanna Quinn

Manufacturing Coordinator:
Diane Lohman

Media Technology Editor:
Diane Van Bakel

Media Developmental Editor:
Chris Wittmer

Media Production Editor:
Amy Wilson

Printer:
Globus Printing

For more information
contact South-Western,
5191 Natorp Boulevard,
Mason, Ohio 45040.
Or you can visit our Internet site at:
http://www.swcollege.com

For permission to use material from this
text or product, contact us by
Tel (800) 730-2214
Fax (800) 730-2215
http://www.thomsonrights.com

Table of Contents

Chapter 1

Changing Nature of Human Resource Management

Multiple Choice

1. A primary focus of human resource management is
    A. supervising, monitoring, controlling, and disciplining employees.
    B. designing systems to effectively manage people with their needs, expectations, legal rights, etc.
    C. developing strategic planning models for the effective control of human resource costs.
    D. Implementing and maintaining systems to insure accurate HR record keeping.

    ANSWER: B, 4

2. What was the primary function of HR (or "personnel") management when the field emerged about 1900?
    A. coordinating labor/management relations
    B. compliance with social legislation
    C. coordinating the elimination of child labor
    D. clerical operations concerned with payroll and employee records

    ANSWER: D, 4

3. The text defines _____ as "the design of formal systems in an organization to ensure effective and efficient use of human talent to accomplish organizational goals."
    A. human resource management
    B. personnel administration
    C. strategic management
    D. human capital

    ANSWER: A, 4

4. HR management is the responsibility of
    A. all managers and supervisors in the organization.
    B. the union representatives.
    C. all employees of the organization.
    D. only the organization's HR unit

    ANSWER: C, 5

5.   Who usually takes care of HR issues in a company with an owner and 10 employees?
      A.   a personnel clerk
      B.   the owner
      C.   an outside vendor
      D.   nobody

      ANSWER: B, 5

6.   Through _____, managers attempt to anticipate forces that will influence the future supply of and demand for employees.
      A.   staffing
      B.   HR development
      C.   HR analysis
      D.   HR planning

      ANSWER: D, 6

7.   One activity that affects all other HR activities is
      A.   compliance with equal employment opportunity laws and regulations.
      B.   staffing.
      C.   HR planning and analysis.
      D.   human resources development.

      ANSWER: A, 7

8.   To meet affirmative action requirements, HR plans must
      A.   document compliance with all EEO regulations.
      B.   establish hiring quotas and timetables for meeting affirmative action goals.
      C.   ensure sufficient availability of a diversity of individuals.
      D.   establish a procedure for eliminating unlawful discrimination.

      ANSWER: C, 7

9.   The aim of _____ is to provide an adequate supply of appropriately qualified individuals to fill jobs in an organization.
      A.   diversity assessment and training
      B.   staffing
      C.   HR planning and analysis
      D.   human resource development

      ANSWER: B, 8

10.   _____ identifies paths and activities for individual employees as they develop within the organization.
      A.   Staffing
      B.   HR development
      C.   Performance management
      D.   Career planning

      ANSWER: D, 8

11.   HR development includes which of the following activities?
      A.   performance management
      B.   wage and salary administration
      C.   diversity assessment and analysis
      D.   environmental scanning

      ANSWER: A, 8

12.   A major issue of concern in compensation and benefits is the
      A.   equalization of pay between men and women.
      B.   use of stock options at all levels of the organization.
      C.   rapid increase in the cost of benefits.
      D.   design of early retirement packages.

      ANSWER: C, 8

13.   Employee assistance programs are often used for which of the following?
      A.   career planning and counseling
      B.   to assist employees with substance abuse problems
      C.   pre-retirement planning
      D.   to provide concierge services for busy employees

      ANSWER: B, 8

14.   Workplace _____ has (have) grown in importance in response to the increasing number of acts or workplace violence.
      A.   safety
      B.   monitoring
      C.   employee assistance programs
      D.   security

      ANSWER: D, 8

15.   Employee rights must be addressed in
      A.   all organizations
      B.   primarily unionized organizations
      C.   union-free workplaces to inhibit organizing attempts
      D.   government rather than non-government workplaces

      ANSWER: A, 8

16.   An activity of HR management that is important to facilitating good employee relations is
      A.   a voluntary workplace suggestion system.
      B.   the distribution of a company newsletter.
      C.   the development and communication of HR policies and rules.
      D.   an employee assistance program.

      ANSWER: C, 8

17.   Which of the following has resulted from the explosive growth of information technology?
      A.   Manufacturing facilities have been built off-shore.
      B.   Organizations of all types have had to change.
      C.   Government regulations have changed the way HR is practiced.
      D.   Most businesses have been unable to adapt rapidly enough.

      ANSWER: B, 9

18.   Percentagewise, the fastest growing occupations are related to
      A.   education and skills training.
      B.   the financial industry.
      C.   legal or regulatory compliance.
      D.   information technology.

      ANSWER: D, 9

19.   Approximately _____ of all U.S. jobs are in service industries.
      A.   80%
      B.   60%
      C.   40%
      D.   20%

      ANSWER: A, 9

20.   Temporary workers, independent contractors, and leased employees are collectively referred to as
      A.   part-time workers.
      B.   virtual employees.
      C.   contingent workers.
      D.   non-organizational employees.

      ANSWER: C, 11

21.   Which of the following illustrates why businesses use contingent workers?
      A.   to avoid developing an affirmative action plan
      B.   to stabilize the workforce
      C.   to replace retiring employees
      D.   to encourage employee loyalty

      ANSWER: B, 11

22.   Why are companies increasing their use of contingent workers?
      A.   To avoid minimum wage payments.
      B.   To replace employees taking voluntary early retirement.
      C.   To meet affirmative action goals.
      D.   To reduce legal liability for employers.

      ANSWER: D, 11

23. In the Microsoft case, the court held that their contingent workers were
    A. really employees entitled to benefits under Microsoft's benefit plan.
    B. independent contractors who should file provisional tax returns.
    C. exempt from the provisions of the Fair Labor Standards Act.
    D. entitled to union representation.

    ANSWER: A, 11

24. Immigration of individuals into the United States is heavily weighted towards
    A. males.
    B. non-whites.
    C. Latinos.
    D. Asians.

    ANSWER: C, 12

25. Alternatives such as flexible work schedules and job-sharing primarily benefi
    A. childless couples.
    B. workers who are parents.
    C. older workers.
    D. employed college students.

    ANSWER: B, 13

26. Which of the following activities is NOT usually associated with organizational "rightsizing"?
    A. outplacing workers
    B. closing facilities
    C. merging with other organizations
    D. increasing layers of managers

    ANSWER D, 14

27. A common transformation during organizational restructuring has been to
    A. make organizations flatter by removing several layers of management.
    B. increase managerial control of the workforce.
    C. refocus the organization's attention onto one overriding goal.
    D. change from a bureaucratic structure to one that is less formal.

    ANSWER: A, 14

28. Human costs and benefits associated with downsizing include
    A. increased loyalty for those who remain.
    B. reduced job performance by the survivors.
    C. a survivor's mentality for those who remain.
    D. less likelihood that the employees will seek alternate employment opportunities.

    ANSWER: C, 14

29.   What are the four HR management roles?
       A.   personnel, human relations, labor relations, planning
       B.   administrative, employee advocate, operational, strategic
       C.   staffing, appraisal, compensation, labor relations
       D.   urgent, short term, intermediate term, longer term

       ANSWER: B, 16

30.   The administrative role of HR management is heavily oriented to
       A.   recruitment and selection.
       B.   clerical and administrative support.
       C.   workforce development
       D.   tactical activities.

       ANSWER: D, 16

31.   Which of the following HR activities are more likely to be outsourced?
       A.   background/reference checks
       B.   compensation administration
       C.   labor negotiations
       D.   performance management

       ANSWER: A, 16

32.   Ensuring fair and equitable treatment for employees regardless of personal
       background or circumstances is associated withe the _____ role of HR.
       A.   strategic
       B.   operational
       C.   employee advocate
       D.   administrative

       ANSWER: C, 17

33.   Recruiting and selecting for current openings are typical _____
       activities.
       A.   personnel
       B.   operational
       C.   strategic
       D.   HR planning

       ANSWER: B, 18

34.   Which of the following would NOT be identified as a typical HR operational
       activity?
       A.   government compliance
       B.   HR information systems
       C.   compensation
       D.   crisis management

       ANSWER: D, 18

35. The strategic focus of HR must be on the _____ implications of HR issues.
    A. longer term
    B. maintenance oriented
    C. interpersonal
    D. organizational

    ANSWER: A, 19

36. The _____ role of HR management emphasizes that organizations must manage their human resources as being valuable and in a "business-oriented" manner.
    A. employee advocate
    B. administrative
    C. strategic
    D. operational

    ANSWER: C, 19

37. The human resources in an organization are the ones who
    A. justify their pay and benefits.
    B. design, produce, and deliver products and services to customers.
    C. are hard to quantify in terms of costs and benefits.
    D. usually regarded as expenses by financial managers.

    ANSWER: B, 19

38. It is recommended that HR _____ when organizational strategic planning is being done.
    A. concentrate on personnel issues
    B. leave strategic decisions to financial planners
    C. stress intermediate implications of strategic alternatives
    D. have a "seat at the table"

    ANSWER: D, 20

39. To be viewed as a strategic partner, contributing to organizational performance, HR must demonstrate that
    A. HR activities contribute to the financial results of the organization.
    B. the "right" people are being hired and retained.
    C. the organization is in full compliance with all government laws and regulations.
    D. HR is able to compete in a tight labor market in terms of compensation, benefits and working conditions.

    ANSWER: A, 20

40. The central focus for human resource management must be on
    A. cost efficiency and the design of staffing strategies.
    B. personnel policies.
    C. contributing to organizational success.
    D. ensuring employee satisfaction and personal wellbeing.

    ANSWER: C, 20

41. To be strategic contributors, HR professionals must
     A.   count how many activities and tasks were performed.
     B.   measure their return on investment in human resources.
     C.   limit the organization's exposure to legal liability.
     D.   improve the quality of the human resources available to operational managers.

     ANSWER: B, 21

42. Which of the following activities are included in the administrative role of HR management:
     A.   managing compensation programs
     B.   recruiting and selecting for current openings
     C.   assessing workforce trends and issues
     D.   conducting new employee orientations

     ANSWER: D, 21

43. Preparing equal employment reports is
     A.   an administrative HR role.
     B.   the responsibility of operational managers.
     C.   typically outsourced.
     D.   an employee advocacy role.

     ANSWER: A, 21

44. Recruiting and selecting for current openings is typically
     A.   an administrative role of HR management.
     B.   an employee advocacy responsibility.
     C.   an operational role of HR management.
     D.   a strategic HR responsibility.

     ANSWER: C, 21

45. Which of the following is categorized as an advocacy role of HR management?
     A.   conducting new employee orientations
     B.   resolving employee complaints
     C.   engaging in community workforce development planning
     D.   labor/management negotiations

     ANSWER: B, 21

46. Which issues pose fundamental questions about fairness, justice, and truthfulness?
     A.   legal
     B.   employment-at-will
     C.   social responsibility
     D.   ethical

     ANSWER: D, 21

47.   Ethics deals with
       A.   what ought to be done.
       B.   what is required by law.
       C.   religious values.
       D.   what is acceptable to the general society.

       ANSWER: A, 21

48.   For the HR professional, _____ describes the way in which the manager
       ought to act relative to a given human resource issue.
       A.   situational ethics
       B.   disinterested neutrality
       C.   ethical behavior
       D.   evenhandedness

       ANSWER: C, 21

49.   Deciding whether to relocate a plant to avoid unionization of a workforce is an
       example of an ethical decision with
       A.   mixed outcomes.
       B.   extended consequences.
       C.   uncertain consequences.
       D.   personal effects.

       ANSWER: B, 22

50.   Deciding how much flexibility to offer an employee with family problems, while
       denying other employees similar flexibility, may require considering
       A.   uncertain consequences.
       B.   extended consequences.
       C.   mixed outcomes.
       D.   multiple alternatives.

       ANSWER: D, 22

51.   An example of an ethical issue with mixed outcomes would be
       A.   preserving the jobs of some workers while eliminating the jobs of others.
       B.   terminating a disabled employee to protect the worker from injury on the
             job.
       C.   not permitting an employee with HIV to return to work.
       D.   giving preference in hiring to members of a previously underrepresented
             group.

       ANSWER: A, 22

52.   Determining whether to promote a single parent with three young children would
       be an ethical decision with
       A.   extended consequences.
       B.   multiple alternatives.
       C.   uncertain consequences.
       D.   personal effects.

       ANSWER: C, 22

53.   To respond in situations with ethical dimensions, the HR manager should
       A.   ignore civil law because ethical decisions are at a higher level.
       B.   comply with all organizational standards of ethical behavior.
       C.   investigate how the "typical" manager would respond to a similar situation.
       D.   review the Uniform Guidelines developed by the EEOC.

       ANSWER: B, 22

54.   Which of the following is recommended as a way of addressing ethical issues in organizations?
       A.   reward managers who act ethically, while disciplining unethical behavior
       B.   appoint an "ethics czar" to adjudicate on issues with ethical dimensions
       C.   survey the public to ascertain ethical standards of behavior
       D.   conduct ethical training for all executives, managers, and employees

       ANSWER: D, 22

55.   A person with responsibility for performing a variety of HR activities is an
       A.   HR generalist.
       B.   HR specialist.
       C.   HR professional.
       D.   HR unit manager.

       ANSWER: A, 23

56.   Individuals who have in-depth knowledge and expertise in a limited area of HR are
       A.   HR generalists.
       B.   HR unit manager.
       C.   HR specialists.
       D.   HR professionals.

       ANSWER: C, 23

57.   If HR professionals are to contribute strategically to their organizations, they must
       A.   be professionally certified in human resources.
       B.   have an understanding of the financial, technological, and other facets of the organization.
       C.   be knowledgeable of all relevant laws and regulations.
       D.   have an advanced degree in human resource management.

       ANSWER: B, 23

58.   For generalists, the largest professional HR organization is
       A.   the International Personnel Management Association (IPMA).
       B.   the American Society for Training and Development (ASTD).
       C.   the Human Resource Certification Institute (HRCI).
       D.   the Society for Human Resource Management (SHRM).

       ANSWER: D, 24

59. The _____ administers the most well-known certification program for HR generalists.
    A.   Human Resource Certification Institute
    B.   International Personnel Management Association
    C.   World at Work Association
    D.   American Society for Training and Development

    ANSWER: A, 24

60. The most prevalent HR specialist is
    A.   EEO specialist.
    B.   labor/management relations specialist.
    C.   benefits specialist.
    D.   workforce security specialist.

    ANSWER: C, 25

True and False

61. Human resource management is a technical discipline requiring specialized skills. Accordingly, all HR activities should be carried out by HR professionals.

    ANSWER: False, 5
    In a real sense, *every* manager is an HR manager and engage in HR management activities.

62. Through HR development, managers attempt to anticipate forces that will influence the future supply of and demand for employees.

    ANSWER: False, 6
    It is through HR planning that managers attempt to anticipate forces that will influence the future supply of and demand for employees.

63. Health care jobs are declining as Americans have become more health and fitness conscious and less susceptible to addictive behaviors.

    ANSWER: False, 9
    The number of health care jobs are actually increasing (along with jobs in information technology, financial services, and retail services.)

64. It is estimated that manufacturing jobs will represent only 12% to 15% of all U.S. jobs by the year 2006.

    ANSWER: True, 9

65. Although global and technological changes have changed the workforce and the competition, the way human resource managers do their work remains constant.

    ANSWER: False, 10
    The issues faced by HR management has changed as well.

66.   One consequence of the shift to a service economy is that the number of jobs requiring semi-skilled and less educated workers are expected to grow at a more rapid rate than the number of other jobs.

ANSWER: False, 11
Workforce changes have forced employers to address the deficiencies that many employees have in basic literacy and mathematical skills.

67.   One reason for the growth in contingent workers is the reduced legal liability faced by employers.

ANSWER: True, 11

68.   The percentage of Latinos in the labor force now equals or exceeds the number of African Americans.

ANSWER: True, 12

69.   The number of mothers in the workforce and dual-career couples is declining.

ANSWER: False, 13
Both groups have increased such that 70% of all women with children under age six are in the workforce, and dual-career couples comprise about 60% of all married couples.

70.   Actions by employers to provide family-friendly benefits have produced a backlash from childless employees.

ANSWER: True, 13

71.   Three out of four mergers and acquisitions have failed to achieve their financial and strategic objectives.

ANSWER True, 15

72.   In terms of HR activities, the greatest amounts of outsourcing relate to the administrative role of HR.

ANSWER: True, 16

73.   The operational role of HR management requires HR professionals to identify and implement needed programs and policies in cooperation with operating managers.

ANSWER: True, 18

74.   In terms of strategic planning, human resources is primarily a staff function providing advice and support to the financial, technological, and production functions of the organization.

ANSWER: False, 20
To be a strategic partner, HR must have a "seat at the table", being viewed in the same context as the financial, technological, and other resources that are managed in the organization.

75. In organizations where they are viewed as strategic contributors, HR professionals participate in the discussions prior to top management making final decisions regarding mergers, acquisitions, and downsizing.

ANSWER: True, 20

76. HR professionals must cost justify their existence and administratively deliver HR activities efficiently and responsively.

ANSWER: True, 20

77. Ethics with respect to HR management is primarily concerned with legal compliance to avoid "negative press".

ANSWER: False, 21
For the HR professional, ethics deals with what ought to be done relative to a given human resource issue.

78. A survey of HR professionals indicated that the most common unethical incidents by employees were lying to supervisors, employee drug or alcohol use, and falsification of records.

ANSWER: True, 22

79. "Liking to work with people" is a major qualification necessary for success in HR.

ANSWER: False, 24
This is one of the greatest myths about HR careers. HR professionals must have the technological and education needed for success in this field.

80. Professional certification has grown in importance for HR professionals.

ANSWER: True, 24

Essay

81. Describe changes that are facing organizations with respect to workforce availability and quality. How can HR management help organizations adjust to these changes?

ANSWER: 10-11
Low unemployment, coupled with the need for workers with specialized skills, has caused significant workforce shortages, especially for knowledge jobs. HR management has become active partners with public schools in addition to developing training programs for employees at all levels. Organizations have also increased their use of contingent workers to meet shortfalls in skilled workers and to provide flexibility.

82.   Discuss the challenges of changing demographics facing HR management.

    ANSWER: 12-14
    Major demographic challenges include the increased racial diversity of the
    workforce, more women are in the labor force than ever before, the average age
    of the U.S. workforce is increasing, and a significant number of individuals
    have disabilities. HR managers must ensure that the diverse workforce is
    treated fairly. This impacts all staffing activities and may require diversity-
    oriented training. Problems have emerged in balancing work and family and
    family-friendly benefits offered by employers have led to a backlash from
    childless workers.

83.   Describe the special challenges faced by workers trying to balance work and
    family responsibilities. How can HR assist these workers?

    ANSWER: 13-14
    The decline of the traditional family and the increasing numbers of dual-career
    couples and working single parents place stress on workers trying to balance
    family and work. Many employers have initiated family-friendly programs such
    as child care, elder care, flexible work schedules, job sharing, and time-off
    to attend children's school activities. In some organizations these benefits
    have produced a backlash from single workers and childless couples.

84.   Define and clarify the four roles of HR management.

    ANSWER: 15-21
    Administrative - clerical and record keeping. Advocacy - ensuring fair and
    equitable treatment for all employees. Operational - coordinating the
    management of HR activities with the actions of managers and supervisors
    throughout the organization. Strategic - emphasizes that people are valuable
    resources representing significant organizational investments.

85.   Discuss why ethical issues permeate HR management. Give examples of typical
    ethical decisions faced by an HR manager.

    ANSWER: 21-23
    Ethics deals with what "ought" to be done. Ethical decision making relates to
    questions of fairness, justice, truthfulness, and social responsibility. The
    most common unethical incidents by employees were lying to supervisors, drug and
    alcohol use, and falsification of records. HR managers may be pressured to
    compromise their ethical standards in order to meet financial, scheduling, or
    other operational goals.

Chapter 2

Strategic Human Resource Management

Multiple Choice

1. _____ refers to organizational use of employees to gain or keep a competitive advantage against competitors.
   A. Manpower planning
   B. Strategic HR management
   C. Long-term planning
   D. Operational management
   ANSWER: B, 30

2. A unique capability in an organization that creates high value and that differentiates that organization from its competitors is referred to as
   A. the organizations culture.
   B. a strategic advantage.
   C. a differentiated function
   D. a core competency.

   ANSWER: D, 30

3. Ways that human resources can become a core competency include:
   A. attracting and retaining employees with unique professional and technical capabilities.
   B. recruiting and hiring a diverse workforce that is representative of society at large.
   C. making extensive use of contingent workers to ensure a constant inflow of new employees with contemporary ideas.
   D. encouraging all HR employees to be professionally certified.

   ANSWER: A, 30

4. How can people be an organizational core competency?
   A. when the organization can successfully compete in the labor market for "quality" talent
   B. by successfully maintaining a union-free work place
   C. when they have special capabilities to make decisions and be innovative in ways that competitors cannot easily imitate
   D. by being able to attract top quality employees who work hard and are satisfied with their jobs

   ANSWER: C, 30

5. "The shared values and beliefs of a workforce" is a definition of
    A.   organizational norms.
    B.   organizational culture.
    C.   organizational ethics.
    D.   organizational commitment.

    ANSWER: B, 31

6. Organizational culture comprises the _____ of a workforce.
    A.   ethnic and racial background
    B.   commitment to diversity
    C.   of-the-job pursuits
    D.   shared values and beliefs

    ANSWER: D, 31

7. Which of the following HR activities is affected by the organizational culture,
    as viewed by the people in the organization?
    A.   attraction and retention of competent employees
    B.   performance management
    C.   compensation and employee benefit administration
    D.   EEO compliance and affirmative action planning

    ANSWER: A, 31

8. _____ of a workforce can be measured as the total cost of people per
    unit of output.
    A.   Profitability
    B.   Effectiveness
    C.   Productivity
    D.   Efficiency

    ANSWER: C, 31

9. _____ is computed by dividing the average cost of workers by their
    average levels of output.
    A.   Profitability
    B.   Unit labor cost
    C.   Labor efficiency
    D.   Production effectiveness

    ANSWER: B, 32

10. _____ is contracting with someone else to perform activities that were
    previously done by employees of the organization.
    A.   Rent-a-worker
    B.   Reengineering
    C.   Downsizing
    D.   Outsourcing

    ANSWER: D, 32

11. Which of the following activities would NOT be recommended for productivity improvement?
    A.   recomputing unit labor costs
    B.   outsourcing
    C.   replacing workers with equipment
    D.   redesigning the work

    ANSWER: A, 32

12. Name the American quality expert who argued that getting the job done right the first time is essential to quality production.
    A.   Frederick Winslow Taylor
    B.   Elton Mayo
    C.   W. Edwards Deming
    D.   Henry Ford

    ANSWER: C, 32

13. The text identifies two basic HR strategies, which are
    A.   flexibility and stability
    B.   cost leadership and differentiation
    C.   risk averse and aggressiveness
    D.   planning and spontaneity

    ANSWER: B, 34

14. Wal-Malt is an example of a company following a
    A.   differentiation strategy.
    B.   long-term planning horizon
    C.   spontaneous management process.
    D.   cost-leadership strategy.

    ANSWER: D, 34

15. A cost-leadership strategy is more appropriate in a _____ business environment.
    A.   relatively stable
    B.   highly competitive
    C.   dynamic
    D.   decentralized

    ANSWER: A, 34

16. Which of the following strategies would be more appropriate in a dynamic environment, characterized by the need to continually find new products and new markets?
    A.   aggressiveness
    B.   cost-leadership
    C.   differentiation
    D.   flexibility

    ANSWER: C, 35

17.   The _____ strategy requires an organization to adopt a longer HR
      planning horizon of "building" its own employees to fit its specialized needs.
      A.   flexibility
      B.   cost-leadership
      C.   differentiation
      D.   aggressiveness

      ANSWER: B, 35

18.   Which of the following strategies requires HR planning to have a shorter time
      frame and greater use of outsourcing?
      A.   aggressiveness
      B.   cost-leadership
      C.   flexibility
      D.   differentiation

      ANSWER: D, 35

19.   _____ is the process of analyzing and identifying the need for and
      availability of human resources so that the organization can meet its
      objectives.
      A.   Human resource planning
      B.   Environmental scanning
      C.   Labor market analysis
      D.   Strategic planning

      ANSWER: A, 35

20.   Which of the following best describes the responsibility for HR planning?
      A.   HR planning is the responsibility of the top HR executive.
      B.   Typical HR planning is the responsibility of operating managers.
      C.   The top HR executive and subordinate staff specialists have most of the
            responsibility.
      D.   HR planning is the responsibility of the organization's top management.

      ANSWER: C, 35

21.   The HR unit's responsibilities during the planning process typically include
      A.   review of employee-succession plans in line with HR plans.
      B.   implementation of HR plans as approved by top management
      C.   integration of HR plans with departmental plans.
      D.   monitoring the HR plan to identify changes needed.

      ANSWER: B, 36

22.   One of the top challenges faced by family-owned firms is
      A.   tax planning.
      B.   incorporating non-family managers.
      C.   providing jobs for extended-family members.
      D.   management succession.

      ANSWER: D, 36

23. _____ are the means used to aid the organization in anticipating and managing the supply and demand for human resources.
    A.   HR strategies
    B.   Economic forecasting
    C.   Strategic forecasting
    D.   Labor market analyses

    ANSWER: A, 37

24. Scanning the external environment especially affects HR planning because
    A.   the corporate culture is the responsibility of the HR unit.
    B.   of the demographic patterns of the internal workforce.
    C.   the organization must draw from the same labor market that supplies all other employers.
    D.   the organization must meet certain affirmative action quotas.

    ANSWER: C, 38

25. The ability of an organization to compete for a sufficient supply of human resources with the appropriate capabilities
    A.   governed by EEO regulations.
    B.   one measure of organizational effectiveness.
    C.   a test of how well management provide competitive wages.
    D.   one input to the environmental scanning process.

    ANSWER: B, 38

26. External environmental factors that affect the labor supply include
    A.   life-style choices of employees.
    B.   corporate philosophy and mission.
    C.   environmental scanning.
    D.   government influences.

    ANSWER: D, 38

27. Tax credits for employee day care and financial aid for education may affect
    A.   employer practices in recruiting and retraining workers.
    B.   retirement patterns.
    C.   EEO compliance.
    D.   an expanding array of government rules.

    ANSWER: A, 39

28. As the unemployment rate declines,
    A.   the need for overtime also declines.
    B.   early retirement plans become more attractive.
    C.   people available for work may be less educated, less skilled, or unwilling to work.
    D.   it becomes easier to fill jobs.

    ANSWER: C, 39

29.   Which of the following has been a geographic trend within the last decade that
      has forced changes in HR plans?
      A.   the movement of better educated workers to the Southwest
      B.   the reluctance of many workers with working spouses to accept geographic
              relocation
      C.   the deterioration of inner cities
      D.   the influx of foreign workers into certain regions

      ANSWER: B, 39

30.   A business that fails to offer competitive pay scales will often
      A.   have a generous benefits package.
      B.   attract a committed workforce.
      C.   employ "protected-class" workers.
      D.   have a much lower-quality workforce

      ANSWER: D, 40

31.   One geographic factor affecting the supply of human resources is the
      A.   impact of international competition
      B.   urban/rural ratio.
      C.   gross population profile.
      D.   total labor workforce audit.

      ANSWER: A, 40

32.   Independent contractors, job sharing, and outsourcing are all examples of
      A.   part-time staffing arrangements.
      B.   alternate work schedules.
      C.   flexible staffing arrangements.
      D.   a temporary workforce.

      ANSWER: C, 40

33.   A study by Gramm and Schnell found that one result of higher wages for core
      employees was
      A.   increased union activity.
      B.   more subcontracting.
      C.   a better qualified workforce.
      D.   less job security.

      ANSWER: B, 41

34.   Gramm and Schnell found that in a unionized organization
      A.   core employees received higher wages.
      B.   more workers were classified as "management".
      C.   there was a greater use of part-time employees
      D.   subcontracting increased.

      ANSWER: D, 41

35.   A comprehensive analysis of all current jobs provides a basis for
       A.   forecasting what jobs will need to be done in the future.
       B.   an internal analysis of jobs and people.
       C.   human asset accounting.
       D.   auditing jobs.

       ANSWER: A, 41

36.   Much of the data needed for a comprehensive audit of all current jobs is to be
       found in the
       A.   employee evaluations.
       B.   supervisory files.
       C.   existing staffing and organizational databases.
       D.   personnel update forms completed by employees.

       ANSWER: C, 41

37.   A planner should examine which of the following questions when auditing jobs?
       A.   What is the demographic profile of the current job holders?
       B.   How essential is each job?
       C.   What type of training will be needed to fill each job?
       D.   Who is responsible for staffing the organization?

       ANSWER: B, 41

38.   What is the basic source of data on current employees and their capabilities?
       A.   employee evaluations
       B.   supervisory files
       C.   personnel update forms completed by employees
       D.   HR records in the organization

       ANSWER: D, 41

39.   When general guidelines are applied to a specific situation within the
       organization, which forecasting method is being used?
       A.   rules of thumb
       B.   simulation models
       C.   estimates
       D.   the Delphi technique

       ANSWER: A, 43

40.   Which of the following is a purely judgmental method of forecasting?
       A.   simulation models
       B.   staffing ratios
       C.   the Delphi Technique
       D.   a transition matrix

       ANSWER: C, 43

41.   In the _____, experts meet face to face, generate ideas independently at first, discuss these ideas as a group, then compile a report.
    A.   Delphi technique
    B.   nominal groups
    C.   rules-of-thumb approach
    D.   simulation models

    ANSWER: B, 44

42.   _____ are a forecasting method that uses representations of real situations in abstract form.
    A.   Delphi techniques
    B.   Nominal groups
    C.   Statistical regression analyses
    D.   Simulation models

    ANSWER: D, 44

43.   An intermediate planning range usually projects _____ into the future.
    A.   one to five years
    B.   three to five years
    C.   beyond five years
    D.   six months to one year

    ANSWER: A, 45

44.   Government labor force population estimates and trends in industry are used to
    A.   estimate the internal supply of labor.
    B.   implement a human resource information system (HRIS).
    C.   forecast the external supply of human resources.
    D.   predict terminations, retirements, and deaths of employees.

    ANSWER: C, 45-46

45.   The internal supply of human resources is influenced by
    A.   actions of competing employers.
    B.   training and development programs.
    C.   government regulations and pressures.
    D.   changing workforce composition and patterns.

    ANSWER: B, 46

46.   Succession analysis, one method used to forecast the supply of people for certain positions, relies on
    A.   stand-in potential.
    B.   worker profile analysis.
    C.   succession tables.
    D.   replacement charts.

    ANSWER: D, 46

47. What is purpose of the Worker Adjustment and Retraining Notification (WARN) Act?
    A.   It requires employers to give a 60-day notice before a layoff of facility closing involving more than 50 people
    B.   It mandates job retraining for workers injured in an on-the-job accident.
    C.   It prevents a government official from closing a factory for safety violations without first giving reasonable notice to the owners.
    D.   It establishes a school-to-work program for the "hardcore unemployed."

    ANSWER: A, 47

48. Reducing the size of an organizational work force is called
    A.   re-engineering.
    B.   downshifting.
    C.   downsizing.
    D.   reorganizing.

    ANSWER: C, 48

49. _____ occurs when individuals who quit, die, or retire are not replaced.
    A.   Downsizing
    B.   Attrition
    C.   A buyout
    D.   A hiring freeze

    ANSWER: B, 50

50. In which of the following are employees put on unpaid leaves of absence, and may be called back if business improves?
    A.   attrition
    B.   buyouts
    C.   outplacement
    D.   layoffs

    ANSWER: D, 51

51. _____ is (are) a group of services provided to displaced employees to give them support and assistance.
    A.   Outplacement
    B.   Career guidance
    C.   Job counseling
    D.   Buy-outs

    ANSWER: A, 51

52. A(n) _____ is a formal research effort that evaluates the current state of HR management in an organization.
    A.   HRIS
    B.   personnel assessment
    C.   HR audit
    D.   HR research

    ANSWER: C, 54

53.   _____ is the analysis of data from HR records to determine the
        effectiveness of past and present HR practices.
        A.   Strategic assessment
        B.   HR research
        C.   A performance review
        D.   An HR audit

        ANSWER: B, 54

54.   Attitude surveys, questionnaires, interviews, and experiments are all examples
        of _____ research methods.
        A.   experimental
        B.   interactive
        C.   secondary
        D.   primary

        ANSWER: D, 54

55.   One approach to assessing HR effectiveness is _____, which compares
        specific measures of performance against data on those measures in "best
        practice" organizations.
        A.   benchmarking
        B.   compa-valuation
        C.   HR appraisal
        D.   HR imitation

        ANSWER: A, 55

56.   A(n) _____ is an integrated system designed to provide information
        used in HR decision making.
        A.   human capital operating system
        B.   management tracking and evaluation system
        C.   human resource information system
        D.   strategic personnel management system

        ANSWER: C, 57

57.   Which of the following is the most basic use of an HRIS in an organization?
        A.   centralization of all job postings
        B.   automation of payroll and benefit activities
        C.   maintaining job description and job specification information
        D.   EEO and affirmative action tracking

        ANSWER: B, 57

58.   "What information is available?" "to what uses will the information be put?" and
        "who needs the information?" are questions about
        A   the design, implementation, and training elements of an HRIS.
        B.   the capacity and capabilities of the HRIS equipment.
        C.   HRIS security and privacy.
        D.   the data to be included in the HRIS.

        ANSWER: D, 58

59. _____ is an Internet-linked network that allows employees access to information provided by external entities.
    A.   An extranet
    B.   E-mail
    C.   An intranet
    D.   A listserve

    ANSWER: A, 60

60. Why is security necessary for both extranets and intranets?
    A.   to enable employees readily access their personal files
    B.   to enable supervisors access to update the files of their subordinates
    C.   to prevent unauthorized or inappropriate access and usage
    D.   to prevent access to the system by "computer illiterates"

    ANSWER: C, 60

True and False

61. Human resources can be an organizational core competency when they have special capabilities to make decisions and be innovative in ways that competitors cannot easily imitate.

    ANSWER: True, 30

62. A strong organizational culture is a core competency because the people are committed to the organization's success.

    ANSWER: False, 31
    Not necessarily. The culture might be incompatible with the organization's strategy.

63. The differentiation strategy requires an organization to "build" its own employees to fit its specialized needs.

    ANSWER: False, 35
    This strategy is appropriate for the cost-leadership strategy.

64. In most organizations that do HR planning, the responsibility for this planning is shared by the top HR executives and subordinate staff specialists.

    ANSWER: True, 35

65. HR management and ultimately HR planning are critical in small and entrepreneurial organizations.

    ANSWER: True, 36

66. Family-owned businesses are relieved from most HR planning responsibilities when the business is passed on from one generation to another.

     ANSWER: False, 36
     Management succession is a key issue requiring HR planning.

67. The most telling evidence of successful HR planning is an organization in which the human resources are consistently aligned with the needs of the business over a period of time.

     ANSWER: True, 38

68. One measure of organizational effectiveness is the ability of an organization to compete for a sufficient supply of human resources with the appropriate capabilities.

     ANSWER: True, 38

69. Environmental scanning becomes futile when rapid changes are occurring.

     ANSWER: False, 38-39
     Just the opposite. Environmental scanning is crucial in a dynamic environment.

70. The starting point for evaluating internal strengths and weaknesses is an audit of the jobs currently being done in the organization.

     ANSWER: True, 41

71. Once a person has been hired, an employer can maintain records on that employee without being limited by civil rights and labor laws.

     ANSWER: False, 42
     The data and their use must meet the same standards of job-relatedness and nondiscrimination as when the employee was initially hired.

72. Because of the high degree of uncertainty in the environment, it is virtually impossible to forecast with enough accuracy to benefit an organization's long-range plans.

     ANSWER: False, 43
     Usually experienced people are able to forecast with enough accuracy to benefit organizational long-range planning.

73. Simulation models use input from a group of experts.

     ANSWER: False, 44
     The Delphi technique, a judgmental method, uses input from a group of experts. Simulation models are representations of real situations in abstract form.

74. The internal supply of human resources is influenced by technological development and economic forecasts.

     ANSWER: False, 46
     Promotions, lateral moves, and terminations influence internal supply.

75.   The Worker Adjustment and Retraining Notification (WARN) Act requires employers to give a 60-day notice before a layoff or facility closing involving more than 50 people.

      ANSWER: True, 47

76.   A transition stay bonus is extra payment for employees whose jobs are being eliminated, thereby motivating them to remain with the organization for a period of time.

      ANSWER: True, 48

77.   Research has concluded that those who are still around after downsizing are so glad to have a job that they pose no problems to the organization.

      ANSWER: False, 49
      Performance of survivors and the communications throughout the organization may be affected as the survivors experience guilt because they were spared while their friends were not.

78.   HR professionals interested in benchmarking try to locate organizations that do certain activities particularly well and thus become the "benchmarks."

      ANSWER: True, 55

79.   Human resource information systems (HRIS) are merely HR record-keeping systems that have been computerized.

      ANSWER: False, 57
      An HRIS is an integrated system designed to provide information used in HR decision making. It is useful for both record keeping and strategic planning.

80.   An intranet is an organizational network that operates over the Internet.

      ANSWER: True, 60

ESSAY

81.   Why is strategic HR management essential for organizational success? Describe some of the ways human resources can become a core competency.

ANSWER: 30-35
Strategic HR management is the organizational use of employees to gain or keep a competitive advantage against competitors. HR management can be a core competency through attracting and retaining employees with unique professional and technical capabilities, investing in training and development, and compensating them in ways to keep them competitive with their counterparts in other organizations.

82.   What is organizational culture? Why must HR managers consider the culture of the organization?

ANSWER: 31
Organizational culture is the pattern of shared values and beliefs of a workforce. Culture affects the attraction and retention of competent employees. The culture of an organization may be incompatible with otherwise excellent strategies.

83.   Discuss the impact of the external environment on HR planning.

ANSWER: 38-41
Government influences include rules and regulations, tax credits, educational policies, and immigration policies. Economic conditions such as inflation, growth, and unemployment affects labor supply. Geographic and competitive concerns impact the supply of labor, in addition to changes in the composition of the workforce and the use of flexible staffing.

84.   What strategies are available to an organization with a human resource surplus?

ANSWER: 47-51
The WARN Act requires notice before a layoff or facility closing involving more than 50 people. A reduction in force, or downsizing, may involve a combination of attrition and hiring freezes, early retirement buyouts, and layoffs.

85.   What is the purpose of a human resource information system (HRIS)?

ANSWER: 57-60
An HRIS is an integrated system providing information used in HR decision making. It serves two major purposes: (1) administrative and efficiency - to improve the efficiency with which data on employees and HR activities are compiled; (2) effectiveness - having accessible data enables HR planning and managerial decision making to be based to a greater degree on information rather than relying on managerial perceptions and intuition.

Chapter 3

Individual Performance and Retention

Multiple Choice

1. The three factors, individual ability, effort level expended, and organizational support, affect
    A.   organizational efficiency.
    B.   individual performance.
    C.   organizational effectiveness.
    D.   individual motivation.

    ANSWER: B, 68

2. Performance is a function of
    A.   aptitude and motivation.
    B.   goals and the rewards associated their achievement.
    C.   goals, motivation, and rewards.
    D.   ability, effort, and support.

    ANSWER: D, 68

3. _____ is the desire within a person causing that person to act.
    A.   Motivation
    B.   Loyalty
    C.   Precept
    D.   Attitude

    ANSWER: A, 69

4. Which one of the following is the correct order of Maslow's hierarchy of needs?
    A.   basic, security, self-esteem, social, achievement
    B.   psychological, security, recognition, love, self-actualization
    C.   physiological, safety, belonging, esteem, self-actualization
    D.   existence, relatedness, growth

    ANSWER: C, 69

5. People using Maslow's hierarchy assume that workers in modern, technologically advanced societies
    A.   will rarely reach the top of the hierarchy.
    B.   have basically satisfied their physiological, safety, and belonging needs.
    C.   are concerned primarily with a lack of belonging and love.
    D.   are primarily motivated by money.

    ANSWER: B, 69

6. To motivate workers in today's technologically advanced society, employers should focus on satisfying the following needs.
    A.   physiological and safety
    B.   belonging and social
    C.   financial
    D.   esteem and self-actualization

    ANSWER: D, 69-70

7. Based on Herzberg's theory, what happens if all the hygiene factors are satisfactory?
    A.   people may not be motivated to work harder
    B.   workers are motivated
    C.   absenteeism and turnover are likely to increases
    D.   productivity increases

    ANSWER: A, 70

8. Herzberg's theory suggests that managers should
    A.   understand that a satisfied worker is more productive than a dissatisfied worker.
    B.   ignore hygiene factors since they do not motivate workers.
    C.   use motivators as tools to enhance employee performance.
    D.   initially concentrate on higher order needs.

    ANSWER: C, 70

9. Which of the following is a motivator in Herzberg's theory?
    A.   salary
    B.   recognition
    C.   supervision
    D.   interpersonal relations

    ANSWER: B, 70

10. In Frederick Herzberg's theory, interpersonal relationships, company policy, and supervision and identified as
    A.   motivators.
    B.   satisfiers.
    C.   interpersonal factors.
    D.   hygiene factors.

    ANSWER: D, 70

11.   _____ is defined as the perceived fairness of what the person does
       compared with what the person receives.
       A.   Equity
       B.   Procedural justice
       C.   Distributive justice
       D.   Compensation

       ANSWER: A, 70

12.   When considering equity as a motivator, which of the following would NOT be an
       input?
       A.   educational level
       B.   age
       C.   pay
       D.   productivity

       ANSWER: C, 70

13.   In considering equity as a motivator, pay, benefits, recognition, and prestige
       would be listed as
       A.   outputs.
       B.   outcomes.
       C.   inputs.
       D.   incentives.

       ANSWER: B, 70

14.   A perception of inequity occurs when the comparison process results in
       A.   inadequate rewards.
       B.   a salary that is less than market value.
       C.   inputs that are greater than the outcomes.
       D.   an imbalance between inputs and outcomes.

       ANSWER: D, 70

15.   The Porter and Lawler model indicates that if _____, people may feel
       that they have been unfairly treated and consequently become dissatisfied.
       A.   expectations are not met
       B.   hygiene factors are not adequate
       C.   goals are set too high or too low
       D.   good performance is not recognized

       ANSWER: A, 70

16.   The essence of the Porter and Lawler view of motivation is that individuals base
       decisions about their behaviors on
       A.   job design.
       B.   perceived equity of rewards.
       C.   their expectations.
       D.   job satisfaction.

       ANSWER: C, 70-71

17.   According to Porter and Lawler, _____ leads to _____.
      A..   job satisfaction; high performance
      B.   high performance; rewards
      C.   expectations; motivation
      D.   motivation; performance

      ANSWER: B, 71

18.   According to Expectancy Theory, one determinant of employees' willingness to
      exert effort is the degree to which
      A.   the organization pays above average wages.
      B.   they are motivated to work.
      C.   they believe the organization will compensate them for their efforts.
      D.   they value the rewards offered by the organization.

      ANSWER: D, 71

19.   Deciding how to motivate employees requires managerial diagnoses of
      A.   employees' efforts, abilities, and expectations.
      B.   the competitive nature of the organization's rewards.
      C.   the needs, desires, and goals of each employee.
      D.   the strategic plans of the organization.

      ANSWER: A, 72

20.   A(n) _____ is the unwritten expectations employees and employers have
      about the nature of their work relationships.
      A.   employment contract
      B.   applicant assessment
      C.   psychological contract
      D.   biographical sketch

      ANSWER: C, 72

21.   What is a psychological contract?
      A.   The written employment contract between a job applicant and a prospective
             employer.
      B.   The unwritten expectations employees and employers have about the nature
             of their work relationships.
      C.   The sum of a new employee's experiences during the first days on the job.
      D.   The trade-off between wages and benefits in the overall compensation
             package.

      ANSWER: B, 72

22.   _____ are encompassed by psychological contracts.
      A.   Only intangible items such as loyalty, fair treatment, and job security
      B.   Only wages, benefits, employee productivity, and attendance
      C.   All aspects of the working experience
      D.   Both tangible and intangible items

      ANSWER: D, 72

23. Rather than _____, increasingly employers are expecting employees to _____.
    A. paying them to put in time; accomplish organizational results
    B. expecting teams to produce results; work independently
    C. offering long-term employment; accept short-term assignments
    D. giving regular cost-of-living raises; work as independent contractors

    ANSWER: A, 73

24. When writing about generational differences, people born _____ are labeled as "baby boomers."
    A. between 1981 and 1990
    B. between 1966 and 1980
    C. between 1945 and 1965
    D. before 1945

    ANSWER: C, 73

25. Research has confirmed that individuals whose psychological contract "obligations" are not being satisfied are
    A. generally underpaid.
    B. more likely to leave.
    C. psychologically depressed.
    D. more likely to commit acts of workplace violence.

    ANSWER: B, 74

26. _____ is a positive emotional state resulting from evaluating one's job experiences.
    A. Organizational commitment
    B. Job survival intentions
    C. Employee loyalty
    D. Job satisfaction

    ANSWER: D, 75

27. "The degree to which employees believe in and accept organizational goals and desire to remain with the organization" is a definition of
    A. organizational commitment.
    B. employee involvement.
    C. job satisfaction.
    D. loyalty.

    ANSWER: A, 76

28. If an employee is sick, or has a sick child, and is unable to come to work, the resulting time off is usually referred to as
    A. sick-leave time.
    B. explainable absenteeism.
    C. involuntary absenteeism.
    D. recognized time off.

    ANSWER: C, 76

29.   Research has found a close linkage between job satisfaction and
        A.   productivity.
        B.   absenteeism.
        C.   motivation.
        D.   expectations.

        ANSWER: B, 76

30.   Which of the following was suggested as an absenteeism control option?
        A.   negative reinforcement
        B.   perceptual changes
        C.   equity controls
        D.   positive reinforcement

        ANSWER: D, 77

31.   _____ is a process in when employees leave the organization and have
        to be replaced.
        A.   Turnover
        B.   Vacancy
        C.   Attrition
        D.   Changeover

        ANSWER: A, 78

32.   _____ occurs when an employee is terminated for poor performance.
        A.   At-will-termination
        B.   Dehiring
        C.   Involuntary turnover
        D.   Voluntary withdrawal

        ANSWER: C, 78

33.   Turnover that occurs when an employee decides to stay home for family reasons
        is classified as
        A.   controllable turnover.
        B.   uncontrollable turnover.
        C.   functional turnover.
        D.   dysfunctional turnover.

        ANSWER: B, 79

34.   Surveys have consistently identified the primary factors influencing turnover
        and retention are
        A.   child care and health-related issues.
        B.   relationships with co-workers and supervisors.
        C.   perceptions of fair or discriminatory treatment.
        D.   career opportunities and compensation.

        ANSWER: D, 81

35. "A pattern of shared values and beliefs that provides members organizational meaning and rules for behavior" is a definition of
    A.   organizational culture.
    B.   organizational commitment.
    C.   organizational ethics.
    D.   organizational norms.

    ANSWER: A, 82

36. An organization's _____ shapes its members' responses and defines what an organization can or is willing to do.
    A.   mission
    B.   ethics
    C.   culture
    D.   climate

    ANSWER: C, 82

37. Which of the following has had the most impact on employee loyalty and retention?
    A.   a dynamic economy
    B.   corporate downsizing
    C.   affirmative action plans
    D.   career development programs

    ANSWER: B, 83-84

38. Studies have shown that _____ lead the reasons why individuals took their current jobs and why they stay there.
    A.   compensation
    B.   work/family balance
    C.   organizational culture
    D.   opportunities for personal growth

    ANSWER: D, 84

39. _____ lets employees choose how much and what benefits they will have from a "cafeteria" of choices.
    A.   Benefits flexibility
    B.   Competitive benefits programs
    C.   Benefit portability
    D.   Concierge benefits

    ANSWER: A, 85

40. Concierge benefits provide employees with
    A.   benefits that are "portable" when they move to another employer.
    B.   a choice of benefits that meet their individual situations.
    C.   assistance in personal matters at their places of work.
    D.   employee assistance programs.

    ANSWER: C, 85

41. Which of the following was NOT suggested as a reward issue affecting employee retention?

    A.   recognition
    B.   signing bonuses
    C.   competitive benefits
    D.   performance differentiation

    ANSWER: B, 85-86

42. _____ is an example of intangible recognition as a form of reward.
    A.   "Employee of the month"
    B.   Perfect attendance award
    C.   A gift voucher
    D.   Feedback from managers

    ANSWER: D, 86

43. Organizations have found that high employee turnover rates in the first few months of employment are linked to
    A.   inadequate selection screening.
    B.   uncompetitive pay scales.
    C.   work and family conflicts.
    D.   lack of recognition for performance.

    ANSWER: A, 86

44. Realistic job previews
    A.   introduce new employees to the organization.
    B.   should ensure that job applicants have the proper KSAs for the jobs.
    C.   lead to reduced turnover.
    D.   explain the organization's compensation policy.

    ANSWER: C, 86

45. _____ employees go to work from home or other locations with the aid of technology.
    A.   Virtual
    B.   Telecommuting
    C.   Hoteling
    D.   Contingent

    ANSWER: B, 87

46. _____ occurs when a full week's work is accomplished in fewer than five days.
    A.   Flextime
    B.   A virtual office
    C.   Telecommuting
    D.   A compressed workweek

    ANSWER: D, 87

47. The purpose of flexible benefits, alternate work schedules, and flexible HR policies is
    A.   to convey that the employer cares about its employees.
    B.   to minimize the cost of compensation.
    C.   to assist two-career families.
    D.   to maintain a union-free workplace.

    ANSWER: A, 88

48. The increasing demographic diversity of U.S. workplaces makes _____ important, which aids retention.
    A.   affirmative action plans
    B.   knowledge of all Civil Rights laws and EEO regulations
    C.   nondiscriminatory treatment of all employees
    D.   "mandatory English-spoken-here" policies

    ANSWER: C, 88

49. Firms have recognized that proactive management of diversity issues results in
    A.   an increase in EEO complaints.
    B.   greater retention of individuals of all backgrounds.
    C.   an increased number of minority applicants.
    D.   a reduction in the number of white males being considered for promotion.

    ANSWER: B, 88

50. A survey of individuals of a variety of ages and working in a variety of industries found that the most positively cited factor about going to work was
    A.   a disciplinary policy to reduce absenteeism.
    B.   the availability of on-site child-care facilities.
    C.   an incentive scheme to reward perfect attendance.
    D.   the relationship with co-workers.

    ANSWER: D, 88

51. Retention measurement and assessment, retention interventions, and evaluation and follow-up are phases in
    A.   the retention management process.
    B.   the staffing process.
    C.   strategic turnover management.
    D.   managing an HR surplus.

    ANSWER: A, 89

52. The U.S. Department of Labor uses "separation" to mean
    A.   getting fired.
    B.   retention management.
    C.   leaving the organization.
    D.   dehiring.

    ANSWER: C, 90

53. _____ consider(s) hiring costs, training costs, and productivity costs.
    A.   Separation costing
    B.   Turnover costing models
    C.   Retention management
    D.   Staffing surveys

    ANSWER: B, 90-91

54. _____ include exit interview time, unemployment expenses, and legal fees for challenged dismissals.
    A.   Productivity costs
    B.   Hiring costs
    C.   Effectiveness survey costs
    D.   Separation costs

    ANSWER: D, 91

55. Why do employers use attitude surveys?
    A.   to assess employees' feelings and beliefs about their jobs and the organization
    B.   to provide input to supervisor evaluations
    C.   to assure employees that management is genuinely interested in their needs
    D.   to identify jobs that can be eliminated or automated

    ANSWER: A, 91

56. _____ are a specific type of survey that focuses on employees' feelings and beliefs about their jobs and the organization.
    A.   Employee surveys
    B.   Job diagnostic surveys
    C.   Attitude surveys
    D.   Research surveys

    ANSWER: C, 91

57. Only surveys that are _____ can measure attitudes accurately.
    A.   professionally developed
    B.   valid and reliable
    C.   custom-designed for the specific organization
    D.   confidential

    ANSWER: B, 92

58. By asking employees to respond candidly to an attitude survey, management is building up employees' expectations that
    A.   their responses will be kept confidential.
    B.   an organizational restructuring is being considered.
    C.   the HR department is becoming more professional.
    D.   action will be taken on the concerns identified.

    ANSWER: D, 92

59. With regard to exit interviews, which of the following statements is <u>false</u>?
    A.   . Departing employees are eager to use the occasion to voice their "gripes."
    B.   HR specialists are usually better at gaining useful information than supervisors.
    C.   It is often more useful to contact departing employees a month or so after departure when they may be more willing to provide information.
    D.   A major reason employees commonly give for leaving their jobs is an offer for more pay elsewhere.

    ANSWER: A, 93

60. In a(n) _____ interview, individuals are asked to identify reasons for leaving the organization.
    A.   employment
    B.   appraisal
    C.   exit
    D.   retention

    ANSWER: C, 93

True and False

61. Performance and reaction to compensation are affect by and influence motivation.

    ANSWER: True, 69

62. People using Maslow's theory of motivation assume that workers are motivated by the lower order physiological, safety, and belonging needs.

    ANSWER: False, 69
    It is assumed that these needs have been met in modern, technologically advanced societies. They concentrate on the needs for esteem and self-actualization.

63. According to Herzberg, a business can motivate its employees by improving company policy, supervisory behavior, salaries, and working conditions.

    ANSWER: False, 70
    Herzberg argued that by improving these "hygiene" factors, employers can avoid employee dissatisfaction, but the people may not be motivated to work.

64. If all employees in a business who do the same job are paid the same, we can assume that they will be satisfied and motivated.

    ANSWER: False, 70
    People want to be treated fairly at work. Equity is defined as the perceived fairness of what a person does compared with what the persons receives.

65. Porter and Lawler's Expectancy Theory of motivation suggests that individuals' levels of effort (motivation) are not simply functions of rewards.

    ANSWER: True, 71

66.   In Porter and Lawler's model, *performance-reward linkage* refers to how valuable the rewards are to the employee.

      ANSWER: False, 71
      Performance-reward linkage considers the individuals' expectations that high performance actually will lead to rewards.

67.   Psychological contracts include both tangible items (such as wages, benefits, employee productivity, and attendance) and intangible items (such as loyalty, fair treatment, and job security).

      ANSWER: True, 72

68.   In most organizations today, employees exchange their efforts and capabilities for a secure job that offers rising wages, comprehensive benefits, and career progression within the organization.

      ANSWER: False, 73
      The new psychological contract rewards employees for contributing to organizational success in the competitive marketplace for goods and services.

69.   In general, members of the baby-boom generation are mostly concerned about why managers and organizations make the decisions they do.

      ANSWER: False, 73-74
      Baby boomers are primarily concerned about security and experience.

70.   In tight labor markets, turnover of key people occurs more frequently when employee loyalty is low.

      ANSWER: True, 75

71.   Research has consistently found that improving job satisfaction will lead to a more productive workforce.

      ANSWER: False, 75
      There is no consistent relationship between satisfaction and productivity.

72.   If employees are satisfied with their jobs and committed to the organization, they are less likely to withdraw from the organization.

      ANSWER: True, 76

73.   No consistent relationship has been found between absenteeism, job satisfaction, and organizational commitment.

      ANSWER: False, 76
      Studies have indeed found linkage between these variables.

74.   In a paid-time-off program, vacation time, holidays, and sick leave for each employee are combined into a PTO account. Employees use days from their accounts at their discretion for illness, personal time, or vacation.

      ANSWER: True, 78

75.   Turnover is costly and should be avoided.

ANSWER:, False, 79
Not all turnover is negative for the organization. Some workforce losses are quite desirable.

76.   Career opportunities and compensation are the two most important determinants of retention.

ANSWER: True, 81-82

77.   One positive result of corporate downsizing has been the improved level of employee loyalty and retention of the remaining employees who survived the layoffs.

ANSWER: False, 83-84
Downsizing has caused people to start thinking about leaving the organization before they too are cut.

78.   A good way to eliminate voluntary turnover is to improve the employee selection process.

ANSWER: True, 86

79.   Attitude surveys allow employees to air their views about their jobs, their supervisors, their coworkers, and organizational policies and practices.

ANSWER: True, 91

80.   It is recommended that HR departments develop custom-designed surveys for their organization.

ANSWER: False, 92
Often a research survey developed in-house is poorly structured, confusing, and can lead employees to respond in ways that will give favorable results. It is recommended that organizations only use surveys that are valid and reliable.

Essay

81.   If a panel discussion were possible between Maslow, Herzberg, and Porter and Lawler, how would each respond to the statement: "Pay is the most effective tool management has for motivating the performance of its workers?"

ANSWER: 69-72
Maslow would argue that pay was important only to the extent that it helped satisfy unmet needs. Since most workers in developed countries had satisfied their lower-order needs, pay was only useful as a form of recognition to satisfy esteem needs. Herzberg viewed pay as a hygiene factor, not a motivator. Porter and Lawler focused on the value an employee placed on pay, and the perceived equity in which it was awarded.

82. Traditionally, loyalty and long service with one employer were the norm. How has this changed? Why?

ANSWER: 72-75
The psychological contract refers to the unwritten expectations employees and employers have about their work relationships. It is a reciprocal relationship. This idea of reciprocity is very much an issue in the decline of loyalty and length of service by employees. Workers have seen massive lay-offs, mergers and acquisitions, and outsourcing jobs as indications of a loss of job security. They have responded with reductions in loyalty to their employers, and an unwillingness to commit to long-term employment at one organization.

83. What is meant by job satisfaction and organizational commitment? What are the advantages of a satisfied and committed workforce?

ANSWER: 75-76
Job satisfaction is a positive emotional state resulting from evaluating one's job experiences. Organizational commitment is the degree to which employees believe in and accept organizational goals and desire to remain with the organization. Job satisfaction, while not directly linked to productivity, does impact organizational commitment. A satisfied and committed employee is less likely to be absent or to voluntarily leave the organization.

84. Describe the different reasons why employees are absent from work. What are some of the alternatives for controlling voluntary absenteeism?

ANSWER: 76-78
Some absenteeism is unavoidable or involuntary such as illness, death in the family, personal reasons. Avoidable or voluntary absenteeism is closely linked to job satisfaction and organizational commitment.

85. Why should organizations address controllable turnover? What strategies would you recommend for addressing retention?

ANSWER: 79-88
Controllable turnover occurs when people choose to leave the organization for factors that could be influenced by the employer. Strategies for improving retention include: Improve career opportunities and compensation, develop a supportive culture, minimize the negative effects of mergers, acquisitions, and downsizing, redesign work offering work flexibility and schedule, and improve employee relationships.

Chapter 4

Legal Framework for Equal Employment

Multiple Choice

1. Which of the following statements is true about "diversity?"
   A. Diversity requires organizations to initiate affirmative action programs.
   B. Diversity recognizes that a variety of dimensions differentiate people.
   C. Diversity is a natural consequence of civil rights enforcement.
   D. The best response to diversity is to ignore it.

   ANSWER: B, 102

2. _____ is concerned with developing organizational initiatives that value all people equally, regardless of their differences.
   A. Affirmative action
   B. Cultural diversity
   C. Equal employment opportunity (EEO)
   D. Diversity management

   ANSWER: D, 102

3. _____ is a broad concept holding that individuals should have equal treatment in all employment-related actions.
   A. Equal employment opportunity
   B. Affirmative action
   C. Diversity management
   D. Cultural diversity

   ANSWER: A, 102

4. "Recognizing differences among items or people" is a definition of
   A. diversity.
   B. EEO status.
   C. discrimination.
   D. cultural awareness.

   ANSWER: C, 103

5. Individuals who fall within a group identified for protection under equal employment laws and regulations, are members of a(n)
    A.   affirmative action category.
    B.   protected class.
    C.   EEO classification.
    D.   minority group.

    ANSWER: B, 103

6. Which of the following is <u>not</u> a basis for protection under federal laws?
    A.   military experience
    B.   age
    C.   gender
    D.   sexual orientation

    ANSWER: D, 103

7. "A process in which employers identify problem areas, set goals, and take positive steps to enhance opportunities for protected-class members" is a definition of
    A.   affirmative action.
    B.   cultural diversity.
    C.   diversity management.
    D.   equal employment opportunity.

    ANSWER: A, 103

8. Affirmative action focuses on hiring, training, and promoting protected-class members when they are _____ in an organization in relation to their availability in the labor market.
    A.   discriminated against
    B.   economically deprived
    C.   underrepresented
    D.   placed

    ANSWER: C, 103

9. Employers are required to _____ when they are government contractors with more than 50 employees and over $50,000 in government contracts annually.
    A.   eliminate employment discrimination
    B.   institute affirmative action
    C.   hire protected-class members
    D.   use quotas in hiring minorities

    ANSWER: B, 103

10. _____ may exist when a person is denied an opportunity because of preferences given to protected-class individuals who may be less qualified.
    A.   Employment quotas
    B.   Unlawful discrimination
    C.   Affirmative action
    D.   Reverse discrimination

    ANSWER: D, 103

11. In the _____ case, a federal appeals court ruled that the use of race in admissions for diversity in higher education contradicts, rather that furthers, the aims of equal protection.
    A. Hopwood v. State of Texas
    B. Griggs v. Duke Power
    C. Bakke
    D. Adarand

    ANSWER: A, 104

12. Which of the following types of organizations does <u>not</u> fall under Title VII?
    A. public educational institutions
    B. private employers of 15 or more persons
    C. federal government departments
    D. national labor unions

    ANSWER: C, 105

13. A practice necessary for safe and efficient organizational operations is called
    A. a 4/5ths rule.
    B. a business necessity.
    C. a validity generalization.
    D. a *bona fide* occupational qualification

    ANSWER: B, 106

14. A _____ is a characteristic providing a legitimate reason why an employer can exclude persons on otherwise illegal bases of consideration.
    A. 4/5ths rule
    B. business necessity
    C. validity generalization
    D. *bona fide* occupational qualification

    ANSWER: D, 106

15. _____ occurs when protected-class members are treated differently from others.
    A. Disparate treatment
    B. Discriminatory intent
    C. Disparate impact
    D. Adverse impact

    ANSWER: A, 106

16. _____ occurs when there is a substantial under representation of protected-class members resulting from employment decisions that work to their disadvantage.
    A. Disparate treatment
    B. Adverse treatment
    C. Disparate impact
    D. Discriminatory intent

    ANSWER: C, 106

17. The landmark case that established the importance of disparate impact as a legal
     foundation of EEO law is
     A.   *Adarand Constructors v. Pena*
     B.   *Griggs v. Duke Power*
     C.   *University of California at Davis v. Bakke*
     D.   *University of Texas Law School*

     ANSWER: B, 106

18. When does the burden of proof fall on the employer?
     A.   when there was no Affirmative Action Plan in place
     B.   when it is a class action suit
     C.   the burden of proof always remains on the complainant
     D.   when the court rules that a *prima facie* case has been made

     ANSWER: D, 107

19. Which of the following would be defined as retaliation by EEO laws?
     A.   An employer takes punitive actions against individuals who exercise their
           legal rights.
     B.   An employer fires a supervisor who discriminates against a protective-
           class member.
     C.   A dismissed employee files a false complaint of discrimination with the
           EEOC.
     D.   The EEOC targets an employer with a history of unlawful discrimination.

     ANSWER: A, 107

20. The Civil Rights Act of 1991 emphasized the importance of _____ in
     establishing validity.
     A.   test reliability
     B.   affirmative action
     C.   business necessity
     D.   job descriptions

     ANSWER: C, 107

21. The 1991 Civil Rights Act requires that plaintiffs bringing discrimination
     charges must
     A.   show a pattern of discrimination.
     B.   identify the particular employer practice being challenged.
     C.   identify majority-group members who benefited from the illegal actions.
     D.   provide evidence of financial harm caused by the employer's actions.

     ANSWER: B, 107

22. Under the 1991 Civil Rights Act, employers must show that an individual's race,
     color, religion, sex, or national origin
     A.   was not the deciding factor in the employment decision.
     B.   did not limit that individual's employment options.
     C.   caused no financial hardship to the individual.
     D.   played no factor in their employment practices.

     ANSWER: D, 107

23. The _____ allows victims of discrimination on the basis of sex, religion, or disability to receive both compensatory and punitive damages in cases of intentional discrimination.
    A.   Civil Rights Act of 1991
    B.   *Griggs v. Duke Power* decision
    C.   Civil Rights Act of 1964
    D.   *Price Waterhouse v. Hopkins* decision

    ANSWER: A, 107

24. _____ is the practice of adjusting employment test scores on the basis of the race of test takers.
    A.   Discriminatory intent
    B.   Affirmative adjustment
    C.   Race norming
    D.   Business necessity

    ANSWER: C, 107

25. With respect to U.S. citizens working abroad, the 1991 Civil Rights Act
    A.   requires corporations to abide by local laws and customs.
    B.   extended coverage of U.S. EEO laws, except where local laws conflict.
    C.   does not apply internationally.
    D.   takes precedence over local· laws.

    ANSWER: B, 108

26. A(n) _____ is issued by the president of the United States to provide direction to government departments on a specific area.
    A.   authorized bill
    B.   presidential directive
    C.   legislative initiative
    D.   executive order

    ANSWER: D, 108

27. Which agency is responsible for enforcing nondiscrimination in government contracts?
    A.   The Office of Federal Contract Compliance Programs
    B.   The U.S. Contracts and Agreements Agency
    C.   The Equal Employment Opportunity Commission
    D.   The Executive Orders Group

    ANSWER: A, 108

28. Who is required to have an affirmative action plan?
    A.   all government contractors
    B.   all government agencies
    C.   an employer with at least 50 employees and over $50,000 in government contracts annually
    D.   an employer with at least 20 employees and who has a history of unlawful discrimination

    ANSWER: C, 108

29. _____ identifies the number of protected-class members available to work in the appropriate labor markets in given jobs.
     A.   A labor market survey
     B.   An availability analysis
     C.   A labor-trends analysis
     D.   An affirmative action analysis

     ANSWER: B, 108

30. Identifying the number of protected-class members employed and the types of jobs they hold in an organization is the purpose of a(n)
     A.   equal opportunity investigation.
     B.   availability determination.
     C.   affirmative action assessment.
     D.   utilization analysis.

     ANSWER: D, 108

31. The _____ describes actions that will be taken to recruit, hire, promote, and train more protected-class individuals.
     A.   affirmative action plan
     B.   workforce analysis
     C.   OFCCP report
     D.   EEOC audit

     ANSWER: A, 109

32. The major provision of the Pregnancy Discrimination Act of 1978 was that
     A.   pregnant employees are to be given 12 weeks family leave without pay.
     B.   pregnant employees are entitled to 12 weeks of paid maternity leave.
     C.   maternity leave was to be treated the same as other personal or medical leaves.
     D.   employers could not discriminate against employees based on family status.

     ANSWER: C, 110

33. Which of the following is required by the Family and Medical Leave Act of 1993?
     A.   maternity leave was to be treated the same as other medical leaves.
     B.   Individuals are to be given up to 12 weeks of family leave without pay.
     C.   employers could not discriminate against employees based on family status.
     D.   both male and female employees are entitled to paid family leave following the birth of a child.

     ANSWER: B, 110

34. Which of the following has been a general ruling in cases filed under the Pregnancy Discrimination Act?
     A.   Employers are not required to accommodate the needs of pregnant employees.
     B.   Pregnancy is a disability requiring special accommodation.
     C.   Women must be assignment less strenuous tasks during pregnancy.
     D.   Employers must treat pregnant employers the same as non-pregnant employees with similar abilities or inabilities.

     ANSWER: D, 110

35. The Equal Pay Act, enacted in 1963, requires employers to
     A. pay similar wage rates for similar work without regard to gender.
     B. establish pay rates based upon merit rather than seniority.
     C. conduct wage and salary surveys to ensure pay equity.
     D. ensure that older employees are not discriminated against in compensation.

     ANSWER: A, 110

36. The courts have ruled that a female employee with the same job title as a male
     A. must be paid the same salary and benefits as the male.
     B. must be paid the same unless the male employee has more seniority.
     C. may be paid less than the male if there are seniority differences.
     D. is not eligible for leave under the Family and Medical Leave Act.

     ANSWER: C, 110

37. According to the concept of _____, the pay for jobs requiring comparable levels of knowledge, skill, and ability should be similar even if actual duties differ significantly.
     A. equal pay
     B. pay equity
     C. comparable pay
     D. pay fairness

     ANSWER: B, 110

38. "Actions that are sexually directed, are unwanted, and subject the worker to adverse employment conditions or create a hostile work environment," is a definition of
     A. *quid pro quo* discrimination.
     B. gender discrimination.
     C. sexual assault.
     D   sexual harassment.

     ANSWER: D, 111

39. Title I of the ADA prohibits employment-related discrimination against
     A. persons with disabilities.
     B. employees who are pregnant.
     C. disabled Vietnam-era veterans.
     D. individuals unable to perform certain essential job functions.

     ANSWER: A, 112

40. Which of the following would be considered disabled persons under the ADA?
     A. current users of illegal drugs
     B. compulsive gamblers
     C. individuals infected with HIV
     D. pregnant women

     ANSWER: C, 113

41. The fundamental job duties of the employment position that an individual with a disability holds or desires are called
     A.   job specifications.
     B.   essential job functions.
     C.   reasonable accommodations.
     D.   minimum job requirements.

     ANSWER: B, 113

42. A _____ is the modification or adjustment to a job or work environment that enables a qualified individual with a disability to enjoy equal employment opportunity.
     A.   creating access
     B.   workplace essential job function
     C.   job modification
     D.   reasonable accommodation

     ANSWER: D, 113

43. If making reasonable accommodation for a disabled person imposes significant difficulty or expense on an employer, the employer
     A.   can claim undue hardship exists.
     B.   will have to make the accommodation anyway.
     C.   will be responsible for finding alternate work for the disabled person.
     D.   may reduce the salary of the disabled person to compensate.

     ANSWER: A, 113

44. The Age Discrimination in Employment Act protects individuals over the age of
     A.   65.
     B.   50.
     C.   40.
     D.   70.

     ANSWER: C, 113

45. What is the legal position regarding mandatory retirement?
     A.   There can be no mandatory retirement age.
     B.   It is permitted if age is a job-related occupational qualification.
     C.   A company can set its own maximum age, based on company tradition.
     D.   ADEA-protected individuals may not be fired.

     ANSWER: B, 114

46. The Immigration Reform and Control Act
     A.   permits employers to hire only U.S. citizens.
     B.   permits employers to require more documentation for some prospective employees than for others to ensure that illegal aliens are not hired.
     C.   prevents employers from discriminating against undocumented aliens.
     D.   makes it illegal for an employer to discriminate based on national origin.

     ANSWER: D, 115

47. Which of the following is a requirement of the Immigration Reform and Control Act, as revised?
    A.   Employers who knowingly hire illegal aliens must be penalized.
    B.   Civil Rights Act protection must be extended to undocumented workers.
    C.   Employers are required to verify the citizenship and/or immigration status of job candidates suspected of being foreign born.
    D.   Employers cannot require workers speak only English in the workplace.

    ANSWER: A, 115

48. Under the Immigration Reform and Control Act, employers are required to examine identification documents
    A.   before a job offer is extended.
    B.   after a job offer is extended but before the new employee begins work.
    C.   within 72 hours of hiring the new employee.
    D.   never.

    ANSWER: C, 115

49. In *TWA v. Hardison*, the Supreme Court ruled that an employer must make reasonable accommodation for
    A.   a disabled person.
    B.   an employee's religious beliefs.
    C.   an employee infected with HIV.
    D.   the domestic partner of an employee.

    ANSWER: B, 115

50. Which of the following is true with respect to the physical appearance of employees?
    A.   Attractiveness may be a valid selection criterion.
    B.   Obesity may be considered as an employment variable.
    C.   Minorities with health problems are exempt from some appearance policies.
    D.   Courts have allowed dress codes as long as they are applied uniformly.

    ANSWER: D, 115

51. Which of the following statements is true with regard to sexual orientation and gay rights?
    A.   the Supreme Court has not decided whether gay men and lesbians have rights under the equal protection amendment to the U.S. Constitution.
    B.   transvestites are considered disabled under the ADA.
    C.   federal law prohibits discrimination based on sexual orientation.
    D.   sex discrimination covers people who have had gender-altering operations.

    ANSWER: A, 116

52. Which of the following is true with regard to conviction and arrest records?
    A.   Using conviction records has been shown to be discriminatory.
    B.   All convictions may be considered in employment decisions.
    C.   In general, only job-related convictions may be considered.
    D.   Recent job-related arrests may be considered in employment decisions.

    ANSWER: C, 117

53. Which agency, created by the 1964 Civil Rights Act, has enforcement authority for charges brought under a number of federal laws?
     A.   The OFCCP
     B.   The EEOC
     C.   The U.S. Justice Department
     D.   The U.S. Civil Rights Commission

     ANSWER: B, 119

54. The major purpose of the OFCCP is
     A.   to evaluate the comparable worth of federal government jobs.
     B.   to help the victims of unlawful discrimination to file claims and obtain relief.
     C.   to monitor labor market changes.
     D.   to require that federal contractors and subcontractors take affirmative action to overcome the effects of prior discriminatory practices.

     ANSWER: D, 120

55. Under the Uniform Guidelines on Employee Selection Procedures, the 4/5ths rule is used to determine if
     A.   disparate impact has occurred.
     B.   illegal discrimination exists.
     C.   the employer is guilty of preferential treatment.
     D.   a protected-class member has suffered from disparate treatment.

     ANSWER: A, 121

56. A test has _____ if it reflects an actual sample of the work done on the job in question.
     A.   reliability
     B.   criterion validity
     C.   content validity
     D.   validity generalizability

     ANSWER: C, 124

57. In measuring criterion-related validity, a test is the _____ and the desired KSAs and measures of job performance are the _____.
     A.   validator; job statistics
     B.   predictor; criterion variables
     C.   X-variable; Y-variables
     D.   measure; performance scores

     ANSWER: B, 125

58. The validation strategy that tests current employees and correlates the scores with their performance ratings is called
     A.   predictive validity.
     B.   construct validity.
     C.   criterion validity.
     D.   concurrent validity.

     ANSWER: D, 125

59. _____ validity shows a relationship between an abstract characteristic inferred by research and job performance.
    A.   Construct validity
    B.   Predictive validity
    C.   Concurrent validity
    D.   Criterion

    ANSWER: A, 126

60. In order to effectively defend itself against a charge of discrimination in the recruiting and selection of members of protected classes, organizations should
    A.   provide exit interview summaries.
    B.   keep job evaluation data.
    C.   maintain applicant flow data.
    D.   design objective applications.

    ANSWER: C, 128

True and False

61. Affirmative action occurs when employers identify problem areas, set goals, and take positive steps to guarantee equal employment opportunities for people in a protected class.

    ANSWER: True, 103

62. The burden of proof shifts to the defendant once the court rules that a *prima facie* case of discrimination has been made.

    ANSWER: True, 107

63. Under the 1991 Civil Rights Act, an employer cannot simply require that all job applicants have a minimum level of education, such as a high school diploma. They must be able to defend the requirement as job related for the position.

    ANSWER: True, 107

64. The Civil Rights Act of 1991 differs from the Civil Rights Act of 1964 in that the 1991 act permits jury trials to determine liability and to assess punitive damages.

    ANSWER: True, 107

65. The Civil Rights Act of 1991 permits the adjustment of employment test scores on the basis of the race and gender of test takers to achieve affirmative action goals.

    ANSWER: False, 107-108
    The practice, called "race norming," is prohibited by the Act.

66.   The 1991 Civil Rights Act extended coverage of U.S. EEO laws to U.S. citizens working abroad, except where local laws conflict.

      ANSWER: True, 108

67.   Although the Pregnancy Discrimination Act requires employers to treat maternity leave the same as other medical leaves, it does not require insurance coverage for prescription contraceptives under employer-provided health plans.

      ANSWER: False, 110
      The U.S. Equal Employment Commission has ruled that the denial of prescription contraceptives violates the PDA.

68.   The Equal Pay Act prohibits employers from having different pay rates based on race.

      ANSWER: False, 110
      The Equal Pay Act prohibits differences in pay based on sex.

69.   Sexual harassment can occur among non-employees who have business contacts with employees.

      ANSWER: True, 111

70.   Obesity may be considered as a disability under the ADA.

      ANSWER: True, 112

71.   The ADA does not require an employer to hire a disabled person who is unable to perform all the requirements of the job.

      ANSWER: False, 113
      ADA guidelines require employers to identify essential job functions of each position. These do not include marginal functions of the position.

72.   The Immigration Reform and Control Act makes it illegal for an employer to discriminate in recruiting, hiring, or termination based on an individual's national origin or citizenship.

      ANSWER: True, 115

73.   The purpose of the Immigration Reform and Control Act is to penalize illegal aliens who work in the United States, rather than to penalize the employers.

      ANSWER: False, 115
      The act requires that employers who knowingly hire illegal aliens be penalized, not the employees.

74. Federal law prohibits employers from using genetic test results to exclude individuals from certain jobs if they have genetic conditions that increase health risks.

    ANSWER: False, 115-116
    While legislation has been proposed, there is currently no federal restrictions on the use of genetic testing.

75. Federal employment laws prohibit discrimination based on sexual orientation.

    ANSWER: False, 116
    Although some states and cities have passed laws making it unlawful to discriminate based on sexual orientation, there are no federal laws.

76. The EEOC is part of the Department of Labor, and is responsible for requiring that federal contractors take affirmative action to overcome the effects of prior discrimination practices.

    ANSWER: False, 120
    It is the task of the OFCCP to require federal contractors and subcontractors take affirmative action. The EEOC is an independent agency responsible for enforcing employment-related provisions of the 1964 Civil Rights Act.

77. The Uniform Guidelines are used by enforcement agencies to examine recruiting, hiring, promotion, and many other employment-related practices.

    ANSWER: True, 121

78. An "employment test" is defined as any paper-and-pencil test that an employer may use prior to making a hiring decision.

    ANSWER: False, 123
    The Uniform Guidelines defines an employment test as any employment procedure used as the basis for making an employment decision.

79. Content validity is a logical, non-statistical method used to identify the KSAs and other characteristics necessary to perform a job.

    ANSWER: True, 124

80. Concurrent validity studies use a sample of current applicants for the data collection.

    ANSWER: False, 125
    Concurrent validity tests current employees and correlates the scores with their performance ratings.

Essay

81.   Discuss the interrelationships among equal employment opportunity, affirmative action, and reverse discrimination.

ANSWER: 102-104
Equal employment requires that individuals be treated equally in employment-related actions. Affirmative action focuses on hiring, training, and promotion of protected-class members where they are under represented in an organization. Reverse discrimination may exist when a person is denied an opportunity because of preferences given to protected-class members.

82.   Discuss the following statement with reference to EEO laws and regulations: *"This is my business ... I founded it ... I can hire and fire whomever I choose without interference from the government."*

ANSWER: 104-108
An assortment of federal, state, and local laws limit the ability of a business to hire and fire at will. Regulations prohibit discrimination based on disability, age, race, color, religion, sex, ethnic and national origin, etc.. A business owner acting upon the sentiment expressed could face legal actions and possibly social and business consequences.

83.   Discuss in some detail two gender-based discrimination issues, other than sexual harassment. What, if any, legislation exists to address these issues?

ANSWER: 109-111
Discrimination in pay and benefits, discrimination in jobs and careers. Legislation includes Equal Pay Act (1963), Pregnancy Discrimination Act (1978), and Family and Medical Leave Act (1993).

84.   What are the major requirements of the Americans with Disabilities Act? How has the ADA impacted both employers and individuals with disabilities? What actions should an employer take to insure compliance with the ADA?

ANSWER: 112-113
Employers with 15 or more employees are to make reasonable accommodation for individuals with disabilities. Jobs must be analyzed to identify essential job functions. An undue hardship is a significant difficulty or expense imposed on an employer in making an accommodation for individuals with disabilities.

85.   How could a plant manager validate a new employment test that has been developed to select machine operators?

ANSWER: 123-127
The concurrent validity approach would test current operators and correlate the scores with their performance ratings. To measure predictive validity, test results of applicants are compared with their subsequent job performance. Content validity would identify the KSAs needed to perform the job and check that the test measured these KSAs.

Chapter 5

Managing Diversity and Equal Employment

Multiple Choice

1. Which of the following statements about diversity is true?
   A. Diversity is about racial preferences.
   B. Diversity is about the differences among people.
   C. Diversity occurs as the result of natural human interaction.
   D. Diversity recognized that conflict is inevitable.

   ANSWER: B, 138

2. Which of the following occurs as a result of diversity?
   A. Diversity initially leads to reduced tensions and conflicts in the workplace.
   B. Outright hostility and physical resistance have been common occurrences.
   C. Reverse discrimination is a common occurrence when organizations embrace diversity.
   D. Organizations find that a more diverse workplace is a strategic HR consideration.

   ANSWER: D, 138

3. Which of the following statements is true about demographic diversity in the workforce?
   A. The average age of the workforce is now considerable older than ever before.
   B. Asian women are the fastest growing segment of the workforce.
   C. Whites now make up less than 50% of the workforce.
   D. The number of women in the workforce is beginning to decline.

   ANSWER: A, 138

4. _____ is(are) seen as the primary way of overcoming hostility towards protected-class members.
   A. An affirmative action plan
   B. Flexible job assignments
   C. Diversity management programs
   D. Increased legal action

   ANSWER: C, 139

5.   Organizations that have proactively addressed diversity have experienced
     A.   strategic advantages in marketing their products globally.
     B.   success in recruiting and retaining workers from diverse backgrounds.
     C.   increased discrimination complaints and costs.
     D.   limitations in their range of decision alternatives.

     ANSWER: B, 141

6.   A study found that one-third of minority and female job candidates will rule out
     an employer because of
     A.   a lack of diversity-training programs.
     B.   inequitable salaries and benefits.
     C.   overt discrimination and prejudice related to sex or race.
     D.   perceived lack of diversity.

     ANSWER: D, 141

7.   For diversity management to succeed, the most crucial component is
     A.   organization-wide commitment beginning with top management.
     B.   a set of rewards for diversity efforts.
     C.   clearly defined outcomes for managers who fail to embrace diversity.
     D.   a strategic focus embracing diversity.

     ANSWER: A, 141

8.   What is the purpose of diversity training?
     A.   to teach the necessary behaviors for getting along in a diverse workforce
     B.   to draw attention to differences
     C.   to eliminate discrimination and harassment lawsuits
     D.   to implement affirmative action programs

     ANSWER: C, 141

9.   The components of diversity training include each of the following except
     A.   legal awareness.
     B.   harassment training.
     C.   cultural awareness.
     D.   sensitivity training.

     ANSWER: B, 141-142

10. A common complaint about diversity training is
     A.   it fosters resentment due to perceptions of reverse discrimination.
     B.   it suggests that white males are the "villains", the beneficiaries of past
             discrimination.
     C.   it costs too much money and produces few or no benefits.
     D.   it draws attention to differences, building walls rather than breaking
             them down.

     ANSWER: D, 143

11. A backlash against diversity efforts comes from _____ who believe they are set up as scapegoats for societal problems.
     A.   white males
     B.   protected-class members
     C.   single mothers
     D.   professional women

     ANSWER: A, 143

12. _____ requires covered employers to submit plans describing their attempts to narrow the gaps between the composition of their workforce and that of labor markets where they obtain employees.
     A.   Diversity strategies
     B.   Preferential selection
     C.   Affirmative action
     D.   Strategic management

     ANSWER: C, 144

13. Which of the following is identified part of affirmative action efforts?
     A.   employers establish quotas for hiring protected-class members
     B.   employers set goals, targets, and timetables
     C.   increased polarization and separation among gender and racial lines
     D.   preferences for certain groups which results in reverse discrimination

     ANSWER: B, 144

14. What is the result when a person is refused employment opportunities because of being the "wrong" race, sex, age, or other classification?
     A.   quota
     B.   unlawful discrimination
     C.   affirmative action
     D.   reverse discrimination

     ANSWER: D, 144

15. One factor that affects the status of affirmative action is the
     A.   composition of the U.S. Supreme Court.
     B.   amount of lobbying being done by special interest groups.
     C.   number of grievances being reported to government agencies.
     D.   mass media's attention and editorials.

     ANSWER: A, 145

16. What was the original purpose of the Civil Rights Act of 1964?
     A.   to end all employment discrimination
     B.   to establish equal pay for equal work
     C.   to address race and national origin discrimination
     D.   to provide legal remedies for victims of unlawful discrimination

     ANSWER: C, 146

17. Which is the fastest-growing segment of the U.S. population?
     A.   multiracial families
     B.   Hispanic population
     C.   persons under age 25
     D.   Americans with disabilities

     ANSWER: B, 147

18. Of the 800,000-900,000 immigrants arriving annually, workers with limited
     educational skills are coming primarily from
     A.   Eastern European countries
     B.   EEC countries, especially the Irish Republic.
     C.   Middle Eastern and Northern African countries
     D.   Mexico and poorer Latin American countries.

     ANSWER: D, 147

19. Why was the American Competitiveness and Workforce Improvement Act passed?
     A.   to increase the number of visas for highly skilled workers
     B.   to restrict the number of visas issued to unskilled and semi-skilled
           workers
     C.   to protect U.S. manufacturers from foreign imports
     D.   to provide fair wages for foreign workers employed by U.S. businesses
           overseas

     ANSWER: A, 147

20. _____ requires employers inspect I-9 forms and verification documents
     such as birth certificates, passports, visas, and work permits.
     A.   The Civil Rights Act
     B.   The American Competitiveness and Workforce Improvement Act
     C.   The Immigration Reform and Control Act
     D.   Executive Order 11246

     ANSWER: C, 148

21. Implications of the increase in racial and ethnic cultural diversity include:
     A.   employer-sponsored cultural awareness and diversity training will become
           less necessary.
     B.   the potential for harassment of racial and ethnic groups will increase.
     C.   English-only workplaces will become necessary.
     D.   enforced dress codes will become common in the workplace.

     ANSWER: B, 148

22. Nepotism refers to
     A.   favoritism in hiring.
     B.   a discriminatory policy.
     C.   an organization specifically selecting protected class individuals.
     D.   the practice of allowing relatives to work for the same employer.

     ANSWER: D, 150

23. The U.S. Department of Labor defines nontraditional jobs for women as
     A.   those in which women comprise 20% or less of the total number employed.
     B.   those jobs from which women have traditionally been excluded.
     C.   jobs where hazardous materials may cause birth defects during pregnancy.
     D.   jobs which traditionally pay low wages for women employees.

     ANSWER: A, 150

24. Policies of reassigning women from hazardous jobs to lower-paying jobs because
     of health-related concerns, including birth defects sustained during pregnancy,
     A.   are recommended as a way of reducing worker compensation premiums.
     B.   are usually left for supervisors to decide on a case-by-case basis.
     C.   have been ruled illegal by the Supreme Court.
     D.   are recommended as good corporate policy.

     ANSWER: C, 150-151

25. The _____ refers to discriminatory practices that have prevented women
     and other protected-class members from advancing to executive-level jobs.
     A.   old boys network
     B.   glass ceiling
     C.   pyramid effect
     D.   glass walls

     ANSWER: B, 151

26. A problem whereby women have tended to advance to senior management in a limited
     number of functional areas has been referred to as
     A.   the old boys network.
     B.   a pyramid effect.
     C.   glass ceiling.
     D.   glass elevators.

     ANSWER: D, 151

27. With regard to workplace relationships and romances, employment attorneys
     generally recommend that the HR manager
     A.   remind both parties of the company policy on sexual harassment.
     B   prohibit all workplace relationships and romances.
     C.   document all such relationships to minimize future harassment claims.
     D.   do nothing, since such romances are a part of human social interaction.

     ANSWER: A, 152

28. Most frequently, sexual harassment occurs in which of the following scenarios?
     A.   a male harasses a female co-worker
     B.   an employee harasses an employee of the same sex
     C.   a male supervisor harasses a woman within his power structure
     D.   a manager of either sex harasses a subordinate of the opposite sex

     ANSWER: C, 152

29. *Quid pro quo* harassment occurs when
     A.   the harassment has the effect of unreasonably interfering with work performance or psychological well-being.
     B.   employment outcomes are linked to the individual's granting sexual favors.
     C.   intimidating or offensive working conditions are created.
     D.   an employee demands sexual preference as a condition of employment.

     ANSWER: B, 153

30. _____ occurs when the individual's work performance or psychological well-being is unreasonable affected by intimidating or offensive working conditions.
     A.   *Quid pro quo* harassment
     B.   Sexual misconduct
     C.   Victimization
     D.   Hostile environment harassment

     ANSWER: D, 153

31. Which of the following is necessary to prove sexual harassment involving the creation of a hostile environment?
     A.   the conduct interfered unreasonably with an employee's work performance
     B.   the complainant suffered loss of earnings or job loss
     C.   the employee is a member of a protected class
     D.   sexual extortion existed

     ANSWER: A, 153

32. A male who continually asks a female co-worker if they could "get together after work" would be an example of
     A.   someone who can't "get the hint."
     B.   romance at work.
     C.   hostile work environment harassment.
     D.   *quid pro quo* sexual harassment.

     ANSWER: C, 153

33. An employer may avoid liability for sexual harassment in which of the following situations?
     A.   the victim and alleged harasser were both heterosexual males
     B.   the employer took reasonable care to prohibit sexual harassment
     C.   the employee did not suffer any tangible employment action
     D.   the employer had no knowledge of the offensive behavior

     ANSWER: B, 155

34. Employers generally are held responsible for sexual harassment
     A.   if the victim reported the incident.
     B.   unless they had no knowledge of the harassment behaviors.
     C.   if they knew of the behavior.
     D.   if the employee suffers tangible employment actions.

     ANSWER: D, 155

35. An employer's defense in a sexual harassment complaint is aided when
   A.   the employer investigates and takes action when complaint are voiced.
   B.   the employer immediately dismisses the alleged harasser.
   C.   the victim is immediately transferred to another supervisor.
   D.   the alleged harasser is moved to a work site remote from the complainant.

   ANSWER: A, 155-156

36. In the U.S., the medium age of the population is
   A.   remaining constant
   B.   exhibits a normal distribution
   C.   increasing
   D.   decreasing

   ANSWER: C, 156

37. The Age Discrimination in Employment Act protects people in what age range?
   A.   under age 25
   B.   over age 40
   C.   40-65 years old
   D.   40-70 years old.

   ANSWER: B, 156

38. The Age Discrimination in Employment Act
   A.   permits mandatory retirement at age 65.
   B.   permits mandatory retirement at age 70.
   C.   regulates early retirement plans.
   D.   forbids mandatory retirement in most circumstances.

   ANSWER: D, 156

39. Why have many organizations offered early retirement plans?
   A.   They reduce employment costs.
   B.   They are the most legal way to downsize.
   C.   The older employees are often unable to adjust to new technology.
   D.   It is one way to "get around" the ADEA.

   ANSWER: A, 156

40. When is it possible to terminate an employee over age 40?
   A.   when downsizing is necessary following a merger
   B.   when the union contract has a mandatory-retirement-age clause
   C.   when there are documented performance deficiencies
   D.   when a more qualified younger worker is hired

   ANSWER: C, 156

41. The Older Workers Benefit Protection Act of 1990 was passed to ensure that
     A.   pension plans were administered fairly regardless of an employee's age.
     B.   equal treatment for older workers occurs in early retirement or severance situations.
     C.   medical insurance would not be denied to retirees
     D.   companies fund retirement benefits in a financially-sound manner.

     ANSWER: B, 156

42. One purpose of the Older Workers Benefit Protection Act (OWBPA) was to
     A.   safeguard the Social Security benefits for retired workers.
     B.   protect older workers from having their medical insurance policies canceled as a cost-saving measure.
     C.   ensure that the Medicare program was fully funded.
     D.   protect older workers when early retirement and downsizing programs include severance agreements and employee wavers.

     ANSWER: D, 156

43. A change in Social Security regulations has
     A.   allowed individuals over age 65 to earn more per year without affecting their Social Security payments.
     B.   increased the employer's share of Social Security contributions.
     C.   removed the automatic cost-of-living adjustments to monthly payments.
     D.   encouraged individuals to retire at age 60 while collecting full Social Security benefits.

     ANSWER: A, 157

44. _____ is an approach in which employees reduce their workloads and pay.
     A.   Early retirement
     B.   Workforce sharing
     C.   Phased retirement
     D.   Voluntary downsizing

     ANSWER: C, 157

45. Which of the following is true about a phased retirement strategy?
     A.   firms rehire their retirees as part-time workers
     B.   it allows older workers to have more personal flexibility
     C.   it is an alternative to mandatory retirement
     D.   it reduces employment costs

     ANSWER: B, 157

46. It is estimated that _____ Americans with disabilities are covered by the ADA.
     A.   about half of all
     B.   more than 80 million
     C.   less than 20 million
     D.   at least 55 million

     ANSWER: D, 157

47. A Society for Human Resource Management survey identified _____ as the major employment barrier faced by people with disabilities.
     A.   lack of experience
     B.   cost of training
     C.   cost of accommodations
     D.   attitudes or stereotypes

     ANSWER: A, 157

48. The majority of ADA complaints filed with the EEOC relate to
     A.   individuals with mental disabilities
     B.   the failure to provide reasonable accommodation
     C.   the discharge of employees with disabilities or who became disabled
     D.   discrimination against individuals with a life-threatening disease

     ANSWER: C, 158

49. A consequence of the Americans with Disabilities Act is that employers must
     A.   redesign jobs to provide employment for persons with a variety of disabilities.
     B.   make reasonable accommodation to provide access to work areas and in the assignment of work tasks.
     C.   establish an affirmative action plan for hiring persons with disabilities.
     D.   revise medical insurance plans to provide coverage for disabled employees.

     ANSWER: B, 158

50. Key to making reasonable accommodations for individuals with disabilities is to
     A.   restructure the staffing function to minimize the probability of hiring a disabled individual.
     B.   ask job candidates about their need for special accommodations.
     C.   redesign jobs to provide employment for persons with a variety of disabilities.
     D.   identify the essential job functions then determine what accommodations are reasonable.

     ANSWER: D, 158

51. According to the Job Accommodations Network, half of all employer accommodations
     A.   cost less than $500.
     B.   can be classified as "causing undue hardship."
     C.   cannot be considered "reasonable."
     D.   cost little or nothing.

     ANSWER: A, 158

52. Which of the following is true about employees claiming mental disabilities?
     A.   Employers should be alert because mental illness is easy to fake.
     B.   There are no ADA guidelines for accommodating non-physical disabilities.
     C.   Employers should obtain medical verification for claims of mental illness.
     D.   Mentally ill employees present a threat to other employees.

     ANSWER: C, 159

53.   It is estimated that _____ of all ADA claims are based on psychiatric
      or mental illness.
      A.   less than 7%
      B.   about 16%
      C.   almost half
      D.   over 25%

      ANSWER: B, 159

54.   When considering accommodation requests for mental disabilities employers should
      A.   suggest that the employee obtain leave under the firm's disability plan.
      B.   inform other employees of the mental disability accommodation request.
      C.   refer the employee to the Employee Assistance Program coordinator.
      D.   treat such requests in the same manner as physical disability requests.

      ANSWER: D, 159

55.   The U.S. Supreme Court has determined that individuals with life-threatening
      illnesses such as AIDS
      A.   are covered by the ADA.
      B.   are to be isolated from other employees.
      C.   are entitled to a medical leave without pay.
      D.   are entitled to leave under the FMLA.

      ANSWER: A, 159

56.   What is true about employees who indicate that they will not work with a victim
      of a life-threatening illness?
      A.   OSHA gives them the right to walk off the job.
      B.   The employers are required to accommodate their fears.
      C.   Their refusal to work is not protected by law.
      D.   ADA regulations require that such persons should be discharged.

      ANSWER: C, 159

57.   Which of the following is true about religious expression in the workplace?
      A.   Employers must accommodate the religious practices of all employees.
      B.   Discriminating against employees for their religious beliefs is
             prohibited.
      C.   Employers are not required to adjust work schedules to accommodate
             religious observances.
      D.   Employers can prohibit employees from religious expression at work.

      ANSWER: B, 160

58.   To comply with Title VII of the Civil Rights Act of 1964 concerning religion,
      employers should
      A.   prohibit all religious expression in the workplace.
      B.   ensure that one employee's religious expression does not interfere with
             other employees.
      C.   establish a dress code that is "religion-neutral."
      D.   make reasonable accommodation of employees' religious beliefs.

      ANSWER: D, 160

59. What is the present situation with respect to legislation protecting individuals with differing sexual orientations?
  A.   Only a few cities and states have passed such laws.
  B.   Sexual orientation can only be considered if it is a *bona fide* occupational qualification.
  C.   Employers cannot inquire into a candidate's sexual behavior.
  D.   Federal law prohibits discrimination based on sexual orientation.

ANSWER: A, 160

60. Which of the following is true regarding transgendered and transsexual individuals?
  A.   Federal court cases have determined that employers must make reasonable accommodation for transgendered and transsexual employees.
  B.   Title VII prohibits discrimination based on sexual identity.
  C.   The EEOC has ruled that sex discrimination under Title VII applies to a person's gender at birth.
  D.   The ADA lists sexual identity disorders as a disability.

ANSWER: C, 160-161

True and False

61. Diversity management is concerned with developing affirmative action initiatives to achieve a workforce that reflects the ethnic, gender, and lifestyle makeup of the surrounding community.

ANSWER: False, 138-138
The purpose of diversity management is to develop HR strategies that value all people equally, regardless of their differences.

62. Diversity training has proven to be an effective use of training expenditures.

ANSWER: False, 142-143
Relatively few studies have been done on the effectiveness of diversity training. There is some concern that the programs may be seen as entertaining but produce few, if any, long-term changes in people's attitudes and behaviors towards others.

63. Affirmative action efforts involve employers setting goals, targets, and time tables to specify how many of which types of individuals they hope to have in their workforce in the future.

ANSWER: True, 144

64. The original purpose of the Civil Rights Act of 1964 was to establish affirmative action programs.

ANSWER: False, 146
The original purpose was to address race and national origin discrimination.

65.   High birthrates in the minority community is responsible for much of the growth
       of racial and ethnic groups in the workforce.

       ANSWER: False 147
       Much of the growth in the various racial and ethnic groups is due to immigration
       from other countries.

66.   The Courts have generally upheld attempts by employers to ban employees from
       speaking foreign languages at all times in work areas.

       ANSWER: False, 148
       EEOC guidelines state that employers may require workers to speak only English
       at certain times or in certain situations, but the business necessity of the
       requirements must be justified.

67.   The Family and Medical Leave Act (FMLA) applies to both male and female
       employees who are new parents, either through birth or adoptions.

       ANSWER: True, 149

68.   Employer anti-nepotism policies have been outlawed by the courts because they
       often discriminate against the female spouses of current employees.

       ANSWER: False, 150
       The courts have upheld anti-nepotism policies.

69.   Employers may not restrict pregnant women from working at jobs that could cause
       birth defects.

       ANSWER: True, 151

70.   An employer would not liable if an employee were harassed by a customer or some
       other non-employee.

       ANSWER: False, 153
       Employees have won sexual harassment complaints against their employers who took
       no action against a third party causing the harassment.

71.   Withholding a raise from someone who refuses to date you is an example of *quid
       pro quo* harassment.

       ANSWER: True, 153

72.   A manager who permits a lewd posters to be displayed in the workplace may be
       creating a hostile work environment leading to complaints of sexual harassment.

       ANSWER: True, 153

73. Mature workers can be legitimately denied employment if they are determined to be overqualified for the specific position.

     ANSWER: False, 156
     The courts have ruled that the term *overqualified* may have been used as a codeword for workers being too old and thus causing them not to be considered for employment.

74. The Older Workers Benefit Protection Act (OWBPA) was passed to safeguard the Social Security benefits for retired workers.

     ANSWER: False, 156
     The act was passed to ensure that equal treatment for older workers occurs in early retirement or severance situations.

75. Employment-related benefits and work schedules must remain unchanged to avoid giving special treatment for individuals with disabilities.

     ANSWER: False, 158
     The Americans with Disabilities Act requires employers to make reasonable accommodations for individuals with disabilities. This may require providing additional benefits and/or flexible work schedules to accommodate the special needs of disabled persons.

76. If an employee develops a disability, a reasonable accommodation may involve shifting that employee to a different job where the disability does not affect job performance as much.

     ANSWER: True, 159

77. If an employee refuses to work with a person inflicted with a life-threatening illness, such as AIDS, that employee could be subject to disciplinary action up to and including discharge.

     ANSWER: True, 159

78. An employer could not prohibit a Muslim employee from having a beard, if such a prohibition would violate the worker's religious standards.

     ANSWER: True, 160

79. Employee who discuss their religious views with other employees at work could be creating a hostile environment requiring employer action.

     ANSWER: True, 160

80. In the absence of national legislation, only a few cities and states have passed laws outlawing discrimination against individuals with differing sexual orientations.

     ANSWER: True, 160

Essay

81.   What is meant by the term "diversity?" Why is diversity training an important concern for HR management?

        ANSWER: 138-143
        Diversity refers to differences among people, including age, race, religion, gender, and national origin. A diverse population affects an organization's application pool, providing an opportunity to tap a broader set of people, ideas, and experiences. This can help an organization better adapt to customer needs. Diversity brings the possibility of conflict. Diversity training has three components: legal awareness, cultural awareness, and sensitivity training. Its purpose is to minimize discrimination and harassment lawsuits.

82.   Describe the purpose and history of affirmative action. How can employers comply with affirmative action requirements?

        ANSWER: 143-146
        Government regulations require federal government contractors to take affirmative action to overcome the effects of past discriminatory practices. Employers must develop an affirmative action plan that attempts to narrow the gap between the composition of their workforce and that of labor markets where they obtain employees. This plan sets goals, targets, and time tables.

83.   What is the "glass ceiling" and the "glass elevator?" How can employers "break the glass?"

        ANSWER: 151
        The glass ceiling refers to discriminatory practices that have prevented women and other protected-class members from advancing to executive-level jobs. Glass elevators refer to the fact that women have tended to advance to senior management in a limited number of functional areas. Suggestions for "breaking the glass" include: mentoring programs, career rotation, Board memberships, and special arrangements for balancing work/family responsibilities.

84.   What is sexual harassment? What actions can an organization take to minimize the probability of sexual harassment charges being filed?

        ANSWER: 152-156
        Sexual harassment - any action that is sexually directed, unwanted, subject the worker to adverse employment conditions or create a hostile work environment. It may be *quid pro quo* or hostile environment harassment, and is not limited to male/female behavior. Organizations may limit liability by producing evidence that it took reasonable care to prohibit sexual harassment.

85.   What are the legal and practical issues associated with mature workers in organizations?

ANSWER: 156-157
As the population has aged, there are many mature workers in organizations. The Age Discrimination in Employment Act prohibits discrimination against workers over age 40. The Older Workers Benefits Protection Act was passed to ensure equal treatment for mature workers in early retirement or severance situations. Some organizations have actively recruited older workers to benefit from their experience, offering part-time, phased retirement, or independent contractor working arrangements.

Chapter 6

Jobs

Multiple Choice

1. Work is defined as
    A.   what a person does for eight hours a day.
    B.   effort directed toward producing or accomplishing results.
    C.   a collection of tasks and duties performed by one person.
    D.   obligations to perform certain tasks and duties.

    ANSWER: B, 168

2. A _____ is a grouping of tasks, duties, and responsibilities that constitutes the total work assignment for employees.
    A.   job family
    B.   position category
    C.   KSA
    D.   job

    ANSWER: D, 168

3. _____ analysis studies the way work moves through the organization.
    A.   Workflow
    B.   Job
    C.   Performance
    D.   Throughput

    ANSWER: A, 169

4. The three phases of business processes re-engineering are
    A.   ideas, technology, people.
    B.   unfreezing, changing, refreezing.
    C.   rethink, redesign, retool.
    D.   job analysis, job description, job specification.

    ANSWER: C, 170

5.   _____ refers to organizing tasks, duties, and responsibilities into
     a productive unit of work.
     A.   Job analysis
     B.   Job design
     C.   Job characteristics
     D.   Job evaluation

     ANSWER: B, 171

6.   Job design addresses the content of jobs and
     A.   the interrelationships among all jobs in the organization.
     B.   the job's requirements.
     C.   the qualifications needed for someone to effectively perform the jobs'
            functions.
     D.   the effect of jobs on employees.

     ANSWER: D, 171

7.   Job enlargement involves
     A.   broadening the scope of a job by expanding the number of different tasks
            to be performed.
     B.   increasing the depth of a job to provide more autonomy.
     C.   increasing the amount of impact the job has on other people.
     D.   shifting a person from job to job to increase variety.

     ANSWER: A, 172

8.   When you increase the depth of a job by adding responsibility for planning,
     organizing, controlling, and evaluating the job, _____ has occurred.
     A.   job enlargement
     B.   task significance
     C.   job enrichment
     D.   task character improvement

     ANSWER: C, 172

9.   Which of the following is <u>not</u> an example of actions that enrich a job?
     A.   Increasing a person's accountability for work by reducing external
            control.
     B.   Rotating a person among different jobs to break the monotony.
     C.   Giving feedback reports directly to employees.
     D.   Giving a person an entire job rather than just a piece of the work.

     ANSWER: B, 172

10. Job _____ is the process of shifting a person from job to job.
     A.   enlargement
     B.   scope
     C.   responsibility
     D.   rotation

     ANSWER: D, 172

11. The extent to which the work requires several different activities for successful completion indicates its
    A.   skill variety
    B.   enlargement.
    C.   task identity.
    D.   enrichment

    ANSWER: A, 173

12. _____ is the amount of impact the job has on other people.
    A.   Experienced responsibility
    B.   Autonomy
    C.   Task significance
    D.   Task identity

    ANSWER: C, 174

13. A organizational team formed to address specific problems, improve work processes, and enhance product and service quality, is called
    A.   shamrock team.
    B.   a special-purpose team.
    C.   a production cell.
    D.   self-directed work team.

    ANSWER: B, 174

14. The _____ is a small group of employees who monitor productivity and quality and suggest solutions to problems.
    A.   TQM
    B.   special-purpose team
    C.   production cell
    D.   quality circle

    ANSWER: D, 174

15. _____ are groupings of workers who produce entire products or components of products.
    A.   Production cells
    B.   Self-directed work teams
    C.   Quality circles
    D.   Shamrock teams

    ANSWER: A, 175

16. The _____ is composed of individuals who are assigned a cluster of tasks, duties, and responsibilities to be accomplished.
    A.   special-purpose team
    B.   quality circle
    C.   Self-directed work teams
    D.   autonomous work group

    ANSWER: C, 175

17. Which of the following has not been identified for the successful use of self-directed work teams?
     A.   Teams have authority to make decisions.
     B.   Teams encourage a high level of organizational commitment.
     C.   Teams value and endorse dissent.
     D.   Teams use "shamrock" structures and have some variation in membership.

     ANSWER: B, 176

18. In which of the following scheduling arrangements do employees work a set number of hours per day but vary starting and ending times?
     A.   virtual office
     B.   compressed workday
     C.   work sharing
     D.   flextime

     ANSWER: D, 177

19. In the _____ arrangement, a full week's work is accomplished in fewer than five days.
     A.   compressed workweek
     B.   virtual office
     C.   telecommuting
     D.   flextime

     ANSWER: A, 177

20. _____ employees go to work via electronic computing and telecommunications equipment.
     A.   Hoteling
     B.   Contingent
     C.   Telecommuting
     D.   Virtual

     ANSWER: C, 178

21. In which of the following work arrangements do workers check in with an office concierge, carry their own nameplates with them, and are assigned to work cubicles or small offices?
     A.   virtual office
     B.   hoteling
     C.   telecommuting
     D.   contingent workplace

     ANSWER: B, 178

22. In the _____ arrangement, work is done anywhere, anytime, and people are judged more on results than on "putting in time."
     A.   telecommuting
     B.   hoteling
     C.   flexiplace
     D.   virtual office

     ANSWER: D, 178

23. Job analysis is a systematic way to
    A. gather and analyze information about the content, context and human requirements of jobs.
    B. analyze the distinct, identifiable work activities involved in a specific job classification.
    C. evaluate the quality of job performance of employees.
    D. evaluate the strategic determination of the relative worth of jobs.

    ANSWER: A, 179

24. A distinctive, identifiable work activity composed of motions is a
    A. duty.
    B. job.
    C. task.
    D. position.

    ANSWER: C, 180

25. A _____ is a larger work segment composed of several tasks that are performed by an individual.
    A. responsibility
    B. duty
    C. position
    D. job

    ANSWER: B, 180

26. _____ are obligations to perform certain tasks and duties.
    A. Positions
    B. Jobs
    C. Job descriptions
    D. Responsibilities

    ANSWER: D, 180

27. In its most basic form, job analysis is necessary for
    A. developing job description and specifications.
    B. planning the design and redesign of jobs.
    C. ensuring pay equity.
    D. developing a performance management system.

    ANSWER: A, 180

28. Why is relying on supervisors for job analysis information not always advisable?
    A. They might tend to inflate the importance of the job.
    B. They might feel threatened providing top management with this type of information.
    C. They might not know what their employees actually do on the job.
    D. They have a unique perspective of the job.

    ANSWER: C, 180

29.   In a typical division of job analysis responsibilities, a manager would
      A.   seek assistance from experts for difficult or unusual analyses.
      B.   identify performance standards based on jab analysis information.
      C.   prepare and coordinate job analysis procedures.
      D.   write job descriptions and specifications for review.

      ANSWER: B, 181

30.   Job analysis data can be gathered by the following methods:
      A.   interviews, historical data, questionnaires.
      B.   questionnaires, experimentation, observations.
      C.   observations, market data, experimentation.
      D.   observations, interviews, questionnaires.

      ANSWER: D, 183

31.   With respect to observations as a job analysis technique,
      A.   the method is limited because many jobs do not have a complete and easily observed job cycle.
      B.   the manager or job analyst should make only one observation to avoid contamination of results.
      C.   avoid repetitive jobs. Concentrate on "knowledge work."
      D.   observation must be continuous, not based on sampling.

      ANSWER: A, 183

32.   The work sampling type of observation
      A.   gives a more detailed picture of the work.
      B.   is better received by the workers since it is less disruptive to their work schedules.
      C.   determines the content and pace of a typical workday through statistical sampling of current actions.
      D.   is better for complex and non-repetitive jobs.

      ANSWER: C, 183

33.   Which of the following is true about the use of group interviews to gather job analysis information?
      A.   They are relatively inexpensive given the information obtained.
      B.   They are probably most appropriate for difficult-to-define jobs.
      C.   They are less likely to result in "job inflation."
      D.   The open structure permits in-depth insights into the job.

      ANSWER: B, 185

34.   What is a major advantage of the questionnaire method of gathering data on jobs?
      A.   A checklist is uncomplicated and easy for the employees to complete.
      B.   Anonymity of questionnaires permit employees to give valid information.
      C.   You obtain such a large body of data that follow-up observations and discussion are unnecessary.
      D.   Information on a large number of jobs can be collected inexpensively in a relatively short period of time.

      ANSWER: D, 185

35. The Position Analysis Questionnaire (PAQ) focuses on the _____ elements that describe behaviors necessary to do the job.
     A. worker-oriented
     B. organization-oriented
     C. market-oriented
     D. job-oriented

     ANSWER: A, 186

36. Which of the following is a characteristic of computerized job analysis?
     A. difficulty in identifying mismatches between job scores and salary survey data.
     B. production of technical reports which make it difficult to identify specific KSAs required in the job.
     C. a reduction in the time and effort involved in writing job descriptions.
     D. results cannot be used to develop job evaluation weights.

     ANSWER: C, 186

37. The Functional Job Analysis (FJA) method examines the three components of
     A. clerical, professional, and technical job elements.
     B. data, people, and things.
     C. activities, knowledge, and skills.
     D. interpersonal, executive, and information job elements.

     ANSWER: B, 187

38. The _____ is a standardized data source provided by the U.S. Department of Labor.
     A. Job Information Guide
     B. Occupational Title Index
     C. Dictionary of Job Titles.
     D. Dictionary of Occupational Titles.

     ANSWER: D, 187

39. How is the Dictionary of Occupational Titles (DOT) useful to a manager or HR specialist?
     A. a starting point when confronted with preparing a large number of job descriptions
     B. a defense in an EEOC suit
     C. to compare technological similarities of different jobs.
     D. to conduct wage classifications.

     ANSWER: A, 187

40. _____ transforms mountains of data into precise, focused, information that anyone can understand and use.
     A. The Dictionary of Occupational Titles
     B. Functional job analysis
     C. O*Net
     D. The Internet

     ANSWER: C, 187

41. Job analysis can be a threatening experience for both managers and employees
    A.   if it highlights discrepancies between a manager's expectations and those of the employee.
    B.   if it identifies the difference between what currently is being performed and what *should* be done.
    C.   if it indicates that the job is no longer necessary for the organization to achieve its goals.
    D.   if it illustrates a poor record of performing the essential job functions.

    ANSWER: B, 187

42. Because job analysis information is often used for compensation purposes, employees and managers have a tendency to
    A.   cooperate with the job analyst.
    B.   resent this examination of their jobs.
    C.   use this as an opportunity to complain about their supervisors.
    D.   inflate the importance and significance of their jobs.

    ANSWER: D, 188

43. Which of the following was identified as an organizational problem that often occurs as part of the job analysis process?
    A.   title inflation
    B.   a managerial conflict between what *is* and what *should be* done
    C.   a focus on the job, rather than on the job incumbent
    D.   an over emphasis on the legal concerns

    ANSWER: A, 188

44. Which of the following is a problem that occurs when conducting a job analysis?
    A.   using the job description only as a broad outline of a job's duties
    B.   modesty when describing a job's importance
    C.   an overemphasis on the current employee
    D.   an emphasis on the employees' job satisfaction and involvement

    ANSWER: C, 189

45. The 1978 Uniform Selection Guidelines make it clear that HR requirements must _____ if employers are to defend their actions as a business necessity.
    A.   not discriminate against protected-class members
    B.   be tied to specific job-related factors
    C.   be limited to actual on-the-job behaviors
    D.   apply to all employees

    ANSWER: B, 190

46. Employers are now placing increased emphasis on developing and maintaining current and accurate job descriptions as a result of the passage of the
    A.   Family and Medical Leave Act.
    B.   Equal Pay Act.
    C.   Civil Rights Act of 1991.
    D.   Americans with Disabilities Act.

    ANSWER: D, 190

47.   _____ are the fundamental duties of a job.
       A.   Essential job functions
       B.   Minimum job elements
       C.   Primary requirements
       D.   Essential KSAs

       ANSWER: A, 190

48.   Marginal functions are those duties that are part of a job
       A.   that a disabled person cannot perform.
       B.   that most disabled individuals can perform with minor assistance.
       C.   but are incidental or ancillary to the purpose and nature of a job.
       D.   and essential to its operation.

       ANSWER: C, 190

49.   A job description identifies
       A.   the knowledge, skills, and abilities an individual needs to do the job
             satisfactorily.
       B.   the tasks, duties, and responsibilities of a job.
       C.   what the job accomplishes and what performance is considered satisfactory.
       D.   the education, experience, and work skill requirements of a job.

       ANSWER: B, 191

50.   A job _____ identifies what is done, why it is done, where it is done,
       and briefly, how it is done.
       A.   analysis
       B.   performance standard
       C.   specification
       D.   description

       ANSWER: D, 191

51.   Performance standards should flow directly from
       A.   a job description
       B.   job specifications
       C.   KSAs.
       D.   the essential elements of the job.

       ANSWER: A, 191

52.   _____ indicate what the job accomplishes and how performance is
       measured in key areas of the job description.
       A.   Job specifications
       B.   Job standards
       C.   Performance standards
       D.   Employee competencies

       ANSWER: C, 191

53.   Job specifications list
       A.   what the job accomplishes and how performance is measured in key areas of
             the job description.
       B.   the knowledge, skills, and abilities an individual needs to perform the
             job satisfactorily.
       C.   the tasks, duties, and responsibilities of a job.
       D.   the education, experience, and work skill requirements of a job.

       ANSWER: B, 192

54.   An example of a _____ for a secretary would be "types 50 words per
       minute with no more than two errors."
       A.   job description
       B.   KSA
       C.   performance standard
       D.   job specification

       ANSWER: D, 192

55.   The _____ section of the job description gives the job title,
       reporting relationships, department, location, and date of analysis.
       A.   identification
       B.   general summary
       C.   essential functions and duties
       D.   specification requirements

       ANSWER: A, 193

56.   Clear, precise statements on the major tasks, duties, and responsibilities
       performed are contained in the _____ section of the job description.
       A.   identification
       B.   general summary
       C.   essential functions and duties
       D.   specification requirements

       ANSWER: C, 193

57.   An accurate _____ gives the qualifications needed to perform the job
       satisfactorily.
       A.   job description
       B.   job specification
       C.   job standard
       D.   performance standard

       ANSWER: B, 193

58.   What information should be provided in the job specification to ensure
       compliance with ADA regulations?
       A.   essential job functions
       B.   disclaimer that it is not a "contract"
       C.   performance standards
       D.   accommodations that might or might not be possible

       ANSWER: D, 193

59. Basic characteristics that can be linked to enhanced performance by individuals or teams, are called
    A. competencies.
    B. responsibilities.
    C. duties.
    D. tasks.

    ANSWER: A, 195

60. The competency approach to job analysis considers
    A. the tasks, duties, knowledge, and skills associated with a job.
    B. the qualifications of the job holder.
    C. how the knowledge and skills are used.
    D. how performance will be assessed.

    ANSWER: C, 195

True and False

61. Job design involves the content of jobs and the effect of jobs on employees.

    ANSWER: True, 171

62. Job enlargement is achieved by adding employee responsibility.

    ANSWER: False, 172
    Job enlargement broadens the scope of a job while job enrichment increases the depth by adding employee responsibility.

63. In the job characteristics model, task identity is defined as the extent of individual freedom and discretion in the work and its scheduling.

    ANSWER: False, 173
    This is, in fact, the definition of "autonomy." Task identity is defined as the extent to which the job includes a whole identifiable unit of work.

64. Production cells are small groups of employees who monitor productivity and quality and suggest solutions to problems.

    ANSWER: False, 174-175
    Quality circles monitor productivity and quality. Production cells are groupings of workers who produce entire products or components of products.

65. The self-directed work team is composed of individuals who are assigned a cluster of tasks, duties, and responsibilities to be accomplished.

    ANSWER: True, 175

66. A shamrock team is composed of a core of members, resource experts who join the team as appropriate, and part-time/temporary members as needed.

    ANSWER: True, 176

67. Hoteling is a work arrangement where employees' offices are wherever they are.

    ANSWER: False, 178
    Hoteling is where workers check in with an office concierge, carry their own nameplates with them, and are assigned to work cubicles or small offices. A "virtual office" is where employees' offices are wherever they are.

68. Job analysis refers to organizing tasks, duties, and responsibilities into a productive unit of work.

    ANSWER: False, 179
    Job analysis is a systematic way to gather and analyze information about the content, context, and the human requirements of jobs.

69. Without the foundation of job analysis, it is difficult for an organization to defend its recruiting and selection procedures, performance appraisal system, employee disciplinary actions, and pay practices.

    ANSWER: True, 179

70. A task is a distinct, identifiable work activity composed of motions, whereas a duty is a larger work segment composed of several tasks that are performed by an individual.

    ANSWER: True, 180

71. One job analysis method requires that employees "observe" their own performance by keeping a diary of their job duties, noting how frequently they are performed and the time required for each duty.

    ANSWER: True, 184

72. The Position Analysis Questionnaire (PAQ) focuses on "worker-oriented" elements that describe behaviors necessary to do the job, rather than on "job-oriented" elements that describe the technical aspects of the work.

    ANSWER: True, 186

73. The primary purpose of job analysis is to comply with government laws and regulations.

    ANSWER: False, 190
    Legal compliance is just one of the purposes of job analysis.

74. Job analysis can help determine whether someone should be classified as exempt or nonexempt under wage/hour laws.

    ANSWER: True, 191

75. A job description tells what a job accomplishes and what performance is considered satisfactory in each area of the job.

     ANSWER: False, 191
     A job description identifies the tasks, duties, and responsibilities of a job. Performance standards indicate what a job accomplishes.

76. The job specification should list the knowledge, skills, and abilities of the ideal candidate.

     ANSWER: False, 192
     Job specifications should reflect what is necessary for satisfactory job performance, not what the "ideal" candidate should have.

77. The current incumbent's job qualifications are usually a good indication of what is necessary to perform the job satisfactorily.

     ANSWER: False, 192
     Actually, the current employee's job qualifications often exceed the minimum KSAs required.

78. The components of job specifications provide information necessary to determine what accommodations might and might not be possible under ADA regulations.

     ANSWER: True, 193

79. The competency approach to job analysis focuses on the educational qualifications needed by potential job candidates.

     ANSWER: False, 195
     The competency approach focuses on how knowledge and skills are used to achieve superior performance.

80. The competency approach meets the legal standard to justify employment decisions.

     ANSWER: False, 196
     While traditional job analysis approaches have been used successfully to substantiate employment decisions, there is little legal precedent regarding competency analysis.

Essay

81.   How has re-engineering affected the design of jobs?

        ANSWER: 170-171
        The purpose of re-engineering is to improve such activities as product
        development, customer service, and service delivery. It may ultimately require
        the use of work teams, training employees to do more than one job, and
        reorganizing operations, workflow, and offices to simplify and speed work. Much
        of the change is made possible by technology.

82.   What are some of the alternatives to the traditional work schedule of a full-
        time, eight-hour day at the employers place of business?

        ANSWER: 177-178
        Alternatives include flextime, compressed workweek, voluntary part-time, shift
        work, telecommuting, hoteling, and virtual office.

83.   Discuss the statement: "Job analysis is the most basic function of human
        resource management."

        ANSWER: 179-180, 190-193
        Job analysis involves collecting information on the characteristics of a job
        that differentiates it from other jobs. It is necessary for all HR activities,
        compliance with ADA regulations, and defense in an EEO complaint.

84.   Describe four common job analysis methods., What are the advantages and
        limitations of each?

        ANSWER: 183-187
        Common methods are observations, interviews, questionnaires, and specialized
        methods of analysis. Combinations of these methods are frequently used.

85.   What impact has the Americans with Disabilities Act has on the job analysis
        process?

        ANSWER: 190-193
        Employers need job analysis to identify the essential functions of each job,
        including the physical demands and environmental condition of jobs. Employers
        must make reasonable accommodation for individuals with disabilities.

Chapter 7

Recruiting in Labor Markets

Multiple Choice

1. The _____ process matches people with jobs.
    A.   HR planning.
    B.   staffing.
    C.   recruiting.
    D.   selection.

    ANSWER: B, 202

2. The process of generating a pool of qualified applicants for organizational jobs is called
    A.   requisitioning.
    B.   acquiring.
    C.   pre-selecting.
    D.   recruiting

    ANSWER: D, 202

3. If the number of available candidates only equals the number of people to be hired
    A.   no real selection is required
    B.   there can be perfect matching of jobs with people.
    C.   the staffing process has been successful.
    D.   the labor market is "tight."

    ANSWER: A 202

4. _____ are the external supply pool from which organizations attract employees.
    A.   Employment offices
    B.   Recruitment sites
    C.   Labor markets
    D.   Applicant pools

    ANSWER: C, 202

5.   The _____ includes all individuals available for selection, if all
     possible recruitment strategies are used.
     A.   manpower pool.
     B.   labor force population
     C.   applicant pool.
     D.   applicant population.

     ANSWER: B, 202

6.   A subset of the labor force population that is available for selection using a
     particular recruiting approach is called the
     A.   manpower pool.
     B.   labor force population.
     C.   applicant pool.
     D.   applicant population.

     ANSWER: D, 202

7.   Recruiting decisions that affect the nature of the applicant population include
     all of the following except
     A.   affirmative action plan.
     B.   recruiting method.
     C.   recruiting message.
     D.   applicant qualifications required.

     ANSWER: A, 202

8.   A(n) _____ labor market exists when the demand for employees exceeds
     the supply of people with the appropriate qualifications.
     A.   loose
     B.   ideal
     C.   tight
     D.   buyers'

     ANSWER: C, 203

9.   The _____ pool consists of all persons who are actually evaluated for
     selection.
     A.   selection
     B.   applicant
     C.   manpower
     D.   recruitment

     ANSWER: B, 202

10. Which of the following was **NOT** listed as ways to identify labor markets?
     A.   geographic area
     B.   industry and occupational
     C.   educational and technical qualifications
     D.   income level

     ANSWER: D, 203-204

11. Which of the following is a typical responsibility of the HR unit in the recruiting process?
    A.   forecasts recruiting needs
    B.   determine KSAs needed from applicants
    C.   anticipate needs for employees to fill vacancies
    D.   provide information about job requirements

    ANSWER: A, 207

12. In larger organizations, managers are usually responsible for _____ in the recruiting process.
    A.   planning and conducting recruiting efforts
    B.   auditing and evaluating recruiting activities
    C.   determining the KSAs needed from applicants
    D.   forecasting recruiting needs

    ANSWER: C, 207

13. Recruiting efforts may be viewed as either continuous or
    A.   continual.
    B.   intensive.
    C.   sporadic.
    D.   targeted.

    ANSWER: B, 207

14. _____ efforts to recruit have the advantage of keeping the employer in the recruiting market.
    A.   Intensive
    B.   Targeted
    C.   Sporadic
    D.   Continuous

    ANSWER: D, 207

15. _____ recruiting may take the form of a vigorous recruiting campaign aimed at hiring a given number of employees, usually within a short time period.
    A.   Intensive
    B.   Targeted
    C.   Sporadic
    D.   Continuous

    ANSWER: A, 207

16. A(n) _____ takes over the staff of a small business and writes the paychecks, pays the taxes, prepares and implements HR policies, and keeps all the required records for a fee.
    A.   employment agency
    B.   payroll executive
    C.   professional employer organization
    D.   trade hire outsourcing firm

    ANSWER: C, 208

17.   One of the advantages for employees of leasing companies is that
       A.   they usually receive many interesting assignments in a variety of start-up
             businesses.
       B.   they may receive better benefits than they would otherwise get in many
             small businesses.
       C.   they are not required to pay social security taxes.
       D.   they can be regarded as self employed for IRS purposes.

       ANSWER: B, 209

18.   _____ makes use of recruiting sources and workers who are not
       traditional employees.
       A.   Flextime
       B.   External recruiting
       C.   Part-time hiring
       D.   Flexible staffing

       ANSWER: D, 209

19.   Which of the following was not given as an example of flexible staffing?
       A.   internships
       B.   independent contractors
       C.   employee leasing
       D.   temporary workers

       ANSWER: A, 209

20.   The use of temporary workers may make sense in which of the following
       situations?
       A.   The industry has a history of high turnover.
       B.   Government regulations make it too expensive to hire permanent employees.
       C.   The work is subject to seasonal or other fluctuations.
       D.   The organization wants to reduce its benefits costs.

       ANSWER: C, 209-210

21.   Workers who perform specific services on a contract basis are called
       A.   flexible staff.
       B.   independent contractors.
       C.   temporary workers.
       D.   internal contractors.

       ANSWER: B, 210

22.   Which of the following is given as an advantage for firms that use independent
       contractors?

       A.   independent contractors are paid lower wages
       B.   it help a firm meet its affirmative action goals
       C.   a professional employer organization handles the payroll
       D.   employers save money by not having to provide benefits

       ANSWER: D, 210

23. Which of the following approaches is credited with successfully diversifying workforces?
    A.   using recruiting sources that target the appropriate types of applicants
    B.   the development of an affirmative action plans
    C.   establishing quotas for hiring from each protected-class group
    D.   the appointment of an HR professional specifically to oversee the hiring of a diverse workforce

    ANSWER: A, 211

24. One key to successfully recruiting employees with disabilities is
    A.   redesigning all job to accommodate individuals with disabilities.
    B.   establishing a separate pay scale that recognizes the individual's capabilities.
    C.   where reasonable, make changes in job duties, work stations, and equipment so that a disabled person can do the job well
    D.   review the total compensation package (pay and benefits) to ensure that individuals with disabilities are not discriminated against.

    ANSWER: C, 211-212

25. In which of the following organizations would promotion from within be more suitable?
    A.   a business with government contracts
    B.   an organization in an environment that changes slowly
    C.   a dynamic high-tech business
    D.   an organization that makes use of independent contractors

    ANSWER: B, 212

26. Which of the following is given as a disadvantage of recruiting internally?
    A.   may not select someone who will "fit" the job
    B.   difficult to assess abilities
    C.   can only hire at entry level
    D.   need for strong management-development program

    ANSWER: D, 212

27. Which of the following was not listed as a disadvantage of internal recruiting?
    A.   longer adjustment or orientation time
    B.   inbreeding
    C.   possible morale problems of those not promoted
    D.   political infighting for promotions

    ANSWER: A, 212

28. Which of the following is given as an advantage of external recruiting?
    A.   better assessment of abilities
    B.   shorter adjustment or orientation time
    C.   may bring industry insights
    D.   having to hire only at entry level

    ANSWER: C, 212

29.   The disadvantages of external recruiting include
       A.   need for a stronger management-development program.
       B.   may cause morale problems for internal candidates not selected.
       C.   inbreeding.
       D.   no group of political supporters in organization already.

       ANSWER: B, 212

30.   The advantages of internal recruiting include
       A.   no need for an expensive management development program.
       B.   cheaper and faster than training professionals.
       C.   inbreeding.
       D.   better assessment of abilities.

       ANSWER: D, 212

31.   Which of the following approaches may add motivation for employees to stay and
       grow in the organization rather than pursuing career opportunities elsewhere?
       A.   filling opening internally
       B.   listing open positions on the organization's web page
       C.   developing an organizational database
       D.   increased commitment to employee development

       ANSWER: A, 213

32.   In terms of recruiting, an advantage of organizational databases is that
       A.   they permit employers to comply more easily with the numerous EEO rules.
       B.   the EEOC guidelines recommend non-biased, automated systems.
       C.   databases maintain background and KSA information on existing employees.
       D.   job candidates have more confidence in systems that minimize the
             possibility of personal bias.

       ANSWER: C, 213

33.   Which of the following statements regarding job posting and bidding is false?
       A.   It gives each employee an opportunity to move to a better job within the
             organization.
       B.   It makes it difficult for supervisors to develop employees long term.
       C.   Job generally are posted before any external recruiting is done.
       D.   In a unionized organization, job posting and bidding often is spelled out
             in the labor agreement.

       ANSWER: B, 213-214

34.   Which of the following was identified as a drawback of promoting from within?
       A.   There may not be any current employees qualified for promotion.
       B.   Additional training and development expenses must be incurred.
       C.   Supervisors often are reluctant to recommend their better employees for
             promotion.
       D.   Performance on one job may not be a good predictor of performance on
             another.

       ANSWER: D, 214

35.   If protected-class individuals are underrepresented, word-of-mouth recruiting
      A.   can violate equal employment regulations.
      B.   will bring in a more diverse group of applicants.
      C.   can be valid affirmative action strategy.
      D.   is less expensive that advertising into the minority community.

      ANSWER: A, 215

36.   What is true about recruiting friends and family of current employees?
      A.   Workers recruited through current employee have high rates of turnover.
      B.   Current employee referrals can reduce the risk of EEO scrutiny.
      C.   Many qualified people can be reached at low cost.
      D.   Current employees are reluctant to refer their family and friends.

      ANSWER: C, 215

37.   What is the principle advantage for hiring former employees?
      A.   most managers are eager to take back a former employee
      B.   their performance and capabilities are known
      C.   they usually cost less in terms of salary and benefits
      D.   their friends usually like to have an old colleague back

      ANSWER: B, 215

38.   Of the following recruiting resources, applicants are most likely to consider
      A.   word of mouth.
      B.   friends and relatives.
      C.   employment agencies.
      D.   newspapers.

      ANSWER: D, 216

39.   Which of the following statements is true about using the Internet for
      recruiting?
      A.   Employers have found Web sites to be effective and efficient.
      B.   It is used by less than 10 percent of organizations.
      C.   Internet recruiting has not lived up to expectations.
      D.   Most managers prefer traditional, face-to-face recruiting methods.

      ANSWER: A, 217

40.   Which of the following is true about Internet recruiting?
      A.   more expensive than traditional media
      B.   used primarily for high-tech jobs
      C.   improves the chances of contacting people not actively seeking work
      D.   regarded as a replacement for newspaper advertising

      ANSWER: C, 218

41.   Which of the following is <u>not</u> a major determinant when deciding at which college an employer will conduct interviews?
       A.   college reputation
       B.   faculty attitudes towards the employer's industry
       C.   organizational budget constraints
       D.   cost of available talent and typical salaries

       ANSWER: B, 219

42.   Which of the following attributes do recruiters seem to value ahead of a high GPA in college graduates?
       A.   extracurricular activities
       B.   family connections and networking possibilities
       C.   part-time and summer work experience
       D.   poise, communication skills, and appearance

       ANSWER: D, 220

43.   Which of the following statements is true regarding college recruiting?
       A.   Employers who show continuing presence and support on a campus are more successful.
       B.   College recruiting is one of the least expensive recruitment methods.
       C.   Recruiters overestimate the importance of extrinsic rewards such as pay and benefits.
       D.   The cost of training decreases due to educational preparedness.

       ANSWER: A, 220

44.   In a cooperative program,
       A.   the HR unit and operating managers conduct joint interviews.
       B.   employees cooperate with the HR unit in recruiting friends for job openings.
       C.   students work part time and receive some school credits.
       D.   the college placement center assists in identifying suitable job candidates.

       ANSWER: C, 221

45.   External recruiting sources include
       A.   former employees.
       B.   labor unions.
       C.   job posting and bidding.
       D.   friends of current employees.

       ANSWER: B, 221

46.   In some industries, such as _____, unions have traditionally supplied workers to employers.
       A.   entertainment
       B.   publishing
       C.   law enforcement
       D.   construction

       ANSWER: D, 221

47. Unions can work to an employer's advantage through
    A.   cooperative staffing programs.
    B.   closed shop agreements.
    C.   less competition for skilled workers.
    D.   establishing wage scales for job candidates.

    ANSWER: A, 221

48. Executive search firms are split into two groups. _____ firms charge
    a fee only after a candidate has been hired by a client company.
    A.   Contract
    B.   Commission
    C.   Contingency
    D.   Retainer

    ANSWER: C, 221

49. Executive search firms classified as _____ charge a client a set fee
    whether or not the contracted search is successful.
    A.   contingency firms
    B.   retainer firms
    C.   employment agencies
    D.   professional societies

    ANSWER: B, 221

50. One advantage of having an executive search firm on retainer is that
    A.   it establishes an on-going professional relationship which enables
          positions to be filled more efficiently.
    B.   search firms give their clients first refusal of an outstanding candidate.
    C.   in the long run, this is less expensive.
    D.   search firms are ethically bound not to approach employees of client
          companies in their search efforts for another client.

    ANSWER: D, 222

51. What is a primary advantage of recruiting through professional and trade
    associations?
    A.   access to specialized professionals needed in an industry
    B.   firms can obtain competitors' secrets
    C.   individuals hired from competitors have enhanced motivation because they
          have decided to take another position in the same industry
    D.   more competitive salaries

    ANSWER: A, 222

52. How can recruiters easily track responses to advertisements in various media?
    A.   advertise different jobs in different media
    B.   ask applicants where they learned of the position
    C.   use different contact names, addresses, or phone numbers
    D.   use specialized codes in different advertisements

    ANSWER: C, 222

53. Job fairs are primarily useful for
     A.   identifying who is currently on the job market.
     B.   filling a large number of jobs quickly.
     C.   assessing the current state of the labor market.
     D.   comparing salaries with competing firms.

     ANSWER: B, 222

54. Evaluating the success of recruiting efforts is important because
     A.   it provides input to the HR unit's compensation system.
     B.   that is one way to measure the firm's reputation on the college campuses.
     C.   it indicates how the employer measures-up against competitors.
     D.   that is the primary way to find out whether the efforts are cost effective
           .
     ANSWER: D, 224

55. Which of the following would be classified as an indirect cost of recruiting?
     A.   involvement of operating managers
     B.   recruiters' salaries
     C.   agency fees
     D.   length of time from contact to hire

     ANSWER: A, 224

56. In evaluating recruiting costs and benefits, direct costs include
     A.   costs of leaving the position unfilled while waiting for a replacement.
     B.   length of time from contact to hire.
     C.   recruiters' salaries.
     D.   involvement of operating managers.

     ANSWER: C, 224

57. Information on job performance, absenteeism, cost of training, and turnover by
     recruiting source help organizations
     A.   develop recruiting sources.
     B.   evaluate recruiting.
     C.   attract job candidates.
     D.   produce a realistic job preview.

     ANSWER: B, 224

58. A _____ is a comparison of the number of applicants at one stage of
     the recruiting process to the number at the next stage.
     A.   selection rate
     B.   success ratio
     C.   hit rate
     D.   yield ratio

     ANSWER: D, 225

59. The _____ equals the number hired divided by the number of applicants.
    A.   selection rate
    B.   success rate
    C.   yield ratio
    D.   hit rate

    ANSWER: A, 226

60. What can a recruiter learn from calculating the acceptance rate?
    A.   the long-term success rate of applicants
    B.   the percentage hired from a given group of candidates
    C.   the organization's success at hiring the candidates it wants to employ
    D.   the competitiveness of the organization's salary structure

    ANSWER: C, 226

True and False

61. Recruitment involves selecting among candidates for a position.

    ANSWER: False, 202
    Recruitment is the process of generating a pool of qualified applicants for organizational jobs.

62. The term "labor market" refers to all individuals looking for a position in the same geographic area.

    ANSWER: False, 202
    Labor markets are the external supply pool from which organizations attract employees.

63. The applicant population includes all individuals who are available for selection if all possible recruitment strategies are used.

    ANSWER: False, 202
    This is the definition of "labor force population." The application population is a subset of the labor force population.

64. Using flexible staffing arrangements enables employers to generate a high degree of employee loyalty by guaranteeing long-term job tenure.

    ANSWER: False, 209
    Just the opposite may result. Flexible staffing allows an employer to avoid some of the costs of full-time benefits.

65. Independent contractors include those who perform specific services on a contract basis.

    ANSWER: True, 210

66.   Disparate impact occurs when there is underrepresentation of protected-class members compared to the labor markets utilized by the employer.

ANSWER: True, 210

67.   To meet affirmative action goals, it is recommended that employers include a specific statement in their advertisements that preference will be given to women and racial minorities.

ANSWER: False, 210
EEOC guidelines state that no direct or indirect references that have gender or race connotations are permitted in advertisements.

68.   Employers are required to modify the workplace and supply needed equipment to accommodate the special needs of disabled persons.

ANSWER: False, 211-212
Employers are only required to make reasonable accommodations for people with disabilities. Not every disability lends itself to every job for accommodation.

69.   If a promotion-from-within policy is followed exclusively, it has the disadvantage of perpetuating old ways of operating.

ANSWER: True, 212

70.   Internal recruiting is faster and less expensive than having to train professionals recruited externally.

ANSWER: False, 212
Internal recruiting has the disadvantage of requiring organizations to operate expensive management-development programs.

71.   Promotions from within are preferred since an employees performance on his/her current job is a good predictor of performance on the new job.

ANSWER: False, 214
Performance on one job may not be a good predictor of performance on another, because different skills may be required.

72.   When an organization has an underrepresentation of a particular protected class, word-of-mouth referral is recommended as a means of recruiting previously underrepresented protected-class employees.

ANSWER: False, 215
Word-of-mouth recruiting has been considered a violation of Title VII of the Civil Rights Act if it perpetuates underrepresentation.

73.   Utilizing current employee referrals is usually one of the most effective methods of recruiting.

ANSWER: True, 215

74. Re-recruiting former employees is an ideal internal source if their performance and capabilities were solid.

    ANSWER: True, 215

75. A primary advantage of Internet recruiting is that many employers have realized cost savings compared to traditional sources such as newspaper advertising and employment agencies.

    ANSWER: True, 217

76. An organization with a strong union may have less flexibility than a nonunion company in deciding where a newly hired person will be placed.

    ANSWER: True, 221

77. Executive search firms are ethically bound not to approach employees of client companies in their search efforts for another client.

    ANSWER: True, 222

78. Job fairs are especially useful for employers in tight labor markets or needing to fill a large number of jobs quickly.

    ANSWER: True, 222

79. The yield ratio is the percentage of candidates hired from a given pool of applicants.

    ANSWER: False, 225
    A yield ratio is a comparison of the number of applicants at one stage of the recruiting process to the number at the next stage. The selection rate is the percentage hired from a given group of candidates.

80. A longer-term measure of recruiting effectiveness is to track the performance and retention of applicants.

    ANSWER: True, 226

Essay

81. Discuss the statement: *"The decisions made about recruiting dictate not only the kinds and numbers of applicants, but also how difficult or successful recruiting efforts may be."*

    ANSWER: 205-211
    Strategic decisions include: how many employees, when, and KSAs needed. Other decisions involve: where to recruit, keeping in touch with outside recruiting sources to maintain visibility, advertising choices, and flexible staffing arrangements.

82.   Describe some of the flexible staffing alternatives available to employers. Why
       are some organizations examining these alternatives?

       ANSWER: 208-210
       Professional employer organizations and leased employees, temporary workers,
       part-time employees, and independent contractors. These alternatives are
       attractive because they provide flexibility and to avoid some of the costs of
       full-time benefits. They also provide some relief from the high costs of
       government regulations.

83.   What are some of the legal restrictions on how organizations can recruit
       employees? How can an employer effectively use the recruiting process to
       achieve a more diverse workforce?

       ANSWER: 210-212
       EEOC guidelines forbid references to age or gender in advertising. If there is
       underrepresentation of protected-class members, affirmative action may be
       required. A diverse workforce may be recruited by directing advertising to
       minority publications, by working with associations representing older or
       disabled individuals, and by making changes in job duties, work stations, and
       equipment to accommodate persons with disabilities.

84.   What are the advantages and limitations of focusing on current employees to fill
       open positions?

       ANSWER: 212-213
       Seen as a reward for good work, serving as a motivator, a better assessment of
       abilities, causes a succession of promotions, and at times may be less costly.
       But perpetuate old ways of operating, EEO concerns, causes possible morale
       problems of those not promoted, may lead to political infighting, and there is
       a need for management-development programs.

85.   Describe some of the external sources of job candidates.

       ANSWER: 218-224
       Colleges and universities, schools, cooperative programs - all are useful for
       entry-level jobs. Labor unions, employment agencies and search firms. Media
       sources including newspapers. Professional and trade associations. The
       Internet. Job fairs and special events. Competitors' employees.

Chapter 8

Selecting and Placing Human Resources

Multiple Choice

1. The process of choosing individuals who have needed qualifications to fill jobs in an organization is called
    A. recruitment.
    B. selection.
    C. staffing.
    D. placement.

    ANSWER: B, 234

2. In the typical division of HR responsibilities for selection, the HR unit will
    A. make the final selection decision.
    B. interview final candidates.
    C. requisition employees with specific qualifications.
    D. obtain background and reference information.

    ANSWER: D, 235

3. _____ involves fitting a person to the right job.
    A. Placement
    B. Orientation
    C. Selection
    D. Staffing

    ANSWER: A, 235

4. More than anything else, placement of human resources should be seen as a(n)
    A. public relations activity.
    B. operating management responsibility.
    C. matching process.
    D. HR unit responsibility.

    ANSWER: C, 235

5. In addition to choosing the best available person, selection and placement also entails
    A. designing a compensation package to be offered to the potential employee.
    B. matching what the applicant can and wants to do with what the organization needs.
    C. the possible impact of the applicants personality on the organization's culture
    D. an applicant's willingness to accept a job.

    ANSWER: B, 235

6. If it is done properly, _____ can provide the basis for identifying KSAs needed in a job.
    A. selection
    B. recruitment
    C. test validation
    D. job analysis

    ANSWER: D, 236

7. If an employer hires at the entry level and promotes from within for most jobs, KSAs might be less important than
    A. general cognitive and problem-solving abilities and work ethic.
    B. personal integrity.
    C. academic qualifications and internal motivation.
    D. natural aptitude as measured by IQ tests.

    ANSWER: A, 236

8. A(n) _____ is a characteristic that a person must have to do a job successfully.
    A. validator
    B. essential element
    C. selection criterion
    D. predictor

    ANSWER: C, 237

9. Measurable indicators of the selection criteria are called
    A. performance standards.
    B. predictors.
    C. essential elements.
    D. validators.

    ANSWER: B, 238

10. In selection, validity refers to the
    A. strength of the correlation between a test score and a predictor.
    B. reliability with which the predictor actually tests the desired construct.
    C. applicant achieving approximately the same score in a test-retest situation.
    D. correlation between a predictor and job performance.

    ANSWER: D, 238

11.   _____ is the extent to which a predictor repeatedly produces the same
      results, over time.
      A.   Reliability
      B.   Test validity
      C.   Accuracy
      D.   Predictability

      ANSWER: A, 238

12.   In the _____ approach, a minimum cutoff is set on each predictor, and
      each minimum level must be passed.
      A.   single predictor
      B.   test validity
      C.   multiple hurdles
      D.   combined

      ANSWER: C, 239

13.   How does the compensatory approach combine predictors?
      A.   a minimum cutoff is set on each predictor
      B.   a higher score on one predictor offsets a lower score on another
      C.   an average of predictor scores for all test takers is used to establish
            cutoffs
      D.   multiple hurdles are set to compensate for the different predictors

      ANSWER: B, 239

14.   In defining who is an applicant, it is recommended that
      A.   all people expressing an interest in employment should complete an
            application form.
      B.   employers do applicant racking on all expressing an interest in
            employment.
      C.   all unsolicited resumes and walk-in applications be kept on file.
      D.   applications be accepted only for existing openings.

      ANSWER: D, 241

15.   What is the purpose of an applicant flow form?
      A.   to obtain EEOC reporting data separately from applicants
      B.   to track candidates through the application process
      C.   to monitor the flow of minority applicants
      D.   to maintain statistics on the impact of different recruiting sources

      ANSWER: A, 241

16.   What can employers do in order to comply with the EEOC requirements of reporting
      the race and sex of applicants?
      A.   Collect the data after the hiring decision has been made.
      B.   Gather the information on the application blank.
      C.   Ask the applicant to provide EEOC reporting data on a separate form.
      D.   Make a visual assessment during the initial selection process and record
            the race and sex of applicants on the application form.

      ANSWER: C, 241

17.   The purpose of a _____ is to inform job candidates of the
       organizational realities of a job, so that they can more accurately evaluate
       their own job expectations.
       A.   practical overview initiation
       B.   realistic job preview
       C.   accurate structured interview
       D.   valid orientation assessment

       ANSWER: B, 242

18.   Some employers use _____ to help prevent unrealistic expectations
       being formed during the selection process.
       A.   organizational job previews
       B.   honest career assessment previews
       C.   internship overviews
       D.   realistic job previews

       ANSWER: D, 242

19.   A review of research on realistic job previews found that
       A.   they help reduce employee disenchantment and ultimately employee
             dissatisfaction and turnover.
       B.   they have little if any impact on employee turnover.
       C.   they significantly reduce employee dissatisfaction and turnover.
       D.   they reduce the size of the applicant pool by making the job and the
             organization less attractive.

       ANSWER: A, 242

20.   What is the purpose of pre-employment screening?
       A.   to provide a realistic job preview
       B.   to encourage potential job candidates to complete application forms
       C.   to determine if applicants meet the minimum qualifications for open jobs
       D.   to obtain information for an EEO report

       ANSWER: C, 242

21.   The purpose of _____ is to compare applicants' qualifications to job
       profiles in order to determine which candidates are likely to be successful.
       A.   application forms
       B.   electronic screening
       C.   applicant flow documentation
       D.   realistic job previews

       Answer: B, 243

22.   Which of the following is a basic purpose of the application form?
       A.   an initial record for the organization's EEO/affirmative action plans
       B.   to provide a defense in an employment discrimination case
       C.   a record of the employer's desire to hire someone for an open position.
       D.   a basic employee record for applicants who are hired.

       ANSWER: D, 243

23.   _____ means that the employer or applicant has the right to terminate the employment relationship at any time with or without notice or cause.
A.   Employment-at-will
B.   Right-of-dismissal
C.   Employee leasing
D.   Contingency employment

ANSWER: A, 243

24.   The Immigration Reform and Control Act of 1986, requires employers to
A.   obtain proof of citizenship before making a hiring decision.
B.   send copies of all documents submitted by employees to the Immigration and Naturalization Service.
C.   determine whether the job applicant is a U.S. citizen, registered alien, or illegal alien, within 72 hours of hiring.
D.   contact the Immigration and Naturalization Service if an illegal alien applies for a job.

ANSWER: C, 245

25.   If an organization uses resumes in place of application forms,
A.   it might be able to use certain "illegal information" that was volunteered by the applicant.
B.   the resume must still be treated as an application form for EEO purposes.
C.   the employer should assume that the information included is less accurate.
D.   the employer will obtain more complete information about the candidate.

ANSWER: B, 245

26.   In _____, questions are weighted to differentiate between satisfactory and poor-performing employees.
A.   scored application forms
B.   in-depth interviews
C.   preparatory interviews
D.   biodata forms

ANSWER: D, 246

27.   What is a "test" as defined by the Uniform Selection Guidelines issued by the EEOC?
A.   any employment requirement
B.   only job assessments that have been validated
C.   all pre-employment inquiries
D.   all paper and pencil assessments that evaluate job skills

ANSWER: A, 247

28.   Tests that assess an individual's ability to perform in a specific manner are
A.   aptitude tests.
B.   knowledge tests.
C.   ability tests.
D.   behavioral tests.

ANSWER: C, 247

29.   Cognitive ability tests measure an individual's
      A.   abilities such as strength, endurance, and muscular movement.
      B.   thinking, memory, reasoning, and verbal and mathematical abilities.
      C.   ability to perform in a specific manner.
      D.   dexterity, hand-eye coordination, and arm-hand steadiness.

      ANSWER: B, 247

30.   _____ measure dexterity, hand-eye coordination, arm-hand steadiness,
      and other factors.
      A.   Physical ability tests
      B.   Work sample tests
      C.   Aptitude tests
      D.   Psychomotor tests

      ANSWER: D, 248

31.   _____ tests require an applicant to perform a simulated job task.
      A.   Work sample
      B.   Vestibule
      C.   Behavioral
      D.   Assessment center

      ANSWER: A, 248

32.   An "in basket" test is an example of a(n) _____ test.
      A.   assessment center
      B.   psychomotor
      C.   work sample
      D.   physical ability

      ANSWER: C, 249

33.   A(n) _____ is a selection and development device composed of a
      series of evaluative exercises and tests.
      A.   evaluative career assessment
      B.   assessment center
      C.   multi-faceted selection process
      D.   "in basket"

      ANSWER: B, 249

34.   The "Big Five" personality trait of _____ has been found to be related
      to job success across most organizations and
      A.   openness/experience
      B.   stability
      C.   extroversion
      D.   conscientiousness

      ANSWER: D, 249

35. The personality trait of _____ predicts success in jobs requiring social interaction, such as many sales jobs.
     A.   extroversion
     B.   conscientiousness
     C.   openness/experience
     D.   emotional stability

     ANSWER: A, 249

36. Which of the following statements is true with regard to personality tests?
     A.   The courts have banned the use of personality tests for privacy reasons.
     B.   Personality tests cannot predict the interpersonal aspects of job success.
     C.   Personality testing requires that a solid job-related link be made.
     D.   Personality tests are rarely used today as a selection device.

     ANSWER: C, 249

37. Which of the following inquire specifically about individual honesty and attitudes and behavior regarding theft?
     A.   personality-oriented honesty tests
     B.   overt integrity tests
     C.   polygraph tests
     D.   theft-intention assessment

     ANSWER: B, 249-250

38. Which of the following statements is true about the use of honesty/integrity tests?
     A.   They are invalid screening devices for organizations.
     B.   They are illegal under the Employee Polygraph Protection Act.
     C.   The public supports their use as a valid way of reducing employee theft.
     D.   Overt integrity tests have high "fake-ability."

     ANSWER: D, 250-251

39. The Employee Polygraph Protection Act
     A.   prohibits polygraph use for pre-employment screening purposes by most employers.
     B.   prohibits employers from using polygraph tests to investigate theft.
     C.   prohibits government agencies from using polygraph tests.
     D.   permits the use of polygraphs, but only when administered by a trained expert.

     ANSWER: A, 251

40. The purpose of a(n) _____ is to obtain additional information on a candidate and to clarify information gathered throughout the selection process.
     A.   polygraph test
     B.   application form
     C.   selection interview
     D.   reference check

     ANSWER: C, 252

41. In a structured interview,
     A.   all candidates meet in the same room with the same interviewer.
     B.   a set of standardized questions are asked of all job applicants.
     C.   each candidate appears before a panel of interviewers.
     D.   computers are used to devise a set of questions.

     ANSWER: B, 253

42. Research on interviews has consistently found that one approach is more reliable
     and valid than the others. What is this approach?
     A.   situational interview
     B.   panel interview
     C.   stress interview
     D.   structured interview

     ANSWER: D, 253

43. In what type of interview might an applicant be asked the following: "How did
     you handle a situation where there were no rules or guidelines for employee
     discipline?"
     A.   behavioral
     B.   negative
     C.   nondirective
     D.   stress

     ANSWER: A, 254

44. In a _____ interview questions would be asked about how applicants
     might handle specific job situations.
     A.   behavioral
     B.   nondirective
     C.   situational
     D.   stress

     ANSWER: C, 254

45. The _____ interview uses general questions from which other questions
     are developed.
     A.   situational
     B.   nondirective
     C.   stress
     D.   flow

     ANSWER: B, 254

46. The interviewer assumes an extremely aggressive and insulting posture in a
     A.   situational interview.
     B.   negative interview.
     C.   aggressive reaction interview.
     D.   stress interview.

     ANSWER: D, 255

47. Several interviewers interview a candidate at the same time in a
     A.   panel interview.
     B.   situational interview.
     C.   team interview.
     D.   structured interview.

     ANSWER: A, 255

48. In a _____ interview, applicants are interviewed by the "team members"
     with whom they will work.
     A.   panel interview.
     B.   situational interview.
     C.   team interview.
     D.   structured interview.

     ANSWER: C, 256

49. The problem of _____ occurs when interviewers make a decision on the
     job suitability of applicants within the first four or five minutes and spend
     the balance of the interview looking for evidence to support it.
     A.   bias
     B.   snap judgments
     C.   devil's horns
     D.   halo effect

     ANSWER: B, 258

50. Research has shown that _____ is the biggest factor considered in
     interviewers' decisions about overall suitability.
     A.   the background investigation report
     B.   an applicant's prior work experience
     C.   intangible information observed during the interview
     D.   unfavorable information about an applicant

     ANSWER: D, 258

51. An interview problem which occurs when an interviewer allows a prominent
     characteristic to overshadow other evidence is called
     A.   the halo effect.
     B.   bias perception.
     C.   negative emphasis.
     D.   the dominant trait error.

     ANSWER: A, 258

52. _____ occurs when the candidate gives responses that are believed to
     be socially acceptable rather than factual.
     A.   Padding
     B.   Prevarication
     C.   Cultural noise
     D.   Judgmental responding

     ANSWER: C, 259

53.   _____ is the ability of interviewers to pick the same capabilities again and again in applicants.
A.   Validity
B.   Reliability
C.   Rater experience
D.   Predictor correlation

ANSWER: B, 259

54.   Which of the following is of little value to a potential employer and should not be used?
A.   academic transcripts
B.   law enforcement reports
C.   credit history
D   personal references

ANSWER: D, 260

55.   Applicants frequently misrepresent their qualifications and backgrounds. Surveys have shown that the most common false information relates to
A.   length of prior employment.
B.   credit history.
C.   marital and family situation.
D.   academic credentials.

ANSWER: A, 261

56.   Which of the following is true about the Fair Credit Reporting Act?
A.   The use of credit reports for employment purposes is forbidden.
B.   A governmental employer must have a signed release from a person before it can give information about that person to someone else.
C.   An employer must disclose that a credit check is being made and obtain written consent from the person being checked.
D.   Credit agencies are liable for damages if false credit information is disclosed about a job candidate.

ANSWER: C, 262

57.   Which of the following is a basic provision of the Federal Privacy Act of 1974?
A.   All employers, both public and private sector, must have a signed, written release from a person before it can give information about that person to someone else.
B.   A governmental employer must have a signed release from a person before it can give information about that person to someone else.
C.   Government agencies must give permission before employers may seek certain critical information.
D.   An organization must have written permission from an applicant before it can seek information about that applicant from other sources.

ANSWER: B, 262

58. An employers may be sued for _____ if a worker commits violent acts on the job.
    A.   insufficient validity
    B.   criminal liability
    C.   security violations
    D.   negligent hiring

    ANSWER: D, 263

59. Which is the current law regarding pre-employment medical examinations?
    A.   A company may require applicants to take a drug test.
    B.   All pre-employment medical exams are prohibited.
    C.   Medical exams can be given only after a candidate reaches the short list.
    D.   Companies may ask questions about the job applicant's current medical condition, but not past medical problems.

    ANSWER: A, 263

60. Which of the following is true about genetic testing?
    A.   Genetic testing minimizes a company's liability for workplace illnesses.
    B.   The public approves of the use of genetic testing for risk screening.
    C.   Genetic testing permits employers to exclude individuals from certain jobs if they have genetic conditions that increase their health risks.
    D.   Federal law prohibits the use of genetic tests to screen applicants.

    ANSWER: C, 263-264

True and False

61. Job analysis can provide the basis for identifying KSAs needed in a job if it is done properly.

    ANSWER: True, 236

62. In selection, a predictor is a characteristic that a person must have to do a job successfully.

    ANSWER: False, 237
    A selection criterion is a characteristic that a person must have to do a job successfully. A predictor is a measurable indicator of that criterion.

63. Reliability is the ability of a test to produce the same results repeatedly over time.

    ANSWER: True, 238

64. A non-union employer is permitted to investigate a job candidate's attitudes towards and past involvement in union activities.

    ANSWER: False, 239
    Questions about union-related information violates federal labor laws.

65.   Unless an organization has a written policy defining conditions that make a person an applicant, any person who calls or sends an unsolicited resume might later claim not to have been hired because of illegal discrimination.

ANSWER: True, 240-241

66.   In order to fulfill EEO reporting requirements, it is recommended that voluntary questions about race and sex be included in application forms.

ANSWER: False, 241-242
The application form cannot contain these questions. It is recommended that applicants provide EEOC reporting data on a form which is filed separately and not used in any other HR activity.

67.   A novel work sample test uses realistic job previews to observe how a job candidate behaves and performs in an actual work situation.

ANSWER: False, 242
In realistic job previews, job applicants are provided an accurate picture of the job.

68.   The Immigration Reform and Control Act of 1986 states that employers can assume that documents submitted by new employees, such as U.S. passports, birth certificates, original Social Security cards, and driver's licenses are genuine.

ANSWER: False, 245
Employers are responsible to make sure that the documents appear to be genuine.

69.   The Uniform Guidelines of the EEOC define application forms as employment tests.

ANSWER: True, 247

70.   Cognitive ability tests measure an individual's thinking, memory, reasoning, and verbal and mathematical abilities.

ANSWER: True, 247

71.   Psychomotor tests measure individual abilities such as strength, endurance, and muscular movement.

ANSWER: False, 248
Psychomotor measure dexterity, hand-eye coordination, and arm-hand steadiness.

72.   Personality tests may be used in selection when there is a solid job-related link.

ANSWER: True, 249

73.   The EEOC has determined that honesty/integrity tests are invalid because they are biased against protected-class members.

ANSWER: False, 250
These tests may be valid as broad screening devices for organizations if used properly.

74. In a behavioral interview, applicants are required to give specific examples of how they have handled a problem in the past.

    ANSWER: True, 254

75. The situational interview uses questions that are developed from answers to previous questions.

    ANSWER: False, 254
    This is a description of the nondirective interview. Situational interviews are structured interviews composed of questions about how applicants might handle specific job situations.

76. Just because someone is personable and likes to talk, there is no guarantee that the person will be a good interviewer.

    ANSWER: True, 256

77. One negative fact may influence the selection decision more than any amount of positive information.

    ANSWER: True, 258

78. Personal references are a useful indication of an applicant's character.

    ANSWER: False, 260
    No applicant would request a recommendation from someone who would give a negative one. Greater reliance should be placed on work-related references.

79. Federal law provides immunity for employers who, in good faith, provide information on a current or past employee to another employer.

    ANSWER: False, 263
    There is no federal protection. Some states have passed laws providing legal immunity for employers providing information to other employers.

80. Drug tests are the only pre-employment medical exams permitted by the Americans with Disabilities Act (ADA).

    ANSWER: True, 263

Essay

81. Who is an applicant? Why must an employer develop a policy defining who is an "applicant?"

    ANSWER: 240-242
    An employer must not discriminate against an applicant for any reasons that are against the law, and must keep detailed records on applicant flow. An individual submitting an unsolicited resume may be considered an applicant if the employer does not define at what point an inquiry becomes an application for employment.

82.   Briefly describe the steps in a typical selection process. What are the legal considerations, if any, at each step?

ANSWER: 239-240
Applicant job interest and pre-employment screening - define who is an applicant. Application form - can only ask questions that are job related. Testing - all tests must be valid and job related. Interviewing - most widely used test, cannot ask questions that are not job related. Background investigation - Privacy Act, Fair Credit Reporting Act. Conditional job offer. Medical exam/drug test - Other than drug tests, most medical exams may violate the ADA. Job placement.

83.   You are the college recruiter for an investment bank. What selection tests would you use?

ANSWER: 243-263
Application form requesting information on academic achievements and work experience. Assessment center to test skills and management potential. Personality test to assess conscientiousness. Honesty/integrity test. Behavioral and situational interviews. Background investigation. Drug test.

84.   Discuss the statement: *"Interviews are the most widely used, but the least valid, selection method."* What are some of the uses and problems associated with employment interviews?

ANSWER: 252-260
An interviewer can integrate all information obtained from application forms, tests, and reference checks, and investigate any conflicting information that may have emerged. The interview has high intrarater reliability and face validity. It can be the final step before a hiring decision is made. Problems include low interrater reliability and poor validity, snap judgment, negative emphasis, halo effect, and biases. Taken alone, the interview is not an especially valid predictor of job performance and success, particularly when using unstructured interviews.

85.   Would you recommend that employers conduct background investigations and medical examinations of job applicants? What are some of the legal issues involved?

ANSWER: 260-263
Background investigations can be used to verify information given on application forms and identify any criminal records. Medical examinations should only be used to check for drug use. The Privacy Act, the Fair Credit Reporting Act, and the ADA limit what can be investigated.

Chapter 9

Training Human Resources

Multiple Choice

1. _____ is a process whereby people acquire capabilities to aid in the achievement of organizational goals.
   A. Orientation
   B. Training
   C. Reinforced learning
   D. Employee development

   ANSWER: B, 272

2. Viewed narrowly, _____ provides employees with specific, identifiable knowledge and skills for use in their present jobs.
   A. orientation
   B. learning
   C. employee development
   D. training

   ANSWER: D, 272

3. Development is distinguished from training, in that
   A. development is broader in scope, focusing on individuals gaining new capabilities useful for both present and future jobs.
   B. EEO laws and regulations apply primarily to training not development.
   C. training is used mostly for management positions.
   D. development provides people with specific, identifiable knowledge and skills for use on their present jobs.

   ANSWER: A, 272

4. A growing number of companies have recognized that training and HR development are
   A. expensive substitutes for public education.
   B. primarily associated with orienting new employees to the organization and their jobs.
   C. integral to competitive business success.
   D. an expense that can be cut when times get tough.

   ANSWER: C, 272

5. Which is the best way to determine if training is cost effective?
    A.   measure improvements in performance resulting from training
    B.   compare costs and benefits associated with training
    C.   identify attitude changes following the training programs
    D.   assess any reductions in voluntary turnover

    ANSWER: B, 273

6. In what ways have some organizations identified training as a source of business revenues?
    A.   establishing "universities" for customers.
    B.   ensuring that the measurable benefits of training and development programs exceed their costs.
    C.   setting up for-profit training departments within the HR unit.
    D.   bundling training as part of sales packages of products and services for customers.

    ANSWER: D, 273

7. The performance consulting approach to training
    A.   compares desired and actual organizational results and desired and actual employee performance.
    B.   bundles training as part of a sales package of products and services for customers.
    C.   uses outside vendors to design and implement training programs.
    D.   directs all training issues to the organization's Chief Learning Officer (CLO)

    ANSWER: A, 274

8. With respect to training, the HR unit
    A.   has a more shorter-term view of employee careers than operating managers.
    B.   should conduct on-the-job training.
    C.   serves as a source of expert training assistance and coordination.
    D.   is the best source of technical info used in skill training.

    ANSWER: C, 275

9. In a typical division of training responsibilities, the HR unit
    A.   monitors training needs.
    B.   prepares skill-training materials.
    C.   conducts on-the-job training.
    D.   participates in organizational change efforts.

    ANSWER: B, 275

10. In a typical division of training responsibilities, which of the following would be a primary responsibility of operating managers?
    A.   prepare skill-training materials
    B.   provide input and expertise for organizational development
    C.   conduct or arrange for off-the-job training
    D.   monitor training needs

    ANSWER: D, 275

11. How does training add value to an organization?
    A. by linking training strategy to organizational objectives, goals, and business strategies
    B. by ensuring that the benefits flowing from training exceeds the training and development costs
    C. by creating a Chief Learning Officer (CLO) position to coordinate training
    D. by producing direct "bottom line" results

    ANSWER: A, 276

12. What are the four major stages when developing a strategic training plan?
    A. analyze, plan, implement, monitor
    B. planning, unfreezing, training, refreezing
    C. strategize, plan, organize, justify
    D. planning, implementing, evaluating, changing

    ANSWER: C, 277

13. The benefits of strategic planning include:
    A. cost effectiveness.
    B. HR and training professionals get intimately involved with the business.
    C. more focused training.
    D. recognition that training can solve most employee and organizational problems.

    ANSWER: B, 277

14. What are the four phases of the training process?
    A. planning, unfreezing, training, refreezing
    B. strategize, plan, organize, justify
    C. analysis, development, implementation, control
    D. assessment, design, delivery, evaluation

    ANSWER: D, 278

15. In the _____ phase of the training process, organizational and employee performance issues are considered to determine if training can help.
    A. assessment
    B. implementation
    C. evaluation
    D. accomplishment

    ANSWER: A, 278

16. During the assessment phase, using the performance consulting approach, it is important that _____ be considered.
    A. existing training methods
    B. the separation of training from development
    C. non-training factors such as compensation
    D. the cost of training programs

    ANSWER: C, 278-279

17. Departments or areas with high turnover, high absenteeism, low performance, or other deficiencies can be pinpointed through which level of the training needs assessment?
    A.   job/task analyses
    B.   organizational analyses
    C.   individual analyses
    D.   group analyses

    ANSWER: B, 280

18. During _____ analyses, the requirements of jobs are compared with the knowledge, skills, and abilities of employees to identify training needs.
    A.   organizational
    B.   group
    C.   individual
    D.   job/task

    ANSWER: D, 280

19. Performance appraisal data is the most common approach use in
    A.   individual analyses
    B.   organizational analyses
    C.   group analyses
    D.   job/task analyses

    ANSWER: A, 280

20. A person's ability to learn must be accompanied by
    A.   the right attitude.
    B.   appropriate time.
    C.   a desire to learn.
    D.   organizational support.

    ANSWER: C, 282

21. An instructor's motivation and ability, and the training method used can influence the student's
    A.   ability to learn.
    B.   motivation to learn.
    C.   Gestalt learning.
    D.   perceived valence of results.

    ANSWER: B, 282

22. Self-Efficacy refers to
    A.   a person's desire to learn training content.
    B.   learners possessing the basic skills and sufficient cognitive abilities.
    C.   the perceived ability of the instructor to transfer the knowledge to the student.
    D.   a person's belief that he/she can successfully learn the training program content.

    ANSWER: D, 282

23. People vary in their beliefs about their ability to learn things through training. People with low self-efficacy seem to benefit from
    A. one-on-one training.
    B. conventional training.
    C. mentoring programs.
    D. computer-assisted programs.

    ANSWER: A, 283

24. Trainers should consider individual learning styles. _____ learners must "get their hands on" and use the training resources.
    A. Auditory
    B. Action
    C. Tactile
    D. Visual

    ANSWER: C, 283

25. Dividing the instructions into small elements after employees have had the opportunity to see how all the elements fit together is part of
    A. behavior modification.
    B. Gestalt learning.
    C. assessment evaluation.
    D. vestibule training.

    ANSWER: B, 284

26. _____ occurs when trainees perform job-related tasks and duties during training.
    A. Whole learning
    B. Transfer of training
    C. Positive reinforcement
    D. Active practice

    ANSWER: D, 284

27. _____ occurs when several practice sessions are spaced over a period of hours or days.
    A. Spaced practice
    B. Massed practice
    C. Alternate practice
    D. Active practice

    ANSWER: A, 284

28. For memorizing tasks, _____ is usually the more effective training design.
    A. cognitive practice
    B. spaced practice
    C. massed practice
    D. alternative practice

    ANSWER: C, 284

29. The most elementary way in which people learn is _____, or copying someone else's behavior.
     A.   behavior modification
     B.   behavior modeling
     C.   cognitive practice
     D.   positive reinforcement

     ANSWER: B, 284

30. When people repeat responses that give them some type of positive reward and avoid actions associated with negative consequences, they are demonstrating the concept of
     A.   modification.
     B.   behavior.
     C.   learning.
     D.   reinforcement

     ANSWER: D, 285

31. The concept of reinforcement is based on the law(s) of
     A.   effect
     B.   behavior.
     C.   learning.
     D.   modification.

     ANSWER: A, 285

32. The learning concept of _____ indicates that people learn best if reinforcement is given as soon as possible after training.
     A.   behavior modeling
     B.   positive reinforcement
     C.   immediate confirmation
     D.   active practice

     ANSWER: C, 285

33. One conditions that must be met for effective transfer of training is the
     A.   existence of positive reinforcement for applying the skills on the job.
     B.   employees must maintain their use of the learned material over time.
     C.   trainees must be able to recall the training as needed.
     D.   trainees must understand the practical applications of the training.

     ANSWER: B, 285

34. One way to aid transfer of training to job situations is to ensure that
     A.   positive reinforcement occurs.
     B.   immediate confirmation is provided.
     C.   the trainees are able to see the "big picture."
     D.   the training mirrors the job context as much as possible.

     ANSWER: D, 285

35. "The planned introduction of new employees to their jobs, coworkers, and the organization" is a definition of
    A. orientation.
    B. organizational entry.
    C. employee development.
    D. socialization.

    ANSWER: A, 286

36. In a small organization without an HR department, new employee orientation becomes the responsibility of
    A. the new employer him/herself.
    B. a well-written employee handbook.
    C. the new employee's supervisor or manager.
    D. the new employee's coworkers.

    ANSWER: C, 286

37. Which of the following was not given as a special key purpose of the orientation process?
    A. establish a favorable employee impression of the organization
    B. enhance positive employee expectations of life in the organization
    C. ensure employee performance and productivity begin more quickly
    D. improve employee retention rates

    ANSWER: B, 286

38. Training is an area targeted by EEO laws and regulations. A primary concern centers on the
    A. methods by which mentors are selected and allocated.
    B. diversity content of training programs.
    C. expectations of participants in the training programs.
    D. criteria used to select individuals for inclusion in training programs.

    ANSWER: D, 288

39. _____ is an internal source of training that occurs through interactions and feedback among employees.
    A. Informal training
    B. Vestibule training
    C. Employee development
    D. New employee orientation

    ANSWER: A, 289

40. The most common type of training at all levels in an organization is
    A. simulation exercises.
    B. role playing.
    C. on-the-job training.
    D. classroom instruction.

    ANSWER: C, 289

41.   Which of the following is true about on-the-job training?
       A.   It is less disruptive to the work flow.
       B.   It is flexible and relevant to what employees do.
       C.   It is more expensive as compared to classroom training.
       D.   Supervisors are better prepared to teach their own subordinates.

       ANSWER: B, 289

42.   Which of the following is a problem with on-the-job training (OJT)?
       A.   uncontrolled environment
       B.   professional trainers not managers do OJT
       C.   OJT emphasizes learning not doing
       D.   OJT can disrupt regular work

       ANSWER: D, 289

43.   _____ involves the use of vendors to train employees.
       A.   Outsourcing
       B.   Informal training
       C.   On-the-job development
       D.   Certification

       ANSWER: A, 290

44.   What is the purpose of the Workforce Investment Partnership Act (WIPA)?
       A.   fund school-to-work programs
       B.   assist ex-prisoners to become productive members of the workforce
       C.   target adult education, disadvantaged youth, and family literacy
       D.   provide tax credits for work-release study programs

       ANSWER: C, 290

45.   _____ is defined as the use of the Internet or an organizational
       intranet to conduct training on-line.
       A.   Computer-assisted learning
       B.   E-learning
       C.   Cooperative learning
       D.   Simulation learning

       ANSWER: B, 291

46.   Which of the following would be identified as a form of cooperative training?
       A.   simulations
       B.   E-learning
       C.   vestibule training
       D.   school-to-work

       ANSWER: D, 293

47. _____ combine(s) job training with classroom instruction.
    A. Internships
    B. Simulations
    C. Vestibule training
    D. Trade education

    ANSWER: A, 293

48. Apprenticeships are used most often to train people for jobs in
    A. management development.
    B. the construction industry.
    C. skilled crafts.
    D. technology-related areas.

    ANSWER: C, 293-294

49. Which of the following training methods use a wide array of multimedia technologies to tap multiple learner senses?
    A. distance learning
    B. computer-based training
    C. E-learning
    D. cooperative training

    ANSWER: B, 294

50. Computer-supported _____ can replicate the psychological and behavioral requirements of a task.
    A. reality
    B. classroom training
    C. E-learning
    D. simulations

    ANSWER: D, 294

51. _____ creates an artificial environment for trainees so they can participate in the training
    A. Virtual reality
    B. Vestibule training
    C. New Age training
    D. A simulator

    ANSWER: A, 294

52. When a university asks students to complete an instructor-evaluation survey, it is evaluating training at the _____ level.
    A. results
    B. learning
    C. reaction
    D. behavior

    ANSWER: C, 295-296

53.   When a school gives trainees a test on the training material, it is evaluating
       training at the
       A.   results level.
       B.   learning level.
       C.   reaction level.
       D.   behavior level.

       ANSWER: B, 296

54.   The _____ level of evaluation involves measuring the effect of
       training on job performance through interviews of trainees and their coworkers
       and observing job performance.
       A.   reaction
       B.   learning
       C.   results
       D.   behavior

       ANSWER: D, 296

55.   The difficulty with evaluating results by measuring the effect of training on
       the achievement of organizational objectives is
       A.   pinpointing whether it actually was training that caused the changes.
       B.   that organizational results are not clearly quantifiable.
       C.   the criteria is hard to obtain.
       D.   being able to interpret subjective performance measures.

       ANSWER: A, 296

56.   Training can be examined on the basis of costs and benefits associated with the
       training through a
       A.   return on investment (ROI) analysis.
       B.   return on expectations (ROE) comparison.
       C.   cost-benefit analysis.
       D.   results-oriented evaluation.

       ANSWER: C, 296

57.   _____ to evaluate training, HR professionals in an organization gather
       data on training and compare them to data on training at other organizations in
       the industry and of their size.
       A.   In the results approach
       B.   To do benchmarking
       C.   To use a cost/benefit analysis
       D.   Using the reaction level of trainees

       ANSWER: B, 297

58.   A problem with the pre/post measure of evaluating training, is
       A.   the difficulty of constructing a good test.
       B.   being able to eliminate cultural discrimination.
       C.   being able to intervene in the workplace at the appropriate times.
       D.   knowing if the training was responsible for the changes.

       ANSWER: D, 298

59. One way to determine if the training caused the change in performance, or whether it was some other factor, is to use
    A.   a control group.
    B.   a pre-test measure.
    C.   benchmarking.
    D.   pre-/post-measure.

    ANSWER: A, 298

60. Which of the following is the best design for evaluation training?
    A.   benchmarking
    B.   a cost-benefit analysis
    C.   pre-/post-measure with control group
    D.   a rigorous evaluation of expectations

    ANSWER: C, 299

True and False

61. A distinction may be made between training and development, with training being broader in scope and focusing on individuals gaining new knowledge and skills useful for both present and future jobs.

    ANSWER: False, 272
    Actually it is development that is broader in scope with a longer-term focus.

62. Employers that invest in training and developing their employees do so as part of their retention efforts.

    ANSWER: True, 273

63. In a typical division of training responsibilities, operating managers prepare skill-training materials.

    ANSWER: False, 275
    The HR unit is responsible for preparing skill-training materials.

64. Strategic training focuses on efforts that develop competitive advantages for the organization.

    ANSWER: True, 276

65. A danger with strategic training is the temptation for HR professionals and trainers to chase the hottest type of training gimmick.

    ANSWER: False, 277
    One of the advantages of strategic training is that it prevents HR professionals and trainers from chasing fads or latest type of training gimmick.

66.   It is essential that objectives for training be related to the budgetary priorities identified in the organizational analysis.

ANSWER: False, 281
Training objectives and priorities are set to close the gap between where an organization is with its employee capabilities and where it needs to be.

67.   Self-efficacy refers to a person's desire to learn training content.

ANSWER: False, 282
Self-efficacy refers to a person's belief that he/she can successfully learn the training program content.

68.   Active practice occurs when the job instructions are divided into small elements after employees have had the opportunity to see how all the elements fit together.

ANSWER: False, 284
This is a description of whole or Gestalt learning. Active practice occurs when trainees perform job-related tasks and duties during training.

69.   Behavior modeling is the most elementary way in which people learn, and it is one of the best.

ANSWER: True, 284

70.   The concept of reinforcement is based on the law of confirmation, which states that people tend to repeat behaviors that receive a positive confirmation.

ANSWER: False, 285
The concept of reinforcement is based on the law of effect which states that people tend to repeat responses that give them some type of positive reward.

71.   People learn best if reinforcement and feedback is given as soon as possible after training.

ANSWER: True, 285

72.   For effective transfer of learning to occur, the use of the learned material must be maintained over time on the job.

ANSWER: True, 285

73.   The primary purpose of an orientation program is to provide information on how to do the job.

ANSWER: False, 286
This is only one of many purposes of orientation which also includes: establishing a favorable impression, enhancing interpersonal acceptance by co-workers, integrating the new employee into the organization, and productivity improvement.

74.   Fair employment laws and regulations also apply to training.

      ANSWER: True, 288

75.   On-the-job training is by far the most commonly used form of training, because it is provides little or no disruption to regular work.

      ANSWER: False, 289
      While OJT is the most common form of training, it can disrupt regular work.

76.   One problem with on-the-job training is the risk that supervisors can transfer bad habits or incorrect information to the trainees.

      ANSWER: True, 289

77.   Internships are a form of training used most often to train people for jobs in skilled crafts, such as carpentry, plumbing, photoengraving, typesetting, and welding.

      ANSWER: False, 293
      An internship is a form of on-the-job training that combines job training with classroom instruction. It is used for a range of jobs from trade to professional. Apprenticeships are primarily used for skilled crafts.

78.   Virtual reality can be used to create an artificial environment for police officers, training them when to use weapons when chasing suspects in darkened and crowded areas.

      ANSWER: True, 294

79.   One way to evaluate training at the behavioral level would be to measure the effect of the training on job performance.

      ANSWER: True, 296

80.   Since most of the benefits of training are intangible (such as attitude changes and safety awareness), it is rarely possible to evaluate the effectiveness of training programs.

      ANSWER: False, 296
      A comparison of the costs and benefits of training, which can often be measured, is the best way to determine if training is cost effective.

Essay

81.   What learning principles would you consider in designing a training program?

       ANSWER: 281-285
       Learning is a continual process and only occurs when information is received, understood, and internalized in such a way that some change or conscious effort has been made to use the information. The ability to learn must be accompanied by motivation to learn, and the belief that the program content can be learned. The principles of reinforcement and behavior modeling apply. Transfer of learning requires that the learning be applied on the job, and its use maintained over time.

82.   What is the purpose of an orientation program? What should be the format and content of an effective orientation?

       ANSWER: 286-288
       Orientation is the planned introduction of new employees to their jobs, coworkers, and the organization. For employers, the purpose is to provide organizational and job information, accelerate socialization and integration, and improve employee performance and productivity. For new employees it can help create a favorable impression and enhance interpersonal acceptance.

83.   What are some of the legal issues associated with training? What actions should an employer take to comply with EEO laws and regulations?

       ANSWER: 288
       EEO laws and regulations apply to training. They are concerned with criteria used to select individuals for inclusion in a training program. The criteria must be job related and not unfairly limit the participation of protected-class members. However, training is a cost, and courts have upheld the practice whereby some firms require trainees to sign training contracts to repay the training costs if the trainee left the firm within a specified time period.

84.   What is cooperative training? Describe its usefulness.

       ANSWER: 293-294
       Internships and apprenticeships are the two most widely used methods of cooperative training. They mix classroom training and on-the-job experience. They help the trainee get first-hand job experience and enables the employer to assess possible future job candidates.

85.   U.S. employers are spending at least $60 billion annually on training. How can an organization determine if its training expenditures are cost effective?

       ANSWER: 295-299
       While some benefits(such as attitude changes) are hard to quantify, the best approach involves a comparison of costs and benefits. Benchmarking training is one way of comparing costs with the benefits received. The pre-/post-measure with control group provides an objective evaluation.

Chapter 10

Careers and HR Development

Multiple Choice

1. As a result of mergers, acquisitions, restructurings, and layoffs, career success is now defined by
   A. the employer.
   B. the individual.
   C. co-workers.
   D. the employee's family.

   ANSWER: B, 306

2. In recent years, the way people look at careers has changed. The individual, not the organization, managers his or her own development. This has been caused by
   A. increased moonlighting.
   B. challenges to traditional ethical values.
   C. corporate growth and international expansion.
   D. mergers, acquisitions, restructurings, and layoffs.

   ANSWER: D, 306

3. A(n) _____ is a sequence of work-related positions a person occupies throughout life.
   A. career
   B. job
   C. profession
   D. occupation

   ANSWER: A, 307

4. Why do people pursue careers?
   A. to sustain life
   B. to achieve personal achievement
   C. to satisfy deeply individual needs
   D. an identification with the Protestant Work Ethic

   ANSWER: C, 307

5. A career plan in which an individual enters the sales department of an organization as a sales counselor, then is promoted to account director, to sales manager, and finally to vice-president of sales, would be an example of
    A.   individual-centered career planning.
    B.   organization-centered career planning.
    C.   lifetime employment.
    D.   career transitions.

    ANSWER: B, 307

6. More and more people are facing career transitions - they are forced to look for another job. Why?
    A.   Their ethical values are inconsistent with those of the organization.
    B.   They are planning for a second career.
    C.   Two career marriages have produced too many personal and job conflicts.
    D.   Organizational retrenchment and downsizing have changed career plans.

    ANSWER: D, 308

7. Individual-centered career planning focuses on
    A.   the individual's goals and skills.
    B.   the career ladder for that employee.
    C.   the replacement chart.
    D.   the internal opportunities for career advancement.

    ANSWER: A, 308

8. Individual characteristics that affect how people make career choices include
    A.   physical and cognitive traits.
    B.   self-identity and self-disclosure.
    C.   interests, self-image, personality, and social backgrounds.
    D.   a desire for certain individual and organizational rewards.

    ANSWER: C, 309

9. How a person chooses a specific organization is often a function of
    A.   the salary and other compensation offered by the organization.
    B.   the availability of a job when the person is looking for work.
    C.   the socioeconomic status and the education and occupation level of the person's parents.
    B.   the personal orientation and personal needs of the individual.

    ANSWER: B, 309

10. Which of the following is a recent characteristic of career progression?
    A.   The number of middle-management positions will continue to grow.
    B.   Small businesses will provide fewer and fewer jobs each year.
    C.   Large companies will be the source of increased career opportunities.
    D.   The typical career will include many different positions, transitions, and organizations.

    ANSWER: D, 309

11. Many theorists in adult development describe the first half of life as the young adult's quest for
    A. competence and a way to make a mark in the world.
    B. possessions, personal wealth, and security.
    C. personal integrity.
    D. challenge and risk taking.

    ANSWER: A, 309

12. During the first half of life, the young adult seeks happiness primarily through
    A. the development of integrity, values, and well-being.
    B. contributions to society.
    C. achievements and the acquisition of capabilities.
    D. a series of highly structured experiences.

    ANSWER: C, 310

13. During the second half of life, the individual's career interests involve
    A. retirement planning and income maintenance.
    B. the need for integrity, values, and well-being.
    C. the need to learn new skills.
    D. external achievements as measured by wealth and achievements.

    ANSWER: B, 310

14. Adult development theorists believe that
    A. lives and careers are predictably linear.
    B. from early childhood, people have preordained careers.
    C. a person's career is the manifestation of the inner values affecting that person's life.
    D. lives and careers must be viewed as cycles of structure and transition.

    ANSWER: D, 310

15. Which of the following was not identified as a common emotional adjustment faced by retirees?
    A. a renewed need for security
    B. a need to belong
    C. territoriality or personal "turf"
    D. pride in achievement

    ANSWER: A, 311-312

16. In an ideal sense, organizations view retirement as
    A. a way of "getting rid of" older workers.
    B. providing opportunities for fast-track younger people to move up in the organization.
    C. an orderly way to move people out at the ends of their careers.
    D. providing an opportunity to recognize people who have provided years of loyal service.

    ANSWER: C, 312

17. Which statement best describes phased retirement?
    A.   The organization strategically schedules retirements to ensure an orderly transition from retiree to replacement.
    B.   For the employee, the workweek is gradually reduced as vacation time increases.
    C.   Forced retirement is one phase of staff reductions as the result of downsizing and organizational restructurings.
    D.   Retirements are strategically phased to ensure that all valued employees do not retire at the same time.

    ANSWER: B, 312

18. A career plateau occurs when
    A.   a technical worker has no prospects for advancement.
    B.   a dual-career couple mutually agrees to put their marriage ahead of their careers.
    C.   when "baby boomers" reach midlife and mid-career.
    D.   employees find themselves "stuck" at a career level.

    ANSWER: D, 312

19. In order to reward talented technical people who do not want to move into management, many companies have established
    A.   dual career ladders.
    B.   portable career paths.
    C.   phased retirement plans.
    D.   the position of technical-professional.

    ANSWER: A, 313

20. Which of the following statements is true about dual-career couples?
    A.   Part-time work, flextime, and work-at-home arrangements are generally unacceptable options for most couples.
    B.   Dual-career couples are more mobile due to their dual income.
    C.   Dual-career couples have more to lose when relocating.
    D.   Their numbers are decreasing as more women opt for the "mommy track."

    ANSWER: C, 314

21. What is the most common concern of a worker whose partner has been transferred?
    A.   having to work with the partner-assistance program offered by the partner's employer
    B.   losing the support network of co-workers, friends, and business contacts
    C.   the prospect of having a "commuter marriage" and only being with the partner on alternate weekends
    D.   not being able to find comparable employment at the new location

    ANSWER: B, 315

22. _____ represents efforts to improve employees' ability to handle a variety of assignments.
     A.   Career planning
     B.   Succession planning
     C.   Employability
     D.   Development

     ANSWER: D, 315

23. What impact does HR development have on individuals' careers?
     A.   The individuals' careers may evolve and gain new or different focus.
     B.   The employees' career goals are subordinated to the organization's goals.
     C.   The employees will become more valuable to their organizations.
     D.   Individual careers will flourish and generate more success.

     ANSWER: A, 315

24. The focus of _____ is learning specific behaviors and actions, while _____ focuses on such areas as judgment, responsibility, decision making, and communication.
     A.   development; training
     B.   training; knowledge
     C.   training; development
     D.   knowledge; development

     ANSWER: C, 315

25. Development should begin with
     A.   an appraisal of the performance of all managers.
     B.   the HR plans of an organization.
     C.   a review of current training and development practices.
     D.   the career plans of current employees.

     ANSWER: B, 316

26. Which of the following statements best describes current trends regarding the hiring of technical and professional people?
     A.   Employers prefer to develop rather than "buy" their human resources.
     B.   There is a growing shortage of managers with technical backgrounds.
     C.   There is no consensus on what is the "best" way to develop technicians for managerial positions.
     D.   Hiring is based on the amount of skill development the candidates have already achieved.

     ANSWER: D, 316

27. What is an assessment center?
     A.   A collection of instruments and exercises designed to diagnose individuals' development needs.
     B.   The place specifically established for selection screening.
     C.   A procedure for evaluating training and development programs.
     D.   The organization's centralized employee performance appraisal system.

     ANSWER: A, 319

28. The advantages of assessment centers include
     A.   the "typical" manager can serve as an assessor.
     B.   they are used as a way of avoiding difficult promotion decisions.
     C.   they help identify employees with potential in a large organization.
     D.   they are not as expensive as traditional selection techniques.

     ANSWER: C, 319

29. Which of the following statements is true about assessment centers?
     A.   Assessment centers are used primarily for selecting management trainees.
     B.   Traits like leadership, initiative, and supervisory skills are more
           accurately assessed.
     C.   The assessment center is a place where employment testing is centralized.
     D.   Unfortunately, assessment centers have the same built-in biases as other
           selection techniques.

     ANSWER: B, 319

30. Which of the following is a concern about the use of assessment centers?
     A.   A clever participant can fake the results.
     B.   The conclusions reached usually are not valid.
     C.   They are subject to the same biases inherent in interview situations.
     D.   Managers may use them as a way to avoid difficult promotion decisions.

     ANSWER: D, 319

31. What is the primary use of psychological paper-and-pencil tests?
     A.   to determine employees' development potential and needs
     B.   to determine the employees' verbal and mathematical reasoning skills
     C.   to measure managerial experience
     D.   to measure general intelligence, verbal fluency, and mathematical ability

     ANSWER: A, 320

32. The biggest problem with psychological testing lies in
     A.   the limited validity of this type of tests.
     B.   how the tests are scored.
     C.   the interpretation of results.
     D.   the administration costs.

     ANSWER: C, 320

33. Which of the following is true regarding psychological testing?
     A.   The EEOC has banned the use of these tests by private-sector employers.
     B.   Such testing is appropriate only when the testing and feedback process is
           closely supervised by a qualified professional.
     C.   Psychological testing is never appropriate for developing employees.
     D.   Psychological tests are valid predictors of motivation, reasoning
           abilities, interpersonal response traits, and job preferences.

     ANSWER: B, 320

34. What is the purpose of succession planning?
    A. prepare for passing wealth from family-business owners to the next generation
    B. measure the success or failure of the strategic planning process
    C. provide for the orderly transition of ownership from one generation to the next
    D. identify a longer-term plan for the orderly replacement of key employees

    ANSWER: D, 321

35. The purpose of replacement charts is to
    A. ensure that the right individuals with sufficient capabilities and experience to perform the targeted jobs are available at the right time.
    B. prepare a collection of instruments and exercises designed for diagnosing a person's development needs.
    C. provide legal cover for an employer needing to replace an employee.
    D. help train and development recruiters in the HR department.

    ANSWER: A, 322

36. A _____ identifies who could take over key jobs if someone leaves, retires, dies unexpectedly, or otherwise creates a vacancy.
    A. succession plan
    B. career path
    C. replacement chart
    D. needs assessment

    ANSWER: C. 322

37. _____ is/are the daily training and feedback given to employees by immediate supervisors.
    A. Performance appraisal
    B. Coaching
    C. Committee assignments
    D. Development exercises

    ANSWER: B, 323

38. Coaching involves
    A. off-site meetings of the management group.
    B. development cascading down a hierarchy.
    C. learning the intellectual component of many skills.
    D. a continual process of learning by doing.

    ANSWER: D, 323

39. Which of the following is a limitation of committee assignments as a development method?
    A. Committee assignments can become time-wasting activities.
    B. Doing the work gets priority over learning.
    C. It can be a broadened experience.
    D. There is no guarantee that the trainee can perform the assignment well.

    ANSWER: A, 324

40.   When opportunities for promotion are scarce, what is an especially good way to keep employees motivated?
       A.   committee assignments
       B.   coaching
       C.   job rotation
       D.   assistant-to position

       ANSWER: C, 324

41.   As a development technique, the best lateral transfers
       A.   provide a continual process of learning.
       B.   move the person into the core business.
       C.   ensure trainees have an opportunity to deal with interesting assignments.
       D.   provide a monetary incentive for taking on new work.

       ANSWER: B, 324

42.   Limitations of job rotation as a development technique include
       A.   Trainees report constant job changes reduce their level of motivation.
       B.   Rotation reduces the potential for learning new skills.
       C.   Job rotation is only appropriate when the organization is growing and can provide increasingly new responsibilities.
       D.   Time is lost when trainees must become acquainted with different people and techniques in each new unit.

       ANSWER: D, 324

43.   Assistant-to positions are useful for development if
       A.   the assignments are challenging or interesting.
       B.   there is no money for outside development activities
       C.   a team of upper management people act as mentors to each individual.
       D.   mature individuals are selected for participation.

       ANSWER: A, 324

44.   _____ allow(s) participation in courses previously out of reach due to geographic, travel, or cost considerations.
       A.   Job rotation
       B.   Career development centers
       C.   On-line development
       D.   Corporate universities

       ANSWER: C, 324

45.   Advantages of off-the-job-site development techniques?
       A.   less disruptive of daily operations
       B.   contact with others concerned with somewhat different problems and coming from different organizations may provide new and different perspectives
       C.   a variety of available programs provided by a variety of educational institutions can provide a cornucopia of development possibilities
       D.   less expensive than on-the-job methods

       ANSWER: B, 325

46.   The lecture system has the following disadvantage:
      A.   Only a limited amount of information can be covered in a lecture.
      B.   The lecturer may be constantly interrupted by questions.
      C.   It is an expensive training and development technique.
      D.   Lectures encourage passive listening and reduced learner participation.

      ANSWER: D, 325

47.   Which of the following is true of classroom instruction?
      A.   Effectiveness depends on the instructors' style and the subject matter.
      B.   The lecture system discourages passive listening.
      C.   Classrooms promote opportunities to ask questions and seek clarification.
      D.   Its effectiveness is independent of the size of the group.

      ANSWER: A, 325

48.   What is the most common reason managers fail after being promoted to management?
      A.   lack of internal political savvy
      B.   deficiency of technical skills
      C.   poor teamwork with subordinates and peers
      D.   inability to balance work and family demands

      ANSWER: C, 326

49.   Which development techniques requires the participant to analyze a situation and decide the best course of action based on the data given?
      A.   case study
      B.   simulation
      C.   psychological analysis
      D.   role-playing

      ANSWER: B, 326

50.   For simulations to be an effective learning experience
      A.   the situation must be as "realistic" as possible.
      B.   facilitators must constantly "coach" the participants.
      C.   the participants must be given the freedom to fail.
      D.   learning must be the focus, not just "playing the game."

      ANSWER: D, 326

51.   A _____ is paid time off the job to develop and rejuvenate oneself.
      A.   sabbatical leave
      B.   leave of absence
      C.   wilderness-survival course
      D.   simulated leave

      ANSWER: A, 326

52. Which of the following is a disadvantage of paid sabbaticals?
    A.   The executives often work so hard during the sabbatical, that they burnout upon their return.
    B.   It is not a viable option for business organizations.
    C.   The nature of the learning experience is not within the control of the organization and is left somewhat to chance.
    D.   Executives often use the sabbatical to look for another job.

    ANSWER: C, 326

53. Wilderness excursions as a development tool
    A.   are an activity enjoyed by everybody involved.
    B.   can create a sense of teamwork via the shared-risks and challenges.
    C.   help work-groups members reevaluate their goals.
    D.   are a fad with very little value for management development.

    ANSWER: B, 326-327

54. Managers learn by behavior modeling, which is defined as
    A.   reinforcing the desirable behaviors exhibited.
    B.   articulate reflection.
    C.   setting an example for junior managers.
    D.   copying someone else's behavior.

    ANSWER: D, 328

55. In the context of management development, _____ involves a relationship between two managers for a period of time as they perform their jobs.
    A.   management coaching
    B.   behavioral modeling
    C.   human relations training
    D.   assistant-to development

    ANSWER: A, 328

56. _____ is a relationship in which experienced managers aid individuals in the earlier stages of their careers.
    A.   Human relations training
    B.   Management coaching
    C.   Mentoring
    D.   Modeling

    ANSWER: C, 329

57. Which of the following has been identified as a problem with mentoring?
    A.   Women are reluctant to serve as mentors.
    B.   Young minority managers frequently report difficulty finding mentors.
    C.   The relationship between mentor and protégé may become more social than work related.
    D.   Successful managers do not have the time to be effective mentors.

    ANSWER: B, 329

58. The glass ceiling refers to
    A. mentors describing the experiences of top management to a younger manager.
    B. the "window" through which the outside world can see inside the organization.
    C. senior managers illustrating the opportunities for younger managers to progress in the organization.
    D. the situation in which women fail to progress into top management positions.

    ANSWER: D, 330

59. Which of the following statements is true regarding mentoring?
    A. One approach to breaking through the glass ceiling is mentoring.
    B. Young minority managers find white managers are willing to help them.
    C. Women are less willing to be mentors than men.
    D. Mentoring is seen as a one-way-street, with the younger manager getting all the benefits from the relationship.

    ANSWER: A, 330

60. When an individual learns new methods and ideas in a development course and returns to a work unit that is still bound by old attitudes and methods,
    A. lost transference occurs.
    B. non-transference has ensued.
    C. encapsulated development occurs.
    D. negative reinforcement is experienced.

    ANSWER: C, 331

True and False

61. Organization-centered career planning focuses on finding opportunities for career growth within the organizational structure.

    ANSWER: False, 307
    It focuses on jobs and on identifying career paths that provide for the logical progression of people between jobs in an organization.

62. The primary reason why people choose one organization rather than another is the compensation package.

    ANSWER: False, 309
    Other than timing, little is know about how people choose organizations.

63. The objective of a phased retirement program is to aid in the transition of individuals to a useful retirement.

    ANSWER: True, 312

64.   Dual career ladders have been established by many large companies to deal with the problems faced by dual-career couples.

ANSWER: False, 313
Dual career paths have been established to enable technical and professional workers to advance in their organizations without having to move into management.

65.   The purpose of a partner-assistance program is to assist in the relocation of dual-career couples.

ANSWER: True, 315

66.   Development involves cultivating capacities beyond those required by the current job.

ANSWER: True, 315

67.   The HR development process should begin with a detailed analysis of the current operations of the organization.

ANSWER: False, 316
Development should begin with the HR plans of an organization because these plans analyze, forecast, and identify current and future organizational needs for human resources.

68.   Assessment centers are specially equipped training facilities that are used to evaluate individual employees.

ANSWER: False, 319
Assessment centers are not places as much as they are collections of instruments and exercises designed to diagnose an individual's development needs.

69.   Psychological testing can furnish useful information to employers about such factors as motivation, reasoning abilities, leadership styles, interpersonal response traits, and job preferences.

ANSWER: True, 320

70.   Succession planning should not be limited just to top executive jobs.

ANSWER: True, 321

71.   In closely-held Family firms (those that are not publicly traded on stock exchanges), most CEOs arrange for the business to be sold following their retirement or death.

ANSWER: False, 321
Many CEOs plan to pass the business on to a family member. Thus succession planning is important.

72.   The purpose of replacement charts is to document who will temporarily take over responsibilities if the person in charge is unavailable.

ANSWER: False, 322
Their purpose is to ensure that the right individuals with sufficient capabilities and experience to perform the targeted jobs are available at the right time.

73.   Coaching is the daily training and feedback given to employees by immediate supervisors.

ANSWER: True, 323

74.   A substantial amount of managerial time is lost when job rotation is used as a management development technique.

ANSWER: True, 324

75.   On-line development is a novel approach whereby staff people work in line positions thus gaining valuable "hands-on" work experience.

ANSWER: False, 324
On-line development involves video conferencing, live chat, document sharing, streamlining video and audio, and Web-based courses.

76.   The purpose of human relations training is to build teamwork among co-workers.

ANSWER: False, 326
The purpose is to equip supervisors with the skills necessary for dealing with "people problems" brought to them by their subordinates.

77.   Simulations and business games are a development technique that require the participant to analyze a situation and decide the best course of action based on the data given.

ANSWER: True, 326

78.   Behavior modeling is defined as copying someone else's behavior.

ANSWER: True, 328

79.   Mentoring may be a useful way to attack the "glass ceiling" since it was found that women with mentors move up faster than those without mentors.

ANSWER: True, 320

80.   Encapsulated development occurs when an individual learns new methods in a development course and is able to incorporate what was learnt upon returning to the work unit.

ANSWER: False, 312
Just the opposite. Encapsulated development occurs when the individual returns to a work unit that is still bound by old attitudes and methods.

Essay

81.   Describe the unique problems faced by dual-career couples. What can an employer do to address these problems?

ANSWER: 313-315
Problems include family issues, recruiting, and transfers. Actions to address family issues include part-time work, flextime, and work-at-home arrangements. For recruitment and relocation, an employer can establish a partner-assistance program, pay employment agency fees, hire the spouse, or develop computerized job banks listing partners available for jobs, to share with other companies.

82.   Define HR development. What is the difference between development and training? What variables enter into the decision to "buy" rather than "make" scarce employees in today's labor market?

ANSWER: 315-317
HR development represents efforts to improve employees' ability to handle a variety of assignments. As contrasted to training, development involves growing capabilities that go beyond those required by the current job. Developing (or making) human resources is expensive and many firms prefer to buy if the resources are available. However buying does not contribute to a strategy of sustained competitive advantage through human resources.

83.   Discuss the concept of lifelong learning as it applies to HR development.

ANSWER: 318
Lifelong learning is a recognition that learning and development do not occur only once during a person's lifetime. Many professions require continuing education for certification. For skilled and semi-skilled employees, it involves training to expand existing skills.

84.   What is an assessment center? What role can an assessment center play in an organization's HR development process?

ANSWER: 319
An assessment center is a collection of instruments and exercises designed to diagnose a person's development needs. They can help identify key variables such as leadership, initiative, and supervisory skills. They are also useful as a selection tool to identify managerial potential and can overcome many of the biases inherent in interviews, supervisor ratings, and written tests.

85.   Describe a typical mentoring relationship. How can mentoring aid women and minorities in their career advancement?

ANSWER: 329-330
Mentoring is a relationship in which experienced managers aid individuals in the early stages of their careers, conveying technical, interpersonal, and organizational skills. Historically, most mentoring relationships have involved white males. Mentoring has been found to be useful in countering the glass ceiling, which is assumed to prevent many protected-class members from advancing in their organizations.

Chapter 11

Performance Management and Appraisal

Multiple Choice

1. A _____ system consists of the processes used to identify, encourage, measure, evaluate, improve, and reward employee performance.
    A.   performance appraisal
    B.   performance management
    C.   organizational analysis
    D.   organizational feedback

    ANSWER: B, 338

2. Performance management links organizational strategy to organizational
    A.   culture.
    B.   goal setting.
    C.   rewards.
    D.   results.

    ANSWER: D, 338

3. Performance is essentially
    A.   what an employee does or does not do.
    B.   limited to what can be effectively measured.
    C.   what a supervisor says it is.
    D.   the quantity and qualify of output.

    ANSWER: A, 338

4. What are job criteria?
    A.   the most important duties and tasks of jobs
    B.   expected levels of performance
    C.   important elements in a given job
    D.   the essential elements of a job

    ANSWER: C, 338

5. _____ define what the organization is paying an employee to do.
    A.   Performance measures
    B.   Job criteria
    C.   Essential job elements
    D.   Expected performance levels

    ANSWER: B, 338

6. _____ information identifies a subjective character trait of the employee, such as attitude, initiative, or creativity.
    A.   Results-oriented
    B.   Behaviorally-anchored
    C.   Personality-factor
    D.   Trait-based

    ANSWER: D, 339

7. Courts have held that the _____ information is too vague to use when making performance-based HR decisions.
    A.   trait-based
    B.   results-based
    C.   behavior-oriented
    D.   productivity-based

    ANSWER: A, 340

8. Which type of performance information is the most difficult to identify?
    A.   trait-based
    B.   results-based
    C.   behavior-based
    D.   productivity-based

    ANSWER: C, 340

9. Which of the following is true about using behavior-based information for evaluating job performance?
    A.   The aim is to identify the one behavior which will lead to job success.
    B.   Behavior-based information clearly specifies the behaviors management wants to see.
    C.   Behavior-based information is the easiest to develop.
    D.   Behavior-based information looks at what the employee has done or accomplished.

    ANSWER: B, 340

10. Results-based information, used for evaluation performance,
    A.   focuses on specific behaviors that lead to job success.
    B.   identifies character traits that result from job success.
    C.   determines how well the employees do their jobs.
    D.   considers employee accomplishments.

    ANSWER: D, 340

11.   A results-based approach works very well for jobs in which
      A.   measurement is easy and obvious.
      B.   performance criteria are multidimensional.
      C.   team work is emphasized.
      D.   employees need little or no supervision.

      ANSWER: A, 340

12.   Performance measures are said to be _____ if they leave out some
      important job duties.
      A.   subjective
      B.   contaminated
      C.   deficient
      D.   unnecessary

      ANSWER: C, 340

13.   Performance measures that include some irrelevant criteria are said to be
      A.   subjective.
      B.   contaminated.
      C.   deficient.
      D.   unnecessary.

      ANSWER: B, 340

14.   Counting the number of invoices that a clerk processes each day would be an
      example of a(n) _____ measure of performance.
      A.   quality
      B.   subjective
      C.   acceptable
      D.   objective

      ANSWER: D, 340

15.   A supervisor's ratings of an employee's attitude is an example of a(n)
      A.   subjective measure.
      B.   objective measure.
      C.   deficient measure.
      D.   acceptable measure.

      ANSWER: A, 340

16.   _____ define the expected levels of performance.
      A.   Job criteria
      B.   Job analyses
      C.   Performance standards
      D.   Essential elements

      ANSWER: C, 341

17.   Performance _____ define the expected levels of performance.
        A.   measures
        B.   standards
        C.   appraisals
        D.   objectives

        ANSWER: B, 341

18.   Requiring that bank tellers balance at the end of each day is an example of a(n)
        _____ standard of performance.
        A.   objective
        B.   subjective
        C.   acceptable
        D.   nonnumerical

        ANSWER: D, 341

19.   _____ is the process of evaluating how well employees perform their
        jobs when compared to a set of standards, and then communicating that
        information to those employees.
        A.   Performance appraisal
        B.   Job evaluation
        C.   Appraisal interview
        D.   Supervisor rating

        ANSWER: A, 342

20.   The two general uses of performance appraisal, which are often in conflict, are
        A.   salary administration and discipline.
        B.   training and development.
        C.   administrative and development.
        D.   coaching and career planning

        ANSWER: C, 343

21.   Which of the following is an example of the administrative role of performance
        appraisal?
        A.   identifying weaknesses to determine coaching needs
        B.   measuring performance for the purpose of making pay decisions
        C.   identifying the organization's training needs
        D.   communicating feedback to the employee

        ANSWER: B, 343

22.   What is the role of appraisal in compensation administration?
        A.   It is the direct determinant of most compensation increases.
        B.   It has very little input into most compensation programs.
        C.   It is perceived by employees as the critical factor in pay raises.
        D.   It is the link between productivity and rewards.

        ANSWER: D, 343

23.   _____ affirms the idea that pay raises should be given for performance accomplishments rather that for seniority.
    A.   Performance-based compensation
    B.   Performance management
    C.   The appraisal interview
    D.   Wage and salary administration

ANSWER: A, 343

24.   Why are performance appraisals necessary when organizations terminate, promote, or pay people differently?
    A.   They help explain the connection between merit and seniority.
    B.   They provide developmental information to the employees.
    C.   They are a crucial defense if employees sue over such decisions.
    D.   They are an important input to the strategic planning process.

ANSWER: C, 344

25.   In addition to compensation administration, performance appraisal
    A.   predicts management success.
    B.   is a primary source of information and feedback for employees.
    C.   helps assess the potential of an employee.
    D.   identifies promotional opportunities.

ANSWER: B, 344

26.   Which of the following best describes the manager's role in the developmental aspect of performance appraisal?
    A.   judge
    B.   father/mother
    C.   teacher
    D.   coach

ANSWER: D, 344

27.   What is the purpose of developmental feedback?
    A.   to change or reinforce individual behavior
    B.   to provide examples of acceptable and unacceptable performance
    C.   to compare individuals
    D.   to prepare candidates for promotion

ANSWER: A, 344

28.   Which of the following would be a development function of performance appraisal?
    A.   linking performance appraisal with promotional opportunities
    B.   permitting the employee to comment on the supervisor's performance
    C.   identifying areas in which the employee might wish to grow
    D.   communication performance expectations to the employee

ANSWER: C, 344

29. How can teams be useful in the appraisal process?
     A.   Teams are equipped to handle administrative appraisal.
     B.   Teams can provide developmental feedback to members.
     C.   Teams can provide useful input in downsizing situations.
     D.   Teams are better able to allocate rewards based on merit.

     ANSWER: B, 344

30. A(n) _____ is conducted as part of the day-to-day working relationship
     between a manager and an employee.
     A.   HR functionary
     B.   systematic appraisal
     C.   HR evaluation
     D.   informal appraisal

     ANSWER: D, 344

31. Which of the following statements is true regarding informal appraisals?
     A.   Frequent informal feedback to employees can prevent surprises later when
           the formal evaluation is communicated.
     B.   When time is an issue, informal appraisals are not as appropriate.
     C.   On-the-spot examinations of a piece of work are an unacceptable practice.
     D.   The day-to-day working relationship between a manager and an employee
           would be disrupted by regular informal appraisals.

     ANSWER: A, 345

32. A(n) _____ is used when the contact between manager and employee is
     formal, and a system is in place to report managerial impressions and
     observations on employee performance.
     A.   HR functionary
     B.   HR evaluation
     C.   systematic appraisal
     D.   informal appraisal

     ANSWER: C, 345

33. In the typical division of appraisal responsibilities, the HR unit is
     responsible for
     A.   rating performance of employees.
     B.   designing and maintaining the formal system.
     C.   reviewing appraisals with employees.
     D.   providing regular informal appraisals.

     ANSWER: B, 345

34. In the appraisal process, managers are typically responsible for
     A.   making sure the reports are in on time.
     B.   training the raters.
     C.   designing the formal appraisal system.
     D.   reviewing appraisals with employees.

     ANSWER: D, 345

35. The timing of performance appraisals and pay discussions should be different because
    A. employees often focus more on the pay amount than on what they need to improve.
    B. each of these activities fall under different HR managers, and need different coordination times.
    C. for maximum reinforcement value, the pay discussion should be conducted at a later time.
    D. most supervisors don't know how much their employees are paid.

    ANSWER: A, 346

36. Traditional ratings of employees by supervisors is based on the assumption that
    A. employees are more receptive to criticism from their immediate supervisors.
    B. they have regular day-to-day opportunities for informal appraisals.
    C. the immediate supervisor is the person most qualified to evaluate the employee's performance realistically, objectively, and fairly.
    D. supervisors are more aware of their subordinates' desires and goals.

    ANSWER: C, 347

37. Which of the following applies to the concept of employees rating superiors and managers?
    A. Supervisors strongly oppose the concept.
    B. It can contribute to the career development effort for the managers.
    C. It decreases internal group conflict since employees now have an outlet for their grievances.
    D. It results in managers catering to employee whims, causing them to be less effective.

    ANSWER: B, 348

38. In which of the following situations would peer ratings be most appropriate?
    A. A group of salespeople meets regularly as a committee to talk about one another's customer relations achievements.
    B. The manager is too busy to meet with each subordinate for a formal appraisal interview.
    C. The members of the work group are drawn from a diverse population.
    D. The supervisor does not have the opportunity to observe each employee's performance, but other work group members do.

    ANSWER: D, 348

39. Total quality management (TQM) emphasizes
    A. team performance rather than individual performance.
    B. a balance between quality and quantity of outcomes.
    C. individual accountability for the quality of work outcomes.
    D. quality of outputs over total quantity.

    ANSWER: A, 348

40. Difficulties with team appraisals include
     A.   team members may not be qualified to judge the performance of others.
     B.   "free riders" will get the same rating as the hardest worker.
     C.   team members may "go easy" on their colleagues to spare feelings.
     D.   the supervisor is unable to observe each team member's performance.

     ANSWER: C, 348

41. _____ is a self-development tool that forces employees to think about
     their strengths and weaknesses and set goals for improvement.
     A.   Supervisory appraisal
     B.   Self-appraisal
     C.   Team evaluation
     D.   Peer evaluation

     ANSWER: B, 349

42. Multisource, or _____, recognizes that the manager is no longer the
     sole source of performance appraisal information.
     A.   team appraisal
     B.   outside raters
     C.   peer evaluation
     D.   360° rating

     ANSWER: D, 349

43. In which appraisal method is feedback obtained from various colleagues and
     constituencies and given to the manager?
     A.   360° appraisal
     B.   supervisors rating their employees
     C.   team members rating each other
     D.   comprehensive appraisal

     ANSWER: A, 349

44. The 360° rating method appears to be more appropriate, and less threatening, for
     A.   employee evaluation purposes.
     B.   top management appraisal.
     C.   development uses.
     D.   the appraisal of mid-level managers.

     ANSWER: C, 351

45. The simplest methods for appraising performance are the
     A.   behaviorally anchored rating scales (BARS).
     B.   category rating methods.
     C.   comparative methods.
     D.   written methods.

     ANSWER: B, 352

46.   The _____ allows the rater to mark an employee's performance on a
      continuum.
      A.   ranking system
      B.   checklist
      C.   forced distribution
      D.   graphic rating scale

      ANSWER: D, 352

47.   Which of the following are characteristics of graphic rating scales?
      A.   Descriptive words used may have different meanings to different raters.
      B.   Interrater reliability is high.
      C.   Raters are forced to choose among several statements to describe an
            employee's performance.
      D.   The descriptors can be modified to assign various weights to ratings.

      ANSWER: A, 352

48.   Which performance appraisal method consists of listing all employees from
      highest to lowest in performance?
      A.   checklist
      B.   graphic rating scale
      C.   ranking
      D.   forced distribution

      ANSWER: C, 354

49.   The forced distribution method of appraisal assumes that
      A.   supervisors understand the theory of individual differences.
      B.   the "bell-shaped curve" of performance exists in a given group.
      C.   supervisors can make the necessary distinctions in their group.
      D.   it is possible to compare each employee with each other in the group.

      ANSWER: B, 396

50.   In the _____ method, the manager keeps a written record of both highly
      favorable and unfavorable actions in an employee's performance during the entire
      rating period.
      A.   checklist
      B.   paired comparisons
      C.   essay
      D.   critical incident

      ANSWER: D, 355

51.   In a(n) _____, an outsider interviews the manager about each
      employee's performance, then compiles the notes from each interview into a
      rating for each employee.
      A.   field review
      B.   external audit
      C.   critical incident appraisal
      D.   essay appraisal

      ANSWER: A, 356

52. Attempting to assess an employee's behaviors instead of other characteristics is the purpose of
    A.   critical incident techniques.
    B.   a management by objectives system.
    C.   behavioral rating approaches.
    D.   job dimension methods.

    ANSWER: C, 356

53. What is the first step in constructing behavioral scales?
    A.   determining a "standard of excellence" for each job dimension
    B.   identifying the most important performance factors in an employee's job description
    C.   assessing the performance of the current job holder(s)
    D.   specifying the performance goals that each employee hopes to attain within an appropriate period of time

    ANSWER: B, 356

54. _____ specifies the performance goals that an individual and his or her manager agree to try to attain within an appropriate length of time.
    A.   Behavioral rating scales
    B.   Strategic performance management
    C.   The critical incident technique (CIT)
    D.   Management by objectives (MBO)

    ANSWER: D, 357

55. Which of the following is a key assumption underlying Management by objectives?
    A.   An employee who is involved in planning and setting objectives and determining the performance measures tend to show a higher level of commitment and performance.
    B.   If supervisors set clearly defined objectives, employees are motivated to increased levels of effort.
    C.   Employees perform better when they don't deviate from clear and precise objectives.
    D.   There should be an emphasis on penalties associated with not meeting objectives.

    ANSWER: A, 357

56. The _____ occurs when a rater gives greater weight to recent events when appraising an individual's performance.
    A.   contrast error
    B.   halo error
    C.   recency effect
    D.   primacy effect

    ANSWER: C, 360

57. A _____ is committed when an appraiser rates all employees within a narrow range (usually the middle or average).
    A.   contrast error
    B.   central tendency error
    C.   generalization error
    D.   leniency error

    ANSWER: B, 360

58. The "tendency to rate people relative to other people rather than to performance standards" is the definition of _____ error.
    A.   central tendency
    B.   generalization
    C.   halo
    D.   contrast

    ANSWER: D, 360

59. A legally defensible performance appraisal system should include which of the following?
    A.   appraisal criteria based on job analysis
    B.   opportunity for self appraisals
    C.   informal evaluation criteria to permit managerial discretion
    D.   input from outsiders who can provide objective feedback

    ANSWER: A, 364

60. Which of the following was identified as an organizational tendency that diminishes the value of many appraisal systems?
    A.   minimizing the time spent on discussing the results
    B.   permitting HR personnel to revise forms based on AAP concerns
    C.   distilling performance appraisals into a single number that can be used to support pay raises
    D.   not allowing employees to participate in designing the appraisal forms

    ANSWER: C, 365

True and False

61. Many court decisions have held that performance evaluations based on traits are too vague to use as the basis for performance-based HR decisions.

    ANSWER: True, 340

62. Subjective measures of performance tend to be more narrowly focused than objective measures, leading to subjective measures being inadequately defined.

    ANSWER: False, 340
    Subjective measures are judgmental and thus difficult to measure. Objective measures are limited to what can be counted and so tend to be narrowly defined.

63.   Realistic, measurable, clearly understood performance standards benefit both the organization and the employees.

      ANSWER: True, 341

64.   The two roles of appraisal, administrative decision making and development, are seen as generally complimentary.

      ANSWER: False, 343
      The two roles are in potential conflict. Evaluations leading to compensation, promotion, or layoff decisions, may conflict with the manager's counselor role.

65.   The purpose of developmental feedback is to compare individuals.

      ANSWER: False, 344
      The is to change or reinforce individual behavior, rather than comparisons.

66.   A systematic appraisal is used when the contact between manager and employee is formal, and a system is in place to report managerial impressions and observations on employee performance.

      ANSWER: True, 345

67.   It is argued that the timing of performance appraisals and pay discussions should be different because managers may manipulate pay adjustments to justify performance ratings.

      ANSWER: False, 346
      The major reason for separating performance appraisals from pay discussions is so that the focus will be on improvement rather than the pay amount. There is the danger that managers may manipulate the ratings to justify the pay decision.

68.   The most common method of performance appraisal involves employees being evaluated by their immediate supervisors.

      ANSWER: True, 347

69.   One advantage of having supervisors and managers rated by their employees is that this type of rating program can help make the managers more responsive to employees.

      ANSWER: True, 348

70.   Peer ratings are best when used for administrative purposes, such as determining equitable pay increases, rather than for developmental purposes.

      ANSWER: False, 348
      Peer ratings are useful for development when supervisors do not have the opportunity to closely observe each team member's performance.

71.   Self-appraisal is essentially a self-development tool that forces employees to think about their strengths and weaknesses and set goals for improvement.

      ANSWER: True, 349

72. The purpose of multisource or 360° feedback is to obtain reliable assessments of an employee's performance from a variety of sources.

ANSWER: False, 349
The purpose is not to increase reliability by soliciting like-minded views, rather it is to capture all of the differing evaluations that bear on the employee's different roles.

73. A graphic rating scale is an example of the category rating method.

ANSWER: True, 352

74. The forced distribution method of performance appraisal lists all employees from highest to lowest in performance.

ANSWER: False, 354
The ranking method consists of listing all employees from highest to lowest.

75. The forced distribution method of appraisal assumes that the widely known bell-shaped curve of performance exists in a given group.

ANSWER: True, 354

76. In the behavioral rating approaches to performance appraisal, the manager keeps a record of both favorable and unfavorable actions in an employee's performance.

ANSWER: False, 356
The behavioral approach assesses an employee's behaviors instead of other characteristics.

77. Management by objectives evaluates managers by the extent to which they have achieved organizational objectives.

ANSWER: False, 357
MBO specifies the performance goals that an individual and his or her manager agree to try to attain within an appropriate length of time. Although these goals are derived from the overall goals of the organization, employees are appraised by the extent to which they meet their individual goals.

78. The recency effect occurs when a rater gives greater weight to recent events when appraising an individual's performance.

ANSWER: True, 360

79. EEOC requires that performance appraisals be job-related and nondiscriminatory.

ANSWER: True, 364

80. The overall aim of an effective system is to distill performance appraisal into a single number that can be used to support pay raises.

ANSWER: False, 365
A system that is focused on pay raises fails to fulfil the developmental role of performance management.

Essay

81.   Describe the role of performance appraisal in administrative decision making. What is the possible impact of poorly conducted appraisals?

ANSWER: 342-344
Performance appraisal is a process of evaluating how well employees perform their jobs. One purpose is for rewarding or otherwise making administrative decisions, such as compensation, promotion, dismissal, downsizing, and layoffs. In the absence of good performance appraisal, ineffective, unfair, and possibly unlawful decisions may be made.

82.   Describe the role of performance appraisal in the development of employees. What appraisal methods are appropriate for this role?

ANSWER: 342-344, 356-358
In the role of development, the manager operates as a coach. The emphasis is on changing or reinforcing individual behavior. Development uses include identifying strengths, identifying areas for growth, developmental planning, and coaching and career planning. Appraisal methods useful for development include behavioral rating approaches and management by objectives.

83.   What is multisource appraisal? Why are some organizations using this approach to performance appraisal?

ANSWER: 349-351
Multisource or 360° rating recognizes that the manager is not the sole source of performance information. Feedback is obtained from various colleagues and constituencies and given to the manager. It is useful for development purposes.

84.   Describe the possible sources of error in the performance appraisal process.

ANSWER: 359-361
Problems of varying standards occur when there are ambiguous criteria and subjective weightings. Recency effect occurs when greater weight is placed on recent events. Central tendency, leniency, and strictness errors occur when a manager rates all employees within a narrow range. Rater bias occurs when a rater's values or prejudices distort the rating. The halo effect occurs when a person is rated high or low on all items because of just one characteristic. The contrast error is the tendency to rate people relative to other people rather than to performance standards.

85.   Discuss the characteristics of a legal appraisal system.

ANSWER: 364
The Uniform Guidelines issued by the EEOC and other federal enforcement agencies make it clear that performance appraisal must be job related and nondiscriminatory. Court decisions have, in effect, stated that the appraisal system must be based on job analysis, have evidence of validity, limit managerial discretion, and not have disparate impact.

Chapter 12

Compensation Strategies and Practices

Multiple Choice

1. Compensation is important. Why must employers provide several types of compensation?
   A. to meet employee needs.
   B. to attract, retain, and reward employees
   C. to reward employees for outstanding performance
   D. to allocate scarce organizational resources

   ANSWER: B, 372

2. Which of the following would be an example of an intrinsic reward?
   A. stock options
   B. additional medical insurance coverage
   C. country club memberships
   D. praise from a supervisor for completing a special project

   ANSWER: D, 372

3. Medical insurance, paid by the employer, is classified as _____ compensation.
   A. indirect
   B. direct
   C. variable
   D. intrinsic

   ANSWER: A, 372

4. Which of the following is identified as the basic compensation an employees receives?
   A. incentive
   B. benefits
   C. base pay
   D. motivator

   ANSWER: C, 373

5.   _____ are payments directly calculated on the amount of time worked.
     A.   Salaries
     B.   Wages
     C.   Incentives
     D.   Bonuses

     ANSWER: B, 373

6.   People who are paid _____ receive consistent payments each period regardless of the number of hours worked.
     A.   compensation
     B.   base pay
     C.   wages
     D.   salaries

     ANSWER: D, 373

7.   Which type of compensation is linked directly to individual, team, or organizational performance?
     A.   variable pay
     B.   motivators
     C.   wages
     D.   salary

     ANSWER: A, 373

8.   A(n) _____ is an indirect reward given to an employee or group of employees as a part of organizational membership.
     A.   incentive
     B.   perk
     C.   benefit
     D.   motivator

     ANSWER: C, 373

9.   In a division of compensation responsibilities, _____ typically conduct(s) job evaluations and wage surveys.
     A.   operating managers
     B.   HR specialists
     C.   senior management
     D.   outside consultants

     ANSWER: B, 373

10. In a typical division of compensation responsibilities, the HR unit would be responsible for
     A.   recommending pay rates and pay increases.
     B.   monitoring attendance and productivity for compensation purposes.
     C.   attempting to match performance with rewards.
     D.   conducting job evaluations.

     ANSWER: D, 374

11. In a typical division of compensation responsibilities, operating managers
     A.   evaluate employee performance for compensation purposes.
     B.   develop and administer the compensation system.
     C.   conduct wage surveys.
     D.   develop wage and salary structures and policies.

     ANSWER: A, 374

12. Because so many organizational funds are spent on compensation-related activities, it is crucial for top management and HR executives to match compensation practices with
     A.   affirmative action guidelines.
     B.   their compensation strategies annually.
     C.   what the organization is trying to do.
     D.   organizational, unit and individual performance.

     ANSWER: C, 374

13. Which of the following would be a recommended compensation practice for a new organization that wishes to create an innovative, entrepreneurial culture?
     A.   offer high starting salaries to attract highly-talented employees
     B.   set base pay at modest levels and offer bonuses and stock equity programs
     C.   establish a highly structured pay and benefits program
     D.   establish pay levels consistent with the results of a salary survey

     ANSWER: B, 374

14. Which of the following would be a recommended compensation practice for a large, static organization?
     A.   offer stock equity programs, while keeping pay at modest levels
     B.   offer high starting salaries to attract highly-talented employees
     C.   establish pay levels consistent with the results of a salary survey
     D.   establish a highly structured pay and benefits program

     ANSWER: D, 374

15. _____ organizations are more likely to design a compensation system that favored recruiting and success over retention.
     A.   Dynamic, rapidly changing
     B.   Traditional, family-owned
     C.   Merit-based
     D.   Union-free

     ANSWER: A, 374

16. The two basic compensation philosophies, which should be seen as opposite ends of a continuum, are the _____ and the _____ orientations.
     A.   merit; seniority
     B.   exempt; non-exempt
     C.   entitlement; performance
     D.   time; productivity

     ANSWER: C, 374

17. Most employees receive the same or nearly the same cost-of-living increase each year in an organization that has a(n) _____ orientation.
   A.   performance
   B.   entitlement
   C.   "don't-rock-the-boat"
   D.   fairness

   ANSWER: B, 375

18. Bonuses are determined very paternalistically in what type of organization?
   A.   entrepreneurial
   B.   strategic
   C.   performance-oriented
   D.   entitlement-oriented

   ANSWER: D, 375

19. In an organization with a performance-oriented philosophy,
   A.   no one is guaranteed increased compensation just for completing another year of service.
   B.   all employees can at least count on an annual cost-of-living adjustment to their salaries.
   C.   commissions and piece-rate incentives replace traditional salaries.
   D.   fairness concerns dominate compensation decisions.

   ANSWER: A, 375

20. The total rewards approach tries to place a value of _____ rather than just
   A.   performance; employees.
   B.   merit; job duties.
   C.   employees; the jobs.
   D.   teams; individuals.

   ANSWER: C, 377

21. Organizations that have specifically stated policies about where they wish to be positioned in the labor market use a
   A.   competitive-position strategy.
   B.   quartile strategy.
   C.   bench marking strategy.
   D.   labor market strategy.

   ANSWER: B, 378

22. Employers may choose to use a _____ if there is an abundance of lower-skilled workers.
   A.   competitive-pricing strategy
   B.   foreign-worker strategy
   C.   third-quartile approach
   D.   first-quartile approach

   ANSWER: D, 378

23. A third-quartile approach is a(n)
     A.   aggressive, above-market approach.
     B.   strategy to pay below market compensation.
     C.   strategy based on merit.
     D.   team-based approach.

     ANSWER: A, 379

24. An organization can benefit from a properly designed and implemented competency-based pay system through
     A.   lower overall labor costs.
     B.   increased retention rates.
     C.   greater workforce flexibility.
     D.   improved participative decision making.

     ANSWER: C, 380

25. Employee-oriented outcomes of competency-based pay systems include
     A.   increased compensation.
     B.   enhanced employee understanding of the organizational "big picture."
     C.   increased employee dissatisfaction, turnover, and absenteeism.
     D.   fewer bottlenecks in the work flow.

     ANSWER: B, 380

26. Which of the following has been the most successful use of team-based compensation?
     A.   pay-for-performance based on team member input
     B.   skill-based pay plus a percentage of base pay
     C.   equal pay for each team member based on team performance
     D.   team-based variable pay on top of base pay

     ANSWER: D, 380

27. Base pay, variable pay, and benefits are the _____ one receives from a job.
     A.   outcomes
     B.   outputs
     C.   inputs
     D.   valances

     ANSWER: A, 381

28. _____ is the perceived fairness of the relation between what a person does and what the person receives.
     A.   Distributive justice
     B.   Procedural justice
     C.   Equity
     D.   Compensation satisfaction

     ANSWER: C, 381

29.   In a discussion of internal equity, _____ are what a person brings to
       the organization, including knowledge, skills, and abilities as well as their
       responsibilities and accomplishments.
       A.   outputs
       B.   inputs
       C.   outcomes
       D.   judicials

       ANSWER: B, 381

30.   The perceived fairness of the process and procedures used to make decisions
       about employees, including their pay, is called
       A.   pay equity.
       B.   distributive justice.
       C.   supervisory protocol.
       D.   procedural justice.

       ANSWER: D, 381

31.   In terms of procedural justice, the process of determining base pay, allocating
       pay increases, and measuring performance all must be seen as
       A.   fair.
       B.   equitable.
       C.   just.
       D.   open.

       ANSWER: A, 382

32.   _____ is the perceived fairness of the amounts given for performance.
       A.   Compensation satisfaction
       B.   Reward-performance perceptions
       C.   Distributive justice
       D.   Procedural justice

       ANSWER: C, 382

33.   The crucial element in an open pay system is that
       A.   it is very easy to understand.
       B.   managers be able to explain satisfactorily the pay differences that exist.
       C.   wages and salaries are competitive with the market.
       D.   employees be able to discuss their wages with each other, promoting
             positive competition.

       ANSWER: B, 382

34.   What is a likely outcome when an organization's compensation is viewed as
       lacking external equity?
       A.   lower than average turnover
       B.   employees discussing their pay with other employees
       C.   pressures for secrecy regarding pay and benefits
       D.   difficulty recruiting qualified and high-demand employees

       ANSWER: D, 382

35.   Which major federal law affects compensation?
      A.   Fair Labor Standards Act
      B.   Wagner Act
      C.   National Compensation Fairness Act
      D.   Equal Pay Act

      ANSWER: A, 383

36.   Which of the following is a major objective of the Fair Labor Standards Act?
      A.   give labor unions the right to organize
      B.   promote safe working conditions
      C.   establish a minimum wage floor
      D.   outlaw child labor

      ANSWER: C, 383

37.   A lower minimum wage level is set for which of the following employee groups?
      A.   interns working in a cooperative training program
      B.   "tipped" employees such as restaurant workers
      C.   minors, that is children aged between 16 and 18 years
      D.   disabled workers

      ANSWER: B, 383

38.   _____ has been identified as the amount needed for a family of four
      to be supported by one worker so that family income is above the officially
      identified poverty level.
      A.   Comparable worth
      B.   Pay equity
      C.   The minimum wage
      D.   The living wage

      ANSWER: D, 384

39.   Under the FLSA, what is the minimum age for employment, with unlimited hours,
      in nonhazardous occupations?
      A.   16 years.
      B.   15 years.
      C.   18 years.
      D.   17 years.

      ANSWER: A, 384

40.   Which of the following are not paid overtime under the Fair Labor Standards Act?
      A.   hourly workers
      B.   salaried workers
      C.   exempt employees
      D.   non-exempt employees

      ANSWER: C, 384

41. Which of the following is a true statement about the overtime provisions of the
     Fair Labor Standards Act?
     A.   A manufacturing firm with a 4-day/10-hour schedule still must pay overtime
          for the two hours above 8 each day.
     B.   Overtime pay is set at one and one-half times the regular pay rate for all
          hours in excess of 40 per week.
     C.   All employees are entitled to overtime payments for working over 40 hours
          a week.
     D.   The work week is defined as 168 hours beginning at 12:01 Monday morning.

     ANSWER: B, 385

42. Under the FLSA, which of the following would be classified as a non-exempt
     employee?
     A.   an outside sales person earning less than $250 per week
     B.   a public school teacher
     C.   a supervisor with discretionary authority for independent action
     D.   an administrator spending about 50 percent of the time doing clerical work

     ANSWER: D, 386

43. Compensatory time-off can be given in the private sector if
     A.   it is given at the rate of one and one-half times the hours worked over
          a 40-hour week.
     B.   it is used up within the next three months by the employee.
     C.   the hourly wage is at least one and one-half times the minimum wage.
     D.   it is given at a rate equivalent to the number of hours worked overtime
          within the same pay period.

     ANSWER: A, 387

44. For an employer, a primary advantage of classifying a worker as an independent
     contractor is that
     A.   independent contractors do not have to pay minimum wage and overtime
          payments.
     B.   independent contractors are exempt from EEO regulations.
     C.   the employer does not have to pay Social Security or unemployment costs.
     D.   the contractor can be dismissed at any time without penalty.

     ANSWER: C, 387

45. The criteria for deciding independent contractor status, as identified by the
     IRS, include all of the following except
     A.   can the individual make a profit or suffer a loss?
     B.   can the individual quit at any time without incurring liability?
     C.   does the individual provide the same service to the general public?
     D.   has the individual made a significant investment in facilities?

     ANSWER: B, 387-388

46.   The Equal Pay Act prohibits wage differentials based on
       A.   race.
       B.   job classification.
       C.   seniority.
       D.   sex.

       ANSWER: D, 387-388

47.   _____ is the concept that the pay for all jobs requiring comparable
       knowledge, skills, and abilities should be similar even if actual duties and
       market rates differ significantly.
       A.   Pay equity
       B.   Wage fairness
       C.   Compensatory pay
       D.   Socialized return

       ANSWER: A, 388

48.   _____ is a court action in which a portion of an employee's wages is
       set aside to pay a debt owed a creditor.
       A.   Alimony
       B.   Creditor protection
       C.   Garnishment
       D.   Debt deduction

       ANSWER: C, 389

49.   In a job evaluation, every job in an organization is examined and ultimately
       priced according to which of the following features?
       A.   the educational qualifications needed for employment
       B.   the relative importance of the job
       C.   the seniority needed to advance to the next level in the hierarchy
       D.   the job's level in the organizational hierarchy

       ANSWER: B, 390

50.   A _____ job is one that is found in many organizations and performed
       by several individuals who have similar duties that are relatively stable and
       require similar KSAs.
       A.   comparable
       B.   red-circled
       C.   key
       D.   benchmark

       ANSWER: D, 390

51.   When using the point method of job evaluation, a _____ factor is used
       to identify a job value that is commonly present throughout a group of jobs.
       A.   compensable
       B.   consideration
       C.   value-related
       D.   KSA

       ANSWER: A, 391

52.   Which of the following is a major drawback to the point method of job
      evaluation?
      A.   does not consider all components of a job
      B.   the complexity of the process
      C.   the time needed to develop a system
      D.   can only be used by HR specialists

      ANSWER: C, 391

53.   When an employer collects data on compensation rates for workers performing
      similar jobs at other organizations, a(n) _____ is being conducted.
      A.   equity study
      B.   pay survey
      C.   compensation study
      D.   competitive evaluation

      ANSWER: B, 394

54.   The _____ shows the relationship between job value, as determined by
      job evaluation points and pay survey rates.
      A.   compa-ratio
      B.   Hay survey
      C.   broadband
      D.   market line

      ANSWER: D, 396-397

55.   Why to organizations use pay grades?
      A.   to group individual jobs having approximately the same job worth
      B.   to insure against pay differentials based on sex or race
      C.   to compare similar jobs across a variety of organizations
      D.   to develop a pay structure that is based on market rates

      ANSWER: A, 397

56.   _____ is the practice of using fewer pay grades with much broader
      ranges than in traditional compensation systems.
      A.   Pay scaling
      B.   Variable scheduling
      C.   Broadbanding
      D.   Pay openness

      ANSWER: C, 397

57.   Which of the following is a benefit of reducing the number of pay grades and
      broadening pay ranges?
      A.   it recognizes the uni-dimensional nature of many of the newly-created
            jobs.
      B.   it is more consistent with the flattening of organizational levels.
      C.   it enhances the distinctions between various jobs.
      D.   it increases the opportunities for upward mobility.

      ANSWER: B, 397

58. Which of the following approaches is recommended for bringing a red-circled employee's pay into line.
    A. Transfer the employee to a lower paying job, while cutting the employee's pay to match the rate for the new job.
    B. Keep pay rates secret.
    C. Cut the employee's pay so it falls within the range.
    D. Freeze the employee's pay until the pay range can be adjusted upward to get the employee's pay rate back into the grade.

    ANSWER: D, 401

59. A person's _____ is that employee's current pay level divided by the midpoint of the pay range.
    A. compa-ratio
    B. average pay rate
    C. mid-grade mark
    D. market price

    ANSWER: A, 402

60. Which of the following is an advantage of a lump-sum increase (LSI) plan?
    A. LSI plans involve less administrative work.
    B. The unions support this concept of merit bonuses.
    C. It heightens employees' awareness of what their performance merited.
    D. It increases the compounding effect of succeeding raises.

    ANSWER: C, 404

True and False

61. Compensation is fundamentally about providing employees with the economic means necessary to meet individual and family living expenses.

    ANSWER: False, 372
    Compensation is an important factor affecting how and why people choose to work at one organization over others. It concerns recruiting, retaining, and rewarding employees.

62. Benefits are indirect rewards given to an employee or a group of employees as a part of organizational membership.

    ANSWER: True, 373

63. In a typical division of compensation responsibilities, the HR unit is responsible for matching performance and rewards.

    ANSWER: False, 374
    Operating managers are responsible for matching performance and rewards.

64. An organization that follows an entitlement philosophy to compensation will find that, as employees continue their employment lives, the employer's costs will increase, regardless of employee performance or organizational competitive pressures.

    ANSWER: True, 375

65. Surveys have shown that most organizations are totally performance-oriented in all facets of their compensation practices.

    ANSWER: False, 375
    In fact, very few organizations are totally performance-oriented in their compensation practices. The entitlement philosophy is dominant.

66. A competency-based pay system rewards employees who are more versatile and have continued to develop their skills.

    ANSWER: True, 377

67. Compensation practices are simplified as organizations shift to using work teams, because everyone on a team is paid the same amount.

    ANSWER: False, 380
    Just the opposite - paying everyone on teams the same amount, even though there are differing competencies and levels of performance, creates equity concerns for individual members.

68. Procedural justice refers to the perceived fairness of the process used to make decisions about employees.

    ANSWER: True, 381

69. An increasing number of organizations are keeping pay information secret, thus avoiding disputes about paycheck fairness.

    ANSWER: False, 382
    A growing number of organizations are opening up their pay systems allowing employees to make more accurate equity comparisons.

70. The Fair Labor Standards Act sets minimum wage standards and hours of work for all employees.

    ANSWER: False, 383-384
    The FLSA set minimum wage and overtime provisions for hourly and non-exempt employees. Salaried-exempt employees are not required to be paid the minimum wage and overtime.

71. The work week, as defined by the FLSA for overtime purposes, does not have to be a calendar week.

    ANSWER: True, 385

72. The Equal Pay Act of 1963 was passed to achieve pay equity..

     ANSWER: False, 387-388
     The Equal Pay Act addresses equal pay for equal work for men and women, not equitable pay for comparable work.

73. Federal law requires that the pay for all jobs requiring comparable knowledge, skills, and abilities should be similar, even if actual duties and market rates differ significantly.

     ANSWER: False, 388
     There is no federal law requiring pay equity, (also known as comparable worth.) Some states have laws requiring pay equity for public-sector jobs.

74. Job evaluation provides a systematic basis for determining the relative worth of jobs within an organization.

     ANSWER: True, 390

75. The point method of job evaluation has been widely used because it is a relatively simple system to use.

     ANSWER: True, 391

76. Employers often use outside consultants to conduct pay surveys to avoid charges that the employers are attempting "price fixing" on wages.

     ANSWER: True, 395

77. Broadbanding is most appropriate in a traditional, hierarchial organization where the managers have been conditioned to expect a broad range of benefits and pay grades.

     ANSWER: False, 397
     Broadbanding is the practice of using fewer pay grades having broader ranges than traditional compensation systems. Structured, traditional, hierarchial organizations lack the flexibility associated with broadbanding.

78. A green-circled employee is an incumbent who is paid above the range set for the job.

     ANSWER: False, 401
     A green-circled employee is paid below the range. Red-circles employees are paid above the range set for the job

79. Pay compression occurs when the range of pay differences among individuals with different levels of experience and performance in the organization become small.

     ANSWER: True, 401

80. A maturity curve depicts the relationship between experience and pay rates.

     ANSWER: True, 403

Essay

81.   Discuss the different roles of base pay, variable pay, and benefits in a compensation package, illustrating the effect of each on employee behavior.

ANSWER: 372-373
Base pay, either wages or salaries, is based on the job or position held. Competitive rates impact hiring and retention. Variable pay, usually bonuses, incentives, or stock options, reward above-expectation performance. Benefits are given as a part of organizational membership.

82.   Is equity an important consideration on compensation? What is meant by equity?

ANSWER: 381-382
Equity is the perceived fairness of the relation between a person's inputs and outcomes. Inputs are what a person brings to the job including KSAs, responsibility, and accomplishments. Outcomes are what the person receives from the organization, including pay, benefits, and recognition. A sense of inequity occurs when there is a perceived imbalance between inputs and outcomes. Comparisons are made both within the organization and externally. Procedural and distributive justice contribute to the perceptions of equity.

83.   Would you recommend that an employer require that all salary information be kept confidential? Why or why not? What would be the impact of a secret pay system?

ANSWER: 382
Organizations sometimes choose to keep pay information secret in "closed" systems. This information includes how much people make, what raises have been received, and what pay grades and ranges exist in the organization. The rationale is often to hide any potential inequities. A growing number of organizations are opening up their pay systems to allow employees to make more accurate equity comparisons. Procedural and distributive justice require the system to be open.

84.   What was the purpose of the Fair Labor Standards Act (FLSA) of 1938? Is it relevant to today's workforce?

ANSWER: 383-388
The FLSA has three major objectives: to establish a minimum wage floor, to discourage oppressive use of child labor, and to encourage limits on the number of weekly hours employees work through overtime provisions. Employees are classified as either exempt or non-exempt. Non-exempt employees must be paid overtime. The FLSA was passed when the majority of workers were males employed in manufacturing jobs. The Equal Pay Act of 1963 prohibits discrimination in compensation based on sex. The increasing numbers of computer-related jobs and independent contractors have led to some changes in the act. The concept of a "living wage" is being debated as an alternate to the minimum wage.

85. Why do organizations conduct job evaluations. Discuss four methods of performing a job evaluation.

ANSWER: 390-393
Job evaluation provides a systematic basis for determining the relative worth of jobs in an organization. Every job in the organization is examined according to the relative importance of the job, the KSAs needed to perform the job, and the difficulty of the job. Job evaluations are used to determine internal job worth. Job evaluation methods include ranking, classification, point, and factor comparison.

Chapter 13

Variable Pay and Executive Compensation

Multiple Choice

1. What is variable pay?
   A. techniques to motivate employees to work harder
   B. additional tangible rewards given to employees for performance beyond normal expectations
   C. psychic satisfaction provided for employees
   D. compensation that reflects the knowledge, skills, and abilities employees bring to the job

   ANSWER: B, 410

2. "Compensation linked to individual, team, and/or organization performance" is a definition of
   A. compa-pay.
   B. benefits.
   C. executive perquisites.
   D. variable pay.

   ANSWER: D, 410

3. Which of the following is an assumption of variable-pay systems?
   A. Some jobs contribute more to organizational success than others.
   B. Time spent each day is the primary measure of short-term contributions.
   C. Differences in individual contributions to the organization are recognized through different base pay levels.
   D. Length of time with the organization is the primary differentiating factor among people.

   ANSWER: A, 410

4. Pay systems based on seniority or length of service assume that
   A. some jobs contribute more to organizational success than others.
   B. some people perform better than others.
   C. time spent each day is the primary measure of contribution.
   D. people should be compensated for above average skill and experience.

   ANSWER: C, 410

5. A feature of variable pay plans is that _____ do not increase the degree of cooperation among individuals.
    A.   benefit programs
    B.   individual incentives
    C.   ESOP plans
    D.   organizational incentives

    ANSWER: B, 411

6. When an entire work group or team is rewarded for its performance,
    A.   employees may withhold information from others and focus only on what is rewarded.
    B.   individual and team competition is reduced and all employees working together can generate financial gain.
    C.   the performance of the entire organization improves.
    D.   cooperation among the members usually increases.

    ANSWER: D, 411

7. What is the purpose of organizational incentives?
    A.   to reward people for the performance of the entire organization
    B.   to aid in recruiting high-potential employees
    C.   to distribute fairly the excess profits of the organization
    D.   to sabotage efforts of competitor organizations

    ANSWER: A, 411

8. Which of the following is classified as an individual variable pay plan?
    A.   gainsharing
    B.   labor-cost reduction
    C.   attendance bonuses
    D.   employee stock options

    ANSWER: C, 411

9. Team incentives include
    A.   safety awards.
    B.   gainsharing.
    C.   employee stock options.
    D.   sales commissions.

    ANSWER: B, 411

10. _____ is a type of organization-wide variable pay plan.
    A.   Bonuses
    B.   Quality improvement
    C.   Gainsharing
    D.   Profit sharing

    ANSWER: D, 411

11. An important factor in the success of any variable pay program is that
    A.   it be consistent with the culture of the organization.
    B.   the employees want to participate.
    C.   all jobs are well defined in terms of the procedures used.
    D.   participation is throughout the organization.

    ANSWER: A, 413

12 It is important to make sure that what is being rewarded ties to organizational objectives, because people tend to
    A.   guess what they think management wants done.
    B.   produce what is convenient.
    C.   produce what is measured and rewarded.
    D.   avoid doing unpleasant tasks.

    ANSWER: C, 413

13. Which of the following was identified as a problem that may limit the effectiveness of variable pay plans?
    A.   organizations pay too much because performance isn't measured
    B.   employees may not understand a complex system
    C.   the wrong people get the rewards
    D.   managers adhere to a Theory X style

    ANSWER: B, 414

14. Successful variable pay plans
    A.   factor in an employee's seniority.
    B.   provide everyone in the organization with regular bonuses.
    C.   pay a large bonus at the end of the year when employees most need it.
    D.   separate the incentive payment from base salary.

    ANSWER: D, 414

15. An individual incentive system will be counterproductive when
    A.   the organization emphasizes teamwork and cooperation.
    B.   there is a dynamic technological environment.
    C.   it results in competition among the employees.
    D.   the organizational culture stresses individualism.

    ANSWER: A, 414

16. Under the _____ system, wages are determined by multiplying the number of units produced by the piece rate for one unit.
    A.   Scanlon
    B.   differential piece-rate
    C.   straight piece-rate
    D.   production commission

    ANSWER: C, 415

17.   A differential piece-rate system pays employees
       A.   one piece-rate wage for standard production, but less if producing below
             quota.
       B.   one piece-rate wage for units produced up to a standard output and a
             higher piece-rate wage for units produced over the standard.
       C.   a higher rate per piece for employees with more experience and seniority.
       D.   differential wages depending on the differing responsibilities in the
             production of each unit.

       ANSWER: B, 415

18.   Bonuses are less costly than general wage increases, because
       A.   they receive preferential tax treatment.
       B.   less money can be given while still increasing employee satisfaction.
       C.   they provide a bigger motivational "bang for the buck."
       D.   they do not become part of employees' base wages.

       ANSWER: D, 415

19.   In most organizations, the bonus recognizes performance by both the employee and
       A.   the company.
       B.   the economy.
       C.   the work group.
       D.   the team.

       ANSWER: A, 415

20.   Which of the following common awards are not based on individual performance?
       A.   recognition awards
       B.   "employee of the month" awards
       C.   service awards
       D.   safe driving awards

       ANSWER: C, 417

21.   A _____ approach is useful when serving and retaining existing
       accounts is emphasized more than generating new sales and accounts.
       A.   straight commission
       B.   salary only
       C.   salary plus commission
       D.   salary draw

       ANSWER: B, 417

22.   When an employee receives no compensation until a sale is totally completed, the
       compensation system is called
       A.   lump sum.
       B.   sales payoff.
       C.   deferred salary.
       D.   straight commission.

       ANSWER: D, 418

23. What is a "draw?"
    A. an amount advanced to an employee and repaid from future commissions.
    B. a special incentive program used widely in sales-related jobs.
    C. a term to represent salary-plus-commission.
    D. a lump-sum payment or bonus at the end of the month.

    ANSWER: A, 418

24. The most frequently used form of sales compensation is the
    A. draw.
    B. straight commission.
    C. salary plus commission.
    D. differential commission.

    ANSWER: C, 418

25. Which of the following is true about a sales commission plan?
    A. sales people who don't sell, don't get paid
    B. the plans dramatically reduce team work
    C. the plans have a positive impact on the climate
    D. employees prefer commissions over bonuses

    ANSWER: B, 419

26. Which of the following is true about team-based variable pay?
    A. it has a negative impact on productivity
    B. it makes it difficult to recruit and retain employees
    C. it overcomes the limitations of individual incentive systems
    D. it improves employee morale

    Answer: D, 420

27. Limitations of team-based incentives include:
    A. a poorly performing individual can negatively influences team results.
    B. overall team productivity can decrease due to the absence of leadership.
    C. it is difficult to measure the team contribution to the organization's performance.
    D. it can produce unproductive competition among the team members.

    ANSWER: A, 421

28. 25. Which of the following characteristics is true about team-based incentives?
    A. Union leaders are usually supportive of the concept.
    B. All groups are encouraged to work towards the organizational goals.
    C. The presence of one or two poor performers can result in the group being denied an incentive payment.
    D. There is no evidence that group incentives improve organizational productivity.

    ANSWER: C, 421

29.   _____ is defined as "the sharing with employees of greater-than-expected gains in profits and/or productivity."
A.   The Rucker Plan
B.   Gainsharing
C.   Profit sharing
D.   ESOP

ANSWER: B, 423

30.   There are two crucial decisions that must be made by the gainsharing task force. These are: How much gain is to be shared with employees? and
A.   What are the minimum standards to be met?
B.   What action(s) should be taken if gains are less than expected?
C.   How to "punish" the employee who contributes minimal performance?
D.   How are the rewards to be distributed?

ANSWER: D, 423

31.   What is an Improshare program?
A.   It is a group piece-rate plan.
B.   It is a group-incentive plan.
C.   It is similar to the Scanlon Plan in that cost savings are rewarded.
D.   It is an organizational-wide profit-sharing plan.

ANSWER: A, 423

32.   In a(n) _____ plan, a standard is calculated and weekly bonuses are paid based on the extent to which the standard is exceeded.
A.   Rucker
B.   organizational-wide profit-sharing
C.   Improshare
D.   Scanlon

ANSWER: C, 423

33.   Which of the following statements best describes the Scanlon Plan?
A.   It is an organization-wide profit sharing plan.
B.   Employees are rewarded for cost savings.
C.   Team members each receive identical reward based on the team's productivity.
D.   Employees receive incentive payments for exceeding predetermined levels of production.

ANSWER: B, 423

34.   To be effective, an organizational incentive program should
A.   only reward the employees whose work produces the profits.
B.   reward the shareholders for investing in the business.
C.   demonstrate a clear link between individual performance and organizational profits.
D.   include everyone from non-exempt employees to managers and executives.

ANSWER: D, 423

35.   A(n) _____ distributes a portion of the organizational profits to employees.
      A.   profit sharing plan
      B.   team-based incentive plan
      C.   gainsharing plan
      D.   employee stock ownership plan (ESOP)

      ANSWER: A, 424

36.   For a profit-sharing plan to be effective, management must
      A.   increase innovative solutions to technical problems.
      B.   recruit employees who are motivated primarily by money.
      C.   be willing to disclose financial and profit information to employees.
      D.   stabilize profits so that the annual payoff is consistent.

      ANSWER: C, 424

37.   What is one of the drawbacks of a profit-sharing plan?
      A.   Most workers prefer a guaranteed pay increase instead of a one-time bonus.
      B.   Employees may not see the link between their efforts and the rewards.
      C.   Unions oppose profit sharing plans.
      D.   Profit sharing leads to conflict among employees.

      ANSWER: B, 424

38.   Which of the following statements about stock options is true?
      A.   Stock options are exclusively an executive-level compensation option.
      B.   Stock options are taxable when they are given to the employee.
      C.   Stock options operate as "golden handcuffs" to keep executives from leaving the organization.
      D.   Stock options can be used at all levels of an organizations.

      ANSWER: D, 425

39.   A(n) _____ is plan whereby employees gain stock ownership in the organization for which they work.
      A.   employee stock ownership plan
      B.   employee shareholder plan
      C.   shareholder bonus plan
      D.   scanlon stock bonus plan

      ANSWER: A, 425

40.   An organization establishes an ESOP by
      A.   deducting a small amount from each employee's pay for the purchase of stock.
      B.   providing upper management with a special bonus.
      C.   using its stock as collateral to borrow capital from a financial institution.
      D.   having its profits distributed with favorable tax treatment.

      ANSWER: C, 425

41. Which of the following statements about ESOPs is <u>false</u>?
     A.   The firm can receive favorable tax treatment of the earnings earmarked for use in the ESOP.
     B.   Many employees opt-out of being involved in the company's ESOP.
     C.   Employees are motivated to work harder because they have a "piece of the action."
     D.   Employees place their financial future at greater risk.

     ANSWER: B, 426

42. New rules on ESOPs by the Financial Accounting Standards Board (FASB) require companies to
     A.   list the stock transfers as an expense.
     B.   first seek approval from the IRS before making any future stock transfers.
     C.   report the value of the stock options as income to the individual employees.
     D.   report the value of the stock options they give employees.

     ANSWER: D, 427

43. An executive typically is defined as someone
     A.   in the top two levels of an organization.
     B.   earning more than $250,000 a year.
     C.   whose salary puts them in the top quartile of the organization.
     D.   in the top two positions in each of the functional areas.

     ANSWER: A, 427

44. After adjusting for age and experience, the pay for female executives is about _____ less than that of men.
     A.   50%
     B.   15%
     C.   5%
     D.   25%

     ANSWER: C, 427

45. At the heart of most executive compensation plans is the idea that
     A.   base pay is not as important as the other benefits and perks.
     B.   executives should be rewarded if the organization grows in profitability and value over a period of years.
     C.   executives should be rewarded for their current performance.
     D.   outstanding executives are hard to keep unless they are well compensated.

     ANSWER: B, 428

46. On average, salaries make up about _____ of the typical top executive's annual compensation total.
     A.   20 percent
     B.   two-thirds
     C.   ninety percent
     D.   40% to 60%

     ANSWER: D, 429

47. A provision of the 1993 tax act prohibits a publicly traded company from
    A. deducting pay of more than $1 million for each of its top five officers unless that pay is based on approved performance criteria.
    B. deducting that portion of an executive's compensation that is more than ten times the compensation of the lowest paid full-time employee.
    C. providing special non-taxable benefits for the top executives.
    D. offering compensation to executives that defers income tax liability.

    ANSWER: A, 429

48. To be meaningful, annual bonus compensation must
    A. be competitive with what executives at similar firms receive.
    B. be awarded to all employees at the firm.
    C. reflect some performance measures.
    D. reflect the employee's level of seniority in the firm.

    ANSWER: C, 429

49. Some organizations award executive bonuses based on subjective judgments of the CEO and the Board of Directors. Which statement best describes this approach?
    A. It is not always possible to have objective measures of performance.
    B. The absence of formal, measurable targets is a major drawback.
    C. The executive is aware of the discretionary reasons for the bonus.
    D. A discretionary system permits the board to account for non-controllables.

    ANSWER: B, 429

50. Which of the following is used to emphasize the long-term growth and success of the organization?
    A. executive perquisites
    B. executive bonus plans
    C. golden parachutes
    D. stock options

    ANSWER: D, 429

51. A(n) _____ is a plan that gives an individual the right to buy stock in a company, usually at a fixed price for a period of time.
    A. stock option
    B. price discretion
    C. investment bonus
    D. appreciation right

    ANSWER: A, 429

52. What is a "phantom stock" plan?
    A. An employee stock ownership plan (ESOP) that a employee cannot receive until retirement.
    B. A means of transferring stock to an employee while avoiding taxes.
    C. A plan that pays recipients the increased value of the stock in the future.
    D. A stock option plan that is only available for Board members.

    ANSWER: C, 429

53. Why do some organizations offer deferred compensation to executives?
     A.   to emphasize long-term performance of the organization
     B.   to help executives with tax liabilities caused by incentive plans
     C.   to place "golden handcuffs" on key executives
     D.   to hide excessive one-time bonuses earned by executives

     ANSWER: B, 430

54. _____ are special benefits for executives that are usually noncash
     items.
     A.   Stock options
     B.   Enhanced benefits packages
     C.   Golden handcuffs
     D.   Perquisites

     ANSWER: D, 430

55. Why do many executives value perks?
     A.   Perks are visible symbols of status.
     B.   Perks are used as incentives to attract and retain senior executives.
     C.   Perks are linked to corporate performance.
     D.   Perks can be used to motivate subordinates.

     ANSWER: A, 430

56. Federal regulatory agencies require that executives compensation packages be
     approved by the
     A.   shareholders.
     B.   Security and Exchange Commission.
     C.   Board of Directors.
     D.   Internal Revenue Service.

     Answer: C, 430

57. What is the usual composition of the compensation committee?
     A.   a subgroup of the board of directors including officers of the firm
     B.   a subgroup of the board of directors who are not officers of the firm
     C.   executives from other companies
     D.   compensation consultants without executive management involvement

     ANSWER: B, 430

58. What is the role of a compensation committee?
     A.   To assist the HR unit is developing overall pay and benefit programs for
           the organization.
     B.   To develop a compensation package that ties overall compensation to
           performance.
     C.   To make recommendations to the shareholders on the compensation formula
           for members of the board of directors.
     D.   To make recommendations to the board of directors on overall pay policies,
           salaries for top officers, bonuses, and additional perks for executives.

     ANSWER: D, 430

59. Golden parachutes provide executives with
     A.   protection and security in the event that they lose their jobs.
     B.   special retirement packages, available only if the executives do not leave
          the firm before a specified date.
     C.   a package of additional perks that is considered very generous.
     D.   larger than usual bonus percentages against company profits.

     ANSWER: A, 432

60. Which of the following was <u>not</u> suggested for determining the "reasonableness"
     of executive compensation?
     A.   Would another company hire this person as an executive?
     B.   What would an investor pay for this level of performance of the executive?
     C.   Is the executive's total compensation more than one hundred times that of
          the lowest paid employee of the company?
     D.   How does the executive's compensation compare with that for other
          executives in similar companies in the industry?

     ANSWER: C, 433

True and False

61. The role of variable pay is to link bonuses with performance.

     ANSWER: False, 410
     Variable pay plans are attempts to tie additional rewards to performance beyond
     normal expectations.

62. Variable pay plans may be very successful if doing the job requires a great deal
     of cooperation among employees.

     ANSWER: False, 411
     Individual incentives increases the level of competition between workers.

63. When an entire work group or team is rewarded for its performance cooperation
     among the members usually increases

     ANSWER: True, 411

64. Most employees prefer incentives such as one-time, lump-sum payments.

     ANSWER: False, 412
     Most employees prefer that performance rewards increase their base pay.

65. People tend to produce what is measured and rewarded.

     ANSWER: True, 413

66.   It is not always appropriate to link pay to performance.

      ANSWER: True, 414

67.   Piece-rate systems are not an appropriate when quality concerns are important.

      ANSWER: True, 415

68.   Bonuses, as individual incentive compensation, are becoming less common because they increase an organization's overall payroll costs.

      ANSWER: False, 415
      Bonuses are increasing in popularity because they do not become part of the employees' base wages. They are less costly to employers than pay increases.

69.   A straight-commission approach is best when an organization emphasizes servicing and retaining existing accounts over generating new sales and accounts.

      ANSWER: False, 417
      A salary-only approach is more useful when the business is emphasizing servicing and retaining accounts over generating new sales and accounts.

70.   Many companies have introduced team-based incentives, finding that teams are eager to handle pay decisions for coworkers.

      ANSWER: False, 421
      Companies have found that in most cases team members are unwilling to make pay decisions about coworkers.

71.   Gain sharing encourages employees to increase their discretionary effort because the extra effort will produce financial gains.

      ANSWER: True, 423

72.   Organized labor continues to oppose profit-sharing plans in which employees' pay increases are tied to improved company performance.

      ANSWER: False, 424
      In recent years, unions have supported profit-sharing plans in which employees' pay increases are tied to improved company performance.

73.   For profit sharing to work, management must be willing to disclose financial and profit information to the employees.

      ANSWER: True, 424

74.   An employee stock ownership plan gives employees the right to purchase a fixed number of shares of company stock at a specific price for a limited period of time.

      ANSWER: False, 425
      An ESOP is designed to give employees stock ownership in the organization for which they work. The above is a definition of stock options.

75. The primary objective of executive compensation plans is to minimize the tax consequences for the executive.

ANSWER: False, 428
The heart of executive compensation is that executives should be rewarded if the organization grows in profitability and value over a period of years.

76. A provision of the 1993 tax act prohibits a publicly traded company from deducting that portion of an executive's pay that exceeds $1 million.

ANSWER: False, 429
The $1 million limit only applies if the pay is not based on performance criteria approved by outside directors and shareholders.

77. A stock option gives an individual the right to buy stock in a company, usually at an advantageous price.

ANSWER: True, 429

78. Perquisites offer substantial tax savings because many perks are not taxed as income.

ANSWER: True, 430

79. Members of the board of directors who are also officers of the firm cannot serve on the firm's compensation committee.

ANSWER: True, 430

80. Golden parachutes are typically included in employment contracts to give special compensation to executives if they are negatively affected in an acquisition or merger.

ANSWER: True, 432

Essay

81. Contrast variable pay plans with a system based on seniority or length of service?

ANSWER: 410
Variable pay is additional compensation linked to individual, team, and/or organizational performance. These plans recognize that some jobs contribute more to organizational success than others, and that some people perform better than others. Systems based on seniority or length of service differentiate among people based on time spent each day and length of service, recognizing that it is not always possible to differentiate individual contributions.

82.   Not all variable pay plans are successful. What conditions must be met for establishing a successful variable pay plan?

ANSWER: 411-414
Be consistent with the organizational culture and goals, make plans understandable, keep plans current, tie variable pay to desired performance, recognize individual differences, and separate variable pay from base pay.

83.   Describe the various methods of compensating sales and marketing employees.

ANSWER: 417-418
Compensation paid to sales or marketing employees is partly or entirely tied to sales performance. Plans include salary only, straight commission, draw system, salary plus commission or bonuses. Each of the plans has different motivating potential.

84.   Describe gainsharing and profit-sharing as organizational incentive systems. Discuss the impact of each system in improving performance.

ANSWER: 423-424
Gainsharing is the sharing with employees of greater-than-expected gains in profits and/or productivity. Employees are rewarded for doing more than the minimum acceptable level of performance. Profit sharing distributes a portion of organizational profits to employees. Both systems require that employees see the link between better performance and rewards.

85.   How does executive compensation differ from the compensation packages provided for other employees in the organization? Describe some of the incentives available for executives.

ANSWER: 428-432
At the heart of most executive compensation plans is the idea that executives should be rewarded if the organization grows in profitability and value over a period of years. Executive salaries are often high and attention is paid to tax consequences. Publicly traded companies are prohibited from deducting pay of more than $1 million for top executives unless that pay is based on performance criteria. Executive pay is often set by outside compensation committees. Executive compensation often includes bonuses, stock options, benefits, perquisites, and golden parachutes in addition to salaries.

Chapter 14

Managing Employee Benefits

Multiple Choice

1. Which statement best describes why employers provide employee benefits to their workers?
    A.   benefits motivate employee performance
    B.   benefits are provided for being part of the organization
    C.   benefits are mandated by government
    D.   benefits are a substitute for low monetary compensation

    ANSWER: B, 440

2. Employee benefits are defined as
    A.   a reward for employee loyalty.
    B.   a right related to organizational membership.
    C.   a performance-related form of compensation.
    D.   a form of indirect compensation.

    ANSWER: D, 440

3. Unlike many other countries, in the United States _____ has/have become a major provider of benefits for citizens.
    A.   employers
    B.   families
    C.   charities
    D.   government

    ANSWER: A, 440

4. Benefits, such as health insurance and retirement contributions, must be viewed as
    A.   the responsibility of each individual employee.
    B.   a right of citizenship.
    C.   influencing employment and retention decisions.
    D.   a governmental responsibility.

    ANSWER: C 440

5. Which of the following is considered a strategic goal of benefits by employers?
    A.   provide the benefits that are mandated by government
    B.   attract and retain employees with the necessary capabilities
    C.   significantly improve the quality of life for employees
    D.   minimize the tax consequences for employees

    ANSWER: B, 440

6. _____ include(s) money paid directly and money paid indirectly.
    A.   Employee benefits
    B.   Membership incentives
    C.   Organizational rewards
    D.   Total compensation

    ANSWER: D, 440

7. Which of the following would be a consequence of hiring predominately younger female employees?
    A.   a family-friendly set of benefits would have to be addressed
    B.   on-site child-care centers have been mandated by federal legislation
    C.   the government has mandated paid parental leave
    D.   most employers are reluctant to hire working mothers

    ANSWER: A, 441

8. A _____ includes a comprehensive look at all aspects of benefits in a firm.
    A.   job evaluation
    B.   job analysis
    C.   benefits needs analysis
    D.   government benefits audit

    ANSWER: C, 441

9. Which is of the following should be considered during a benefits needs analysis?
    A.   What benefits are mandated by government?
    B.   How much total compensation, including benefits, should be provided?
    C.   What benefits significantly improve the quality of life for employees?
    D.   What are the tax consequences for employees of each benefit?

    ANSWER: B, 441

10. Those benefits which employers in the United States are required to provide by law are called _____ benefits.
    A.   obligatory
    B.   required
    C.   compulsory
    D.   mandated

    ANSWER: D, 442

11. Which of the following benefits are <u>not</u> mandated by federal legislation?
    A.   pension plan coverage
    B.   social security
    C.   unemployment insurance
    D.   workers' compensation insurance

    ANSWER: A, 442

12. Social Security, workers' compensation insurance, and Medicare are called
    A.   employment benefits.
    B.   government-sponsored benefits.
    C.   government-mandated benefits.
    D.   social benefits.

    ANSWER: C, 442

13. What are the requirements of the Consolidated Omnibus Budget Reconciliation Act (COBRA) with respect to health care?
    A.   Employers with more than 50 employees must provide medical insurance for all full-time employees.
    B.   Most employers must offer extended health-care coverage to employees after they leave the organization.
    C.   Employer contributions to Medicare were raised to 2.9 percent of payroll.
    D.   Employers offering medical insurance cannot exclude pre-existing conditions from coverage.

    ANSWER: B, 443

14. The Health Insurance Portability and Accountability Act (HIPAA) requires
    A.   employers with more than 50 employees provide medical insurance for all full-time employees.
    B.   insurance companies to offer coverage to contingent workers.
    C.   that most employers offer extended health-care coverage to employees after they leave the organization.
    D.   that most employees be able to obtain health-care insurance coverage if they were previously covered in a health plan.

    ANSWER: D, 443

15. One reason why employers face increasing pressure to provide benefits is that
    A.   federal and state governments want to shift many of the social costs for health care and other expenditures to employers.
    B.   private industry can provide these services more efficiently than government.
    C.   unions are becoming more aggressive in contract negotiations.
    D.   firms need to compete for quality employees in a tight labor market.

    ANSWER: A, 443

16.   Employers provide _____ in order to compete for and retain employees.
      A.   involuntary benefits
      B.   competitive-market benefits
      C.   voluntary benefits
      D.   labor-market benefits

      ANSWER: C, 444

17.   What is workers' compensation?
      A.   the pay and benefits package provided to employees
      B.   benefits provided to persons injured on the job
      C.   law-suit judgments awarded to workers injured on the job
      D.   what a worker receives in compensation for outstanding performance

      ANSWER: B, 444

18.   How is workers' compensation funded?
      A.   by a tax levied by state governments based on size of payroll
      B   by a pool of organizations in the same industry
      C.   through the Social Security Administration
      D.   by insurance purchased from a private carrier or state insurance fund

      ANSWER: D, 444

19.   To be eligible for workers' compensation, the worker must
      A.   suffer a work-related injury or illness.
      B.   be employed by a federally insured employer.
      C.   not have contributed to the cause of the injury.
      D.   prove that the accident was caused by employer negligence.

      ANSWER: A, 444

20.   In exchange for workers' compensation coverage, employees
      A.   forfeit medical insurance coverage.
      B.   can be required to attend safety-awareness seminars.
      C.   give up the right of legal actions and awards.
      D.   are required to pay a portion of the insurance premiums.

      ANSWER: C, 444

21.   How is unemployment compensation administered?
      A.   by the federal government.
      B.   on a state-by-state basis.
      C.   by the states, under U.S. Department of Labor guidelines.
      D.   by a pool of companies engaged in similar industries.

      ANSWER: B, 444

22. How is an employer's cost for unemployment compensation determined?
    A.   the type of business and its known seasonal fluctuations
    B.   the number of covered employees
    C.   the total cost of payroll
    D.   the number of claims filed by workers who leave

    ANSWER: D, 444

23. What is a SUB program?
    A.   It is a benefit, negotiated by a union, requiring an employer to contribute to a fund that supplements unemployment compensation.
    B.   It provides for severance pay in those cases where the company closes down.
    C.   Businesses with seasonal work that use subcontractors rather than hire and lay off people.
    D.   It is a type of benefits program that supervisors have some discretion over.

    ANSWER: A, 445

24. _____ is a security benefit voluntarily offered by employers to employees who lose their jobs.
    A.   Unemployment insurance
    B.   Supplemental unemployment benefit
    C.   Severance pay
    D.   Family security

    ANSWER: C, 445

25. What is the principle requirement of the Worker Adjustment and Retraining Notification Act (WARN) of 1988?
    A.   Employers are to give severance pay to workers who lose their jobs permanently.
    B.   Most employers must give 60 days' notice if a mass layoff or facility closing is to occur.
    C.   Workers are to be given full disclosure regarding and hazardous materials present at the work site.
    D.   Workers under age 60 are entitled to a retraining allowance if their jobs are eliminated.

    ANSWER: B, 445

26. As a result of a 1986 amendment to the Age Discrimination in Employment Act (ADEA), most employees cannot be forced to retire
    A.   before age 60.
    B.   before age 65.
    C.   before age 70.
    D.   at any specific age.

    ANSWER: D, 445

27. The _____ requires equal treatment of older workers in early retirement or severance situations.
    A.   Older Workers Benefit Protection Act (OWBPA)
    B.   Age Discrimination in Employment Act (ADEA)
    C.   Employee Retirement Income Security Act (ERISA)
    D.   Worker Adjustment and Retraining Notification Act (WARN)

    ANSWER: A, 447

28. The Older Worker Benefit Protection Act (OWBPA) sets forth some very specific conditions that must be met when older workers
    A.   are fired for cause or laid off.
    B.   denied coverage under an employers health insurance plan.
    C.   sign waivers promising not to sue for age discrimination.
    D.   apply for supplemental social security benefits.

    ANSWER: C, 447

29. Rule 106 issued by the Financial Accounting Standards Board (FASB)
    A.   permits health-care benefits to be paid out of current yearly income.
    B.   requires that firms establish accounting reserves for funding retiree health-care benefits.
    C.   permits health costs to be taken from after-tax dollars.
    D.   requires a pool of funds that is at least 60 percent of health-care liability costs.

    ANSWER: B, 447

30. Social security can be classified as a(n) _____ benefit.
    A.   voluntary
    B.   insurance
    C.   social
    D.   security

    ANSWER: D, 447

31. Which of the following benefits is not provided by the Social Security system?
    A.   displacement
    B.   disability
    C.   survivor
    D.   old age

    ANSWER: A, 447

32. How are Social Security benefits funded?
    A.   employers are taxed on the amount of wages and salaries paid to employees
    B.   a tax on employee wages and salaries, paid by the employee
    C.   a tax on employee wages and salaries paid equally by employers and employees
    D.   general tax revenues

    ANSWER: C, 447

33.   Retirement benefits established and funded by employers and employees are
       A.   mandated by the Employee Retirement Income Security Act (ERISA).
       B.   called pension plans.
       C.   often treated as "golden handcuffs."
       D.   substitutes for Social Security.

       ANSWER: B, 448

34.   In a _____ plan the employer makes an annual payment to an employee's
       pension account.
       A.   vested
       B.   defined-benefit
       C.   non-contributory pension
       D.   defined-contribution

       ANSWER: D, 448

35.   Which of the following is <u>not</u> a requirement of the Employee Retirement Income
       Security Act (ERISA)?
       A.   Employers must offer retirement benefits for all full-time employees after
             five years' service.
       B.   Plans must meet minimum funding requirements.
       C.   Employers must pay termination insurance to ensure employee pensions will
             be there even if the company goes out of business.
       D.   Accrued benefits must be given to employees when they retire or leave.

       ANSWER: A, 449

36.   In a contributory pension plan, the money for pension benefits is
       A.   deducted from the employees salary pre-tax.
       B.   contributed from the pre-tax earnings of the employer.
       C.   paid by both employees and employers.
       D.   provided by the employer.

       ANSWER: C, 449

37.   In a _____ pension plan, all the funds for pension benefits are
       provided by the employer.
       A.   defined-benefit
       B.   non-contributory
       C.   vested
       D.   defined-contribution

       ANSWER: B, 449

38.   _____ is the right of employees to receive benefits from their pension
       plans.
       A.   Dispatchment
       B.   Portability
       C.   Social security
       D.   Vesting

       ANSWER: D, 449

39. _____ refers to a feature that allows employees to move their pension benefits from one employer to another.
    A.   Portability
    B.   Transference
    C.   Vesting
    D.   Carry-over

    ANSWER: A, 450

40. In *Arizona Governing Committee v. Norris*, the Supreme Court ruled that
    A.   medical examinations may be required before an employee is enroled in a pension plan.
    B.   all participants in a pension plan must be vested.
    C.   pension plan administrators must use unisex mortality tables.
    D.   employers cannot be required to provide pension benefits.

    ANSWER: C, 450

41. A special account in which an employee can set aside funds that will not be taxed until the employee retires is called
    A.   a 401(k) plan
    B.   an individual retirement account
    C.   a super-saver account
    D.   a Keogh plan

    ANSWER: B, 450

42. A(n) _____ is a special type of individualized pension plan for self-employed individuals.
    A.   IRA
    B.   defined-contribution
    C.   401(k) plan
    D.   Keogh plan

    ANSWER: D, 450

43. A 401(k) plan is an agreement in which
    A.   a percentage of an employee's pay is withheld and invested in a tax-deferred account.
    B.   an employee can set aside funds that will not be taxed until retirement.
    C.   individualized pension plans are established for self-employed people.
    D.   both the employee and employee contribute funds to a pension plan.

    ANSWER: A, 450

44. Managed care consists of approaches that monitor and reduce _____ using restrictions and market system alternatives.
    A.   child-care expenses
    B.   elder-care costs
    C.   medical costs
    D.   domestic-partner expenses

    ANSWER: C, 453

45.   A _____ is a health-care provider that contracts with an employer or
      an employer group to provide health-care services to employees at a competitive
      rate.
      A.   contractual medical organization (CMO)
      B.   preferred provider organization (PPO)
      C.   public/private health organization (PPH)
      D.   health maintenance organization (HMO)

      ANSWER: B, 453

46.   A _____ is a managed care plan that provides services for a fixed
      period on a prepaid basis.
      A.   contractual medical organization (CMO)
      B.   preferred provider organization (PPO)
      C   public/private health organization (PPH)
      D.   health maintenance organization (HMO)

      ANSWER: D, 453

47.   A _____ is an audit and review of the services and costs billed by
      health-care providers.
      A.   utilization review
      B.   practice analysis
      C.   operational control
      D.   procedural review

      ANSWER: A, 454

48.   Why are utilization reviews conducted?
      A.   Employers need cost/benefit analyses of services provided by their PPO.
      B.   The government requires an annual audit of health-care expenditures.
      C.   Many employers found that some of the health care provided by doctors and
           hospitals is unnecessary, incorrectly billed, or deliberately overcharged.
      D.   Labor unions need accurate costing of benefits for contract negotiation
           purposes.

      ANSWER: C, 454

49.   _____ try to encourage employees to have more healthy lifestyles.
      A.   In-house dietitians
      B.   Wellness programs
      C.   Physical fitness programs
      D.   Health counseling centers

      ANSWER: B, 454

50.   Long-term disability insurance
      A.   is a mandatory security benefit.
      B.   allows employees to accrue sick leave for emergency needs.
      C.   is rarely provided as part of an employer's benefit package.
      D.   provides continuing income protection for employees who become disabled
           and unable to work.

      ANSWER: D, 457

51.   The Family and Medical Leave Act requires that eligible employees be permitted to take leave for each of the following, <u>except</u>:
       A.   caring for a domestic partner with a serious health condition.
       B.   adoption of a child.
       C.   caring for a parent with a serious health condition.
       D.   serious health condition of the employee.

       ANSWER: A, 459, 461

52.   The Family and Medical Leave Act of 1993, requires that employers allow eligible employees to take a total of _____ during any _____ period.
       A.   1 month's paid leave;   12-month
       B.   3 months' paid leave;   24-month
       C.   12 weeks' unpaid leave;   12-month
       D.   15 weeks' unpaid leave;   24-month

       ANSWER: C, 459

53.   The Family and Medical Leave Act (FMLA) defines a _____ as one requiring in-patient, hospital, hospice, or residential medical care or continuing physician care.
       A.   medical leave emergency
       B.   serious health condition
       C.   life threatening illness
       D.   covered health situation

       ANSWER: B, 459

54.   The Family and Medical Leave Act (FMLA) of 1993 provides that
       A.   employees must be guaranteed a job following the leave, but the scope and status of the job may be different.
       B.   employees are entitled to take family leave after two years' employment.
       C.   the employee is required to return to work following the leave.
       D.   health benefits must be continued during the leave at the same level and conditions.

       ANSWER: D, 459

55.   _____ provides employees with assistance in caring for elderly relatives.
       A.   Elder care
       B.   Family security
       C.   Care giving assistance
       D.   A day-care benefit program

       ANSWER: A, 461

56.   Why do a relatively low percentage of men take paternity leave?
       A.   It is not mandated by the Family and Medical Leave Act.
       B.   Most employers do not offer paternity leave.
       C.   It is not socially acceptable for men to stay home for child-related reasons.
       D.   Most men cannot afford to take unpaid leaves.

       ANSWER: C, 463

57. A(n) _____ plan combines all sick leave, vacation time, and holidays into a total number of hours or days that employees can take off with pay.
     A.   well-pay
     B.   paid time-off
     C.   leaves-of-absence
     D.   earned-time-off benefit

     ANSWER: B, 463

58. The purpose of a flexible benefits plan is to
     A.   allow employees to contribute pre-tax dollars to buy additional benefits.
     B.   continuously update benefit options as employee needs and desires change.
     C.   combine all time-off benefits into a total number of hours that employees can take off with pay.
     D.   allow employees to select the benefits they prefer from groups of benefits established by the employer.

     ANSWER: D, 465

59. A plan that allows employees to contribute pre-tax dollars to buy additional benefits is called a
     A.   flexible spending account.
     B.   benefit incentive plan.
     C.   tax-deferred benefit option.
     D.   cafeteria-style plan.

     ANSWER: A, 465

60. A problem with flexible benefits plans is _____, a situation in which only higher-risk employees select and use certain benefits.
     A.   risk tendency
     B.   augmented liability
     C.   adverse selection
     D.   self-selection

     ANSWER: C, 466

True and False

61. The term "total compensation" refers to the wages and salaries paid by employers to their employees.

     ANSWER: False, 440
     Total compensation also includes money paid indirectly, such as benefits.

62. Benefits generally are not taxed as income to employees.

     ANSWER: True, 442

63.   Benefits mandated by the Fair Labor Standards Act include paid vacations and holidays after one years' full-time service.

ANSWER: False, 442
There is no government mandate regarding vacations or holidays.

64.   A major reason for proposed mandated benefits is that federal and state governments want to shift many of the social costs for health care and other expenditures to employers, thus relieving some of the budgetary pressures.

ANSWER: True, 443

65.   A problem with workers' compensation systems is that an injured employee who collects cash benefits and medical care can also take legal action against the employer for work-related injuries.

ANSWER: False, 444
In exchange for workers' compensation, employees give up the rights of legal actions and awards.

66.   An employee who is out of work, whether laid off or fired for misconduct, either actively seeking employment or not, is eligible for unemployment compensation.

ANSWER: False, 444
Workers fired for misconduct or those not actively seeking employment generally are ineligible for unemployment compensation.

67.   The Worker Adjustment and Retraining Notification Act (WARN) of 1988 requires employers to give severance pay to laid-off and redundant workers.

ANSWER: False, 445
The WARN Act requires 60 day's notice if a mass layoff or facility closing is to occur, but the act does not require employers to give severance pay.

68.   The mandatory retirement age has been increased to 70.

ANSWER: False, 445
A 1986 amendment to the ADEA prohibits mandatory employment at any age for most employees.

69.   ERISA requires many companies to offer retirement plans to all employees if they are offered to any employee.

ANSWER: True, 449

70.   Employee who voluntarily resign or are terminated before being vested, accrue no pension rights except the funds that they have contributed.

ANSWER: True, 450

71.   In *Arizona Governing Committee v. Norris*, the Supreme Court prohibited pension plans from using gender-specific mortality tables when determining benefits.

ANSWER: True, 450

72. A co-payment strategy requires employees to pay a portion of the cost of both insurance premiums and medical care.

    ANSWER: True, 452

73. A health maintenance organization (HMO) is a health care provider that contracts with an employer or employer group to provide health-care services to employees at a competitive rate.

    ANSWER: False, 453
    This is a description of a preferred provider organization (PPO).

74. COBRA allows employees who leave a job, either voluntarily or involuntarily, to continue participation in the employers' group health plan for a period of time.

    ANSWER: True, 455

75. The idea behind social and recreational programs is to promote employee happiness and team spirit.

    ANSWER: True, 458

76. The Family and Medical Leave Act of 1993 includes federal, state, and private employers.

    ANSWER: True, 459

77. A provision of the Family and Medical Leave Act of 1993 permits employers to require that employees take off a block of time rather than intermittent periods to ease employer scheduling problems.

    ANSWER: False, 459
    The act specifies that the leave may be intermittent rather than in one block.

78. Under the FMLA, employees can be required to use all paid-up vacation and personal leave before taking unpaid leave.

    ANSWER: True, 459

79. Employees who use an on-site child-care facility have a more positive attitude towards management and the employer.

    ANSWER: True, 460

80. New federal laws require employers to treat spousal equivalents and domestic partners on the same basis as spouses of married employees when providing benefits.

    ANSWER: False, 461-462
    While some states and cities have passed laws requiring domestic partner benefits, there are no such federal laws.

Essay

81.   Discuss the role of benefits as a component of the total compensation package.

      ANSWER: 440-442
      Spending on benefits exceeds 40% of overall payroll costs. They help an organization compete in a tight labor market, and should be looked as part of the overall compensation strategy of the organization. Changing demographics has focused attention on health-care, retirement, and family-friendly benefits. Benefits provide some tax advantages.

82.   What benefits are mandated by federal law? How are they funded?

      ANSWER: 442-444, 459, 463
      Mandated benefits include social security (funded by payroll taxes on employers and employees), workers' compensation and unemployment compensation insurance (purchased by employers), and family and medical leave, military reserve time off, and election and jury leaves (unpaid, but overhead costs paid by employer). In addition there are mandates for extended and portable health-care insurance.

83.   What are the major provisions of the Employee Retirement Income Security Act? How has this legislation affected retirement benefits?

      ANSWER: 449-450
      ERISA does not mandate pension plans, but regulates plans to assure that employees who have put money into them or depend on a pension for retirement funds actually will receive the money when they retire. ERISA requires that retirement plans must be offered to all employees if they are offered to any, sets minimum funding requirements, and requires termination insurance. Defined-contributions plans are becoming more common.

84.   Explain why health-care cost management has become important. Discuss several strategies available for controlling costs.

      ANSWER: 451-456
      An aging population, government mandates such as COBRA and HIPAA, and increasing medical costs have caused some organizations to drop health-care benefits, while others use managed care plans including PPOs and HMOs. Other strategies for controlling costs include co-payments and utilization reviews.

85.   What family-oriented benefits are being offered by employers? Which of these are mandated by the federal government?

      ANSWER: 458-462
      The FMLA mandates unpaid leaves for eligible employees. Voluntary family-oriented benefits include adoption benefits, child care, elder care, and benefits for domestic partners and spousal equivalents.

Chapter 15

Health, Safety, and Security

Multiple Choice

1. _____ management practices in organizations strive to maintain the overall well-being of individuals.
    A. Safety
    B. Health
    C. Ergonomics
    D. Security

    ANSWER: B, 476

2. Safety is defined as
    A. the protection of employees while on work premises or work assignments.
    B. the protection of employer facilities from unauthorized access.
    C. a general state of physical, mental, and emotional well-being.
    D. a condition in which the physical well-being of people is protected.

    ANSWER: D, 476

3. The main purpose of effective _____ programs in organizations is to prevent work-related injuries and accidents.
    A. Safety
    B. Health
    C. Ergonomics
    D. Security

    ANSWER: A, 476

4. The purpose of _____ is the protection of employees and organizational facilities.
    A. ergonomics
    B. enforcement
    C. security
    D. safety

    ANSWER: C, 476

5.   The primary health, safety, and security responsibilities in an organization
     usually fall on
     A.   safety teams.
     B.   supervisors and managers.
     C.   industrial engineers.
     D.   HR specialists.

     ANSWER: B, 476

6.   In a typical division of health, safety, and security responsibilities, the HR
     unit is responsible for
     A.   monitoring the health and safety of employees daily.
     B.   investigating accidents.
     C.   monitoring the workplace for security problems.
     D.   developing the safety reporting system.

     ANSWER: D, 477

7.   Who is responsible for workers' compensation costs?
     A.   employers
     B.   employees
     C.   employees and employers jointly
     D.   state and local government

     ANSWER: A, 477

8.   What is the purpose of workers' compensation laws?
     A.   to protect employees from dangerous and unhealthy working conditions
     B.   to promote worker safety through the enforcement of safety regulations
     C.   to provide payments to injured workers for lost wages, medical bills, and
          retraining if the worker cannot go back to the current job
     D.   to ensure that employers are held liable for injuries suffered at work

     ANSWER: C, 477 - 478

9.   What has been a major contributor to the increase in workers' compensation
     costs?
     A.   an escalation in the number and seriousness of on-the-job accidents
     B.   higher litigation expenses
     C.   HIV and AIDS-related medical expenses
     D.   employees injured while working at home

     ANSWER: B, 478

10. What could be the impact on employers who make accommodations for injured
     employees through light-duty work?
     A.   They could be liable for increased workers' compensation premiums due to
          the increased risk.
     B.   They would be violating ADA rules.
     C.   They will be held liable for any accidents caused by the injured employee.
     D.   They may be undercutting what really are essential job functions, as
          defined by the ADA.

     ANSWER: D, 479

11. What does the ADA require regarding information from all medical examinations and inquiries?
     A.   It should be maintained separately from all other confidential files.
     B.   It is be given to the employee. No copies may be made or kept by the employer.
     C.   It is to be made available to relevant supervisors who need to make reasonable accommodations for any identified disabilities.
     D.   It should be filed with all other confidential information, with restricted access.

     ANSWER: A, 479

12. Which of the following is a restriction under the child-labor laws, as found in the Fair Labor Standards Act?
     A.   The FLSA has set the minimum age for most employment at 14.
     B.   Individuals from 14-16 years old are restricted to an eight-hour day.
     C.   The minimum age is 18 for hazardous occupations.
     D.   Children under 18 are restricted to an eight-hour day on weekends.

     ANSWER: C, 479

13. _____ was passed to "assure as far as possible every working man or woman in the Nation safe and healthful working conditions and to preserve our human resources."
     A.   Worker's Compensation legislation
     B.   The Occupational Safety and Health Act
     C.   The Fair Labor Standards Act
     D.   The Wagner Act

     ANSWER: B, 480

14. Every employer engaged in commerce with _____ employees is covered by OSHA?
     A.   over 15
     B.   at least 25
     C.   ten or more
     D.   one or more

     ANSWER: D, 480

15. The general duty clause of the Occupational Safety and Health Act refers to
     A.   areas in which no standards have been adopted.
     B.   the philosophy and ideals of safe management.
     C.   strictly following all established standards.
     D.   investigating any and all organizational accidents.

     ANSWER: A, 482

16. The Occupational Safety and Health Act states that employers have a *general duty*
     A.   to obey all rules and regulations developed by the OSHA.
     B.   to inform OSHA when there are no rules to apply in a specific situation.
     C.   to provide safe and healthy working conditions.
     D.   to develop safety and health standards unique to each place of employment.

     ANSWER: C, 482

17. The federal Hazard Communication Standard requires the uses of hazardous chemicals
    A. limit the amount of time that an employee can work in areas where the chemicals are stored.
    B. evaluate, classify, and label these substances.
    C. provide medical insurance for all employees working with the chemicals.
    D. keep detailed records of any accident involving these substances.

    ANSWER: B, 482

18. What is the purpose of a material safety data sheet (MSDS)?
    A. to track the use of hazardous materials on the job
    B. to record accident or injury data
    C. to identify possible consequences of exposure to hazardous substances
    D. to provide information about hazardous substances including antidotes

    ANSWER: D, 482

19. What is the purpose of OSHA's lock out/tab out regulations?
    A. to prevent accidental start-up of defective machinery during repair or adjustment
    B. to deny access to the workplace by unauthorized individuals
    C. to ensure that hazardous substances are kept under lock and key when not being used
    D. to close down a workplace judged unsafe by an OSHA inspector

    ANSWER: A, 482

20. _____ is the study and design of the work environment to address the physiological and physical demands on individuals.
    A. Occupational safety and health
    B. Environmental design
    C. Ergonomics
    D. Industrial physiology

    ANSWER: C, 483

21. An ergonomic study examines such factors as
    A. the social and cultural environment of the job.
    B. fatigue, lighting, tools, equipment layout, and placement of controls.
    C. the environmental quality of the workplace.
    D. job safety and security.

    ANSWER: B, 483

22. _____ occur when workers repetitively use the same muscles to perform tasks, resulting in muscle and skeletal injuries.
    A. Arthritic disorders
    B. Joint failures
    C. Multiple sclerosis
    D. Cumulative trauma disorders

    ANSWER: D, 483

23. Carpal tunnel syndrome is an injury common to people who
    A.   put their hands through repetitive motions.
    B.   spend most of the work day standing or leaning over a counter.
    C.   work in places with constant loud noises.
    D.   perform work that produces constant eye strain.

    ANSWER: A, 483

24. The _____ industry has the highest level of cumulative trauma disorders.
    A.   fast food
    B.   agricultural
    C.   meat-packing industry
    D.   garment

    ANSWER: C, 483

25. In a court case involving reproductive health, the Supreme Court held that Johnson Controls' policy of _____ violated the Civil Rights Act.
    A.   refusing to include abortion services in its medical insurance plan
    B.   keeping women of childbearing capacity out of jobs that might involve lead exposure.
    C.   requiring pregnant women to take unpaid leave prior to giving birth
    D.   not making reasonable accommodation for employees in the later stage of pregnancy

    ANSWER: B, 484

26. Workers have the right to walk off a job and refuse to work if
    A.   they are not receiving fair pay for the hazards presented.
    B.   they have tried at least two alternative procedures which didn't work to solve the problem.
    C.   management has tried to alleviate the problem, but has not succeeded.
    D.   the employee's fear is objectively reasonable.

    ANSWER: D, 485

27. Which employers are not required to keep detailed OSHA records?
    A.   those with good safety records in previous years and those with fewer than 10 employees
    B.   employers not engaged in interstate or foreign commerce
    C.   those with fewer than 25 employees in specified "safe" businesses
    D.   employers with no government contracts or subcontracts

    ANSWER: A, 485

28. Which of the followings organizations are required to complete OSHA Form 300?
    A.   firms with good safety records in previous years and with fewer than 10 employees
    B.   large organizations involved in interstate or foreign commerce
    C.   firms having frequent hospitalizations, injuries, or illnesses and/or work-related deaths
    D.   firms with a record of willful and repeated violations

    ANSWER: C, 485

29.   OSHA representatives who conduct inspections are called
       A.   government safety controllers.
       B.   compliance officers.
       C.   safety and health consultants.
       D.   security officers.

       ANSWER: B, 486

30.   What was the Supreme Court decision in *Marshall v. Barlow's, Inc.*?
       A.   The no-knock provisions are a necessary part of OSHA investigations.
       B.   The Fourth Amendment does not apply to government safety inspections.
       C.   Inspectors must produce reasonable cause before getting a search warrant.
       D.   Safety inspectors must produce a search warrant if an employer refuses to
             allow an inspector into the plant voluntarily.

       ANSWER: D, 486

31.   Whether or not a citation is issued for OSHA violations depends on
       A.   the severity and extent of the problem and on the employer's knowledge of
             them.
       B.   whether the violation is a breach of the *general duty* clause.
       C.   the past record of the employer in correcting previous problems.
       D.   whether a complaint had been filed by an employee.

       ANSWER: A, 487

32.   The nature and extent of the penalty issued by OSHA officials depends on
       A.   whether OSHA had previously notified the employer about the violations.
       B.   the extent to which the employer had cooperated with the OSHA officials.
       C.   the type and severity of the violations.
       D.   whether the employer had prior knowledge of the violations.

       ANSWER: C, 487

33.   The absence of guard railings to prevent employees from falling three stories
       into heavy machinery is an example of a(n) _____ violation.
       A.   serious
       B.   imminent danger
       C.   other than serious
       D.   *de minimis*

       ANSWER: B, 488

34.   When an employer knows of a condition which could probably cause serious
       physical harm, a(n) _____ violation has occurred.
       A.   imminent danger
       B.   other than serious
       C.   *de minimis*
       D.   serious

       ANSWER: D, 488

35. _____ violations could have an impact on employees' health or safety but probably would not cause death or serious harm.
    A.   Other-than-serious
    B.   Serious
    C.   Dangerous
    D.   *De minimis*

ANSWER: A, 488

36. Lack of doors on toilet stalls is a common example of
    A.   an other-than-serious violation.
    B.   a situation that is not an OSHA violation.
    C.   a *de minimis* violation.
    D.   picky OSHA regulations.

ANSWER: C, 488

37. An employer who has been warned of a safety violation, but does not correct the situation would be cited for
    A.   a serious violation.
    B.   a willful and repeated violation.
    C.   a *de minimis* violation.
    D.   an imminent danger violation.

ANSWER: B, 488

38. What can happen if an employer has been warned of a safety violation, but does not correct the situation, and a death occurs,
    A.   the business may be shut down for up to one year.
    B.   the employer can be fined 25 percent of yearly gross income.
    C.   workers' compensation insurance will not pay, leaving the employer liable for civil litigation on the grounds of gross negligence.
    D.   a jail term of six months can be imposed on responsible executives or managers.

ANSWER: D, 488

39. At the heart of safety management is(are)
    A.   an organizational commitment to a comprehensive safety effort.
    B.   routine inspections by OSHA compliance officers.
    C.   safety policies and discipline.
    D.   a safety committee consisting of employees from all departments.

ANSWER: A, 490

40. The _____ approach to safety management focuses on designing jobs, developing and implementing safety policies, and using safety committees.
    A.   engineering
    B.   systems
    C.   organizational
    D.   individual

ANSWER: C, 490

41. Which of the following was __not__ listed as part of the engineering approach to safety management?
    A.   applying ergonomic principles
    B.   designing jobs
    C.   designing work settings and equipment
    D.   reviewing equipment

    ANSWER: B, 490

42. _____ approach safety from the perspective of a proper match of people to jobs and emphasize and employee training in safety methods.
    A.   Safety consultants
    B.   Industrial engineers
    C.   Ergonomists
    D.   Industrial psychologists

    ANSWER: D, 491

43. Which of the following statements is true?
    A.   People who work the "graveyard" shifts have higher accident rates.
    B.   Research has found no relationship between accident rates and the amount of overtime worked.
    C.   People who are dissatisfied with their jobs have higher accident rates.
    D.   "Accident proneness" is a personality disorder.

    ANSWER: A, 491

44. With respect to safety committees, an employer may be in violation of the National Labor Relations Act if
    A.   workers are excluded from participation.
    B.   participation is compulsory.
    C.   managers compose a majority on the committee.
    D.   the committee lacks top management support.

    ANSWER: C, 492

45. _____ is the use of illicit substances or the misuse of controlled substances, alcohol, or other drugs.
    A.   Stress defense
    B.   Substance abuse
    C.   Drug addiction
    D.   Dependency

    ANSWER: B, 494

46. Which of the following groups has the highest incidence of substance abuse?
    A.   white-collar males
    B.   unmarried men and women 45 to 60
    C.   African-American single mothers
    D.   white men aged 19 to 23

    ANSWER: D, 494

47.   Under the Americans with Disabilities Act,
      A.   those addicted to illegal substances are considered disabled.
      B.   recovering substance abusers are not considered disabled.
      C.   current illegal drug users are considered disabled.
      D.   addiction to alcohol is not considered a disability.

      ANSWER: A, 495

48.   What is a fitness-for-duty test?
      A.   an investigation into possible illegal drug and/or alcohol use
      B.   a stress test
      C.   an attempt to detect impairment before putting a person behind dangerous
            equipment
      D.   a medical examination to check for serious illness or disease

      ANSWER: C, 495

49.   The recommended action for supervisors when confronting substance abusers, which
      has been endorsed legally, is
      A.   a probationary period which includes random drug and alcohol testing.
      B.   a firm choice between help and discipline.
      C.   automatic referral to an employee assistance program (EAP).
      D.   disciplinary action.

      ANSWER: B, 495

50.   Which of the following was given as a cause for health problems when working in
      sealed buildings?
      A.   employees open windows which interferes with the ventilation system
      B.   an over dependence on computer-related equipment
      C.   environmental controls are easily manipulated by employees
      D.   air flows are reduced to save energy

      ANSWER: D, 496

51.   The EPA defines _____ as a situation in which occupants experience
      acute health problems and discomfort that appear to be linked to time spent in
      a building.
      A.   sick building syndrome
      B.   employee/work site interactions
      C.   environmental chronic disease
      D.   worker sensitivity effects

      ANSWER: A, 497

52.   Which of the following statements regarding workplace smoking is _false_?
      A.   Employees who smoke tend to adjust to a smoking ban within a few weeks.
      B.   Smoking cessation workshops do seem to reduce smoking by employees.
      C.   Courts have played an active role in addressing the smoking-at-work issue.
      D.   There are many state and local laws banning smoking in the workplace.

      ANSWER: C, 497

53.   _____ are designed to maintain or improve employee health before
       problems arise.
       A.   Preventative programs
       B.   Wellness programs
       C.   Education/awareness programs
       D.   Health maintenance programs

       ANSWER: B, 497

54.   _____ provide(s) counseling and other help to employees having
       emotional, physical, or other personal problems.
       A.   A wellness program
       B.   HR specialists
       C.   An ombudsman
       D.   Employee assistance programs

       ANSWER: D, 498

55.   Which of the following was not listed as a typical area addressed by EAPs?
       A.   educational assistance
       B.   termination/outplacement assistance
       C.   financial counseling
       D.   counseling for marital and family problems

       ANSWER: A, 498

56.   Which of the following occupations experiences the highest rate of workplace
       homicide?
       A.   jewelry store owners
       B.   public school employees
       C.   taxi drivers
       D.   post officers

       ANSWER: C, 500

57.   The most common cause of homicides at work are
       A.   disgruntled employees.
       B.   armed robbery attempts
       C.   former employees.
       D.   domestic relationships.

       ANSWER: B, 500

58.   Which of the following is a recommended approach to the management of workplace
       violence?
       A.   Do not hire job candidates with mental or emotional disabilities.
       B.   Check arrest records of job applicants.
       C.   Discharge employees suspected of behaviors that often precede violence.
       D.   Establish a violence response team.

       ANSWER: D, 501

59. Conducting a comprehensive review of organizational security is the purpose of
    A.   a security audit.
    B.   vulnerability assessment.
    C.   an OSHA inspection.
    D.   stress assessment.

    ANSWER: A, 503

60. Which of the following is true about employee crime?
    A.   Drug use is the cause of most employee theft.
    B.   Employers should screen out all applicants with an arrest record.
    C.   Organization can be held liable if an employee commits a crime.
    D.   Incidents of workplace crime is highest among minority men.

    ANSWER: C, 504

True and False

61. The term "security" refers to protection of the physical well-being of people.

    ANSWER: False, 478
    This is a definition of safety. Security refers to the protection of employees and organizational facilities.

62. Workers' compensation laws were passed as an amendment to the federal Occupational Safety and Health Act of 1970.

    ANSWER: False, 477
    Workers' compensation laws have been passed at the state level of government.

63. Employers are required to provide workers' compensation insurance for employees working at home via telecommuting.

    ANSWER: True, 478

64. The ADA encourages employers, in an attempt to reduce workers' compensation costs, to make accommodations for injured employees through light-duty work.

    ANSWER: False, 479
    Such action may undercut what really are essential job functions. By making accommodations for injured workers, the employer may be required to make accommodations for job applicants with disabilities.

65. The "general duty" clause of the Occupational Safety and Health Act requires that in areas where there are no safety standards, the employer has a general duty to provide safe and healthy working conditions.

    ANSWER: True, 482

66. OSHA requires that material safety data sheets be available in other languages if there are employees for whom English is not their primary language.

    ANSWER: True, 482

67. OSHA has issued regulations to eliminate or minimize occupational exposure to hepatitis B virus (HBV) and human immunodeficiency virus (HIV).

    ANSWER: True, 483

68. Ergonomical studies focus on such factors as fatigue, lighting, tools, equipment layout and placement of controls.

    ANSWER: True, 483

69. Cumulative trauma disorders occur when a worker is required to stand for long periods of time, in the same place, while working.

    ANSWER: False, 483
    CTDs occur when workers repetitively use the same muscles to perform tasks, resulting in muscle and skeletal injuries.

70. Under current OSHA regulations, an employer cannot refuse entry to an OSHA inspector. Instead of allowing an employer time to "tidy up", this *no-knock provision* permits inspection of normal operations.

    ANSWER: False, 486
    In *Marshall v. Barlow's Inc., 1978,* the Supreme Court ruled that safety inspectors must produce a search warrant if an employer refuses to allow an inspector into the plant voluntarily.

71. Other-than-serious violations could have an impact on employees' health and safety but probably would not cause death or serious harm.

    ANSWER: True, 488

72. Many employers pay little attention to OSHA because they have only a small chance of being inspected.

    ANSWER: True, 488

73. Research has found no significant differences in accident rates of employees working different shifts. Day-shift workers had the same rate of accidents as employees who work late-night shifts.

    ANSWER: False, 491
    Employees working the "graveyard" shifts have higher accident rates than those on day or evening shifts.

74. The Americans with Disabilities Act classifies recovering substance abusers as disabled.

    ANSWER: True, 495

75. The Environmental Protection Agency (EPA) defines *sick building syndrome* as a situation in which occupants experience acute health problems and discomfort that appear to be linked to time spent in a building.

     ANSWER: True, 497

76. OSHA has issued regulations which bans all smoking in the workplace.

     ANSWER: False, 497
     There are no national laws regulating smoking in the workplace.

77. A wellness program provides counseling and other help to employees having emotional, physical, or other personal problems.

     ANSWER: False, 497-498
     An EAP provides these programs. A wellness program is designed to maintain or improve employee health before problem arise.

78. To reduce the risk of workplace violence, it is recommended that employers discharge employees for behaviors that often precede violent acts.

     ANSWER: False, 501
     Employers may face legal action under the ADA for discharging employees for behaviors that often precede violent acts.

79. A disaster plan involves conducting a comprehensive review of organizational security.

     ANSWER: False, 503
     A security audit involves such an analysis. A disaster plan addresses how to deal with natural disasters such as floods, fires, and civil disobedience.

80. Firms that do not screen employees adequately may be subject to liability if an employee commits crimes later.

     ANSWER: True, 504

Essay

81. Define the terms "health" and "safety." Discuss the impact of workers' compensation laws, the ADA, and the FLSA on workplace safety.

     ANSWER: 476-479
     Health is a general state of physical, mental, and emotional well-being. Safety refers to protecting the physical well-being of people. Workers' compensation laws, passed by all 50 states, require employers to contribute to an insurance fund to compensate employees for work-related injuries. Under the ADA, action taken to accommodate an injured worker may create a precedent for hiring workers with disabilities. The ADA requires medical data to be kept separate from other confidential files. The FLSA sets the minimum age for hazardous occupations.

82.   What are the basic provisions of the Occupational Safety and Health Act of 1970? What is required of the organization to be in compliance? What is required of managers under this law? What are the responsibilities of individual employees?

ANSWER: 480-488
OSHA states that all private employers have a general duty to provide safe and healthy working conditions, whether there are specific standards or not. The act provides for inspections by compliance officers who can issue citations for violations categorized from *de minimis* to imminent danger. There are extensive record-keeping requirements. The employer is responsible for complying with all OSHA provisions. The individual employees have no such responsibility.

83.   There are three different approaches to safety management - organizational, engineering, and individual. Discuss the focus of each of these approaches, giving examples of actions that can be taken to improve worker safety.

ANSWER: 489-491
The focus of the organizational approach is designing jobs, developing and implementing safety policies, using safety committees, and coordinating accident investigations. The engineering approach involves designing work environments, reviewing equipment, and applying ergonomic principles. The individual approaches attempts to identify and modify behaviors that can lead to accident. It involves safety training and incentive programs.

84.   Would you recommend that an organization ban smoking in the workplace? Discuss your recommendation with respect to OSHA and the ADA.

ANSWER: 497
OSHA requires a healthy work environment, but there are no regulations regarding smoking. The ADA does not identify smoking as a disability. A multiple of state and local laws regulate smoking in the workplace. Many employers have established no-smoking policies and offer smoking cessation workshops.

85.   Define the term "security" with respect to the workplace. What actions can an employer take to minimize the risk of workplace violence?

ANSWER: 500-504
Security involves the protection of employees while on work premises or work assignments, and protection of organizational facilities and equipment from unauthorized access. To minimize the risk of workplace violence, an employer can conduct a security audit/vulnerability analysis, control access to the physical facilities, screen job applicants, and have sufficient security personnel.

Chapter 16

Employee Rights and Discipline

Multiple Choice

1. It has been stated that: "rights do not exist in the abstract. They exist only when
    A. public policy accepts something as a right."
    B. ,someone is successful in demanding their applications."
    C. the judicial system rules that certain activities are rights."
    D. they are fully documented and accepted."

    ANSWER: B, 510

2. _____ belongs to a person by law, nature, or tradition.
    A. Responsibilities
    B. Duties
    C. Lifestyle choices
    D. Rights

    ANSWER: D, 510

3. Rights are offset by
    A. responsibilities.
    B. traditions.
    C. laws.
    D. contracts.

    ANSWER: A, 510

4. Obligations to be accountable for actions are
    A. contracts.
    B. laws.
    C. responsibilities.
    D. rights.

    ANSWER: C, 510

5. If an employee has the right to a safe working environment, the employer has
    A.   the right to expect the employee to assist in providing it.
    B.   an obligation to provide a safe workplace.
    C.   the right to demand compliance with all necessary rules.
    D.   the responsibility to compensate the employee for any workplace injury.

    ANSWER: B, 510

6. The _____ nature of rights and responsibilities suggests that both
    parties to an employment relationship should regard the other as having equal
    rights and should treat the other with respect.
    A.   adversarial
    B.   contractual
    C.   legal
    D.   reciprocal

    ANSWER: D, 510

7. Employees' _____ are the result of specific laws passed by federal,
    state, or local governments.
    A.   statutory rights
    B.   responsibilities
    C.   contractual obligations
    D.   contractual rights

    ANSWER: A, 510

8. An employee's _____ are based on a specific agreement with an
    employer.
    A.   reciprocal rights
    B.   legal rights
    C.   contractual rights
    D.   statutory rights

    ANSWER: C, 511

9. An agreement in which an employee who is being terminated agrees not to sue the
    employer in exchange for specific benefits is called a(n)
    A.   employment contract.
    B.   separation agreement.
    C.   employment-at-will understanding.
    D.   reciprocal agreement.

    ANSWER: B, 511

10. Provisions stating that if the individual leaves the organization intellectual
    property and trade secrets remain, are contained in a(n)
    A.   non-compete covenant.
    B.   contractual right.
    C.   separation agreement.
    D.   employment contract.

    ANSWER: D, 512

11. Provisions stating that if the individual leaves the organization, existing customers and clients cannot be solicited for business for a specific period of time, are contained in a(n)
     A.   non-piracy agreement.
     B.   non-compete covenant.
     C.   separation agreement.
     D.   implied contract.

     ANSWER: A, 512

12. In which of the following are rights and responsibilities of the employee to the employer likely to be spelled out?
     A.   statutory laws
     B.   reciprocal agreements
     C.   a job description
     D.   an employment-at-will understanding

     ANSWER: C, 512

13. A number of court decisions have held that if an employer hires someone for an indefinite period of time
     A.   the employer can terminate the employee at will.
     B.   the employer has created an implied contract.
     C.   the employee has an obligation to remain working for the employer.
     D.   a psychological contract exists.

     ANSWER: B, 512

14. Employment-at-will is a common-law doctrine stating that an
     A.   employee can resign from a job at any time, with notice or without notice.
     B.   employers can fire whomever they please, for any reason or for no reason.
     C.   employee has a guaranteed right to a job until retirement.
     D.   employers have the right to hire, fire, demote, or promote whomever they choose, unless there is a law or contract to the contrary.

     ANSWER: D, 514

15. Which of the following was not given as a defense of employment-at-will (EAW)?
     A.   Challenging EAW violates the employers' right to good faith and fair dealing.
     B.   The right of private ownership of a business guarantees EAW.
     C.   Interfering with EAW reduces productivity in the firm and in the economy.
     D.   EAW defends employees' right to change jobs, as well as employers' rights to hire and fire.

     ANSWER: A, 514

16. Which of the following is an argument defending employment-at-will (EAW)?
     A.   Only a written agreement can provide a contract for life-time employment.
     B.   The right to make a profit is part of our economic system.
     C.   Interfering with EAW reduces productivity in the firm and in the economy.
     D.   The business is located in a right-to-work state.

     ANSWER: C, 514

17.   Which of the following has been recognized by the courts as a rationale for concluding wrongful discharge in an employment-at-will suit?
       A.   The employee is ineligible for unemployment insurance.
       B.   The reason the employee was fired violates public policy.
       C.   Downsizing is for other than economic objectives.
       D.   The probationary employee status is unfair.

       ANSWER: B, 515

18.   When challenging employment-at-will, the _____ approach is based on the premise that an employee will not be fired as long as he or she does the job.
       A.   psychological contract
       B.   union contract
       C.   good faith and fair dealing
       D.   implied employment contract

       ANSWER: D, 515

19.   How have the courts treated unionized workers and employment-at-will actions?
       A.   Unionized workers cannot pursue EAW actions as at-will employees, because they are covered by the grievance-arbitration process.
       B.   Unionized workers can also pursue EAW actions.
       C.   Unionized workers cannot pursue EAW actions in right-to-work states.
       D.   Unionized workers can only be discharged for just cause as spelled out in the union contract.

       ANSWER: A, 516

20.   In the landmark EAW case, *Fortune v. National Cash Register Company*, Fortune was fired shortly after winning a large order which would have earned him a big commission. The courts ruled that
       A.   permitting NCR to fire in these circumstances was against public policy.
       B.   the EAW doctrine gave NCR the right to downsize its workforce at will.
       C.   by firing him, NCR violated the covenant of good faith and fair dealing.
       D.   NCR had a right to fire Fortune in the absence of an employment contract.

       ANSWER: C, 516

21.   _____ is defined as "reasonable justification for taking employment-related actions."
       A.   Constructive discharge
       B.   Just cause
       C.   Due process
       D.   Procedural justice

       ANSWER: B, 516

22.   Dismissal for _____ usually is spelled out in union contracts.
       A.   any reason
       B.   rule breach
       C.   adverse impact
       D.   just cause

       ANSWER: D, 516

23.   Which of the following would be a criterion for determination of just cause for
       disciplinary action?
       A.   Was the employee warned of the consequences of the conduct?
       B.   What is the employee's race, sex, or national origin?
       C.   Did the behavior occur on-the-job?
       D.   What was the performance and discipline record of this employee?

       ANSWER: A, 517

24.   _____ is most often found when an employer deliberately makes
       conditions intolerable in an attempt to get an employee to quit.
       A.   Harassment
       B.   At-will discharge
       C.   Constructive discharge
       D.   Just-cause dismissal

       ANSWER: C, 517

25.   In employment settings, _____ is the means used for individuals to
       explain and defend their actions against charges or discipline.
       A.   progressive discipline
       B.   due process
       C.   legal constraints
       D.   "Georgian" rights

       ANSWER: B, 517

26.   People decide the favorability of their outcomes by comparing them with the
       outcomes of others, given their relative situations. This decision involves the
       concept of
       A.   procedural justice.
       B.   just treatment.
       C.   equitable treatment.
       D.   distributive justice.

       ANSWER: D, 517

27.   Procedural justice deals with which of the following questions?
       A.   Was the decision-making process fair?
       B.   Were the outcome equitably distributed?
       C.   Is the way the outcomes were distributed fair?
       D.   Would a reasonable person agree with the decision?

       ANSWER: A, 518

28.   For unionized employees, due process usually refers to
       A.   protection from arbitrary actions by management.
       B.   a right to participate in union activities.
       C.   the right to use the grievance procedure specified in the union contract.
       D.   the right to sue both the union and management for wrongful discharge.

       ANSWER: C, 518

29. Which of the following is __not__ a common alternative dispute resolution method?
     A.   arbitration
     B.   HR review board
     C.   Peer review panel
     D.   ombudsman

     ANSWER: B, 518

30. _____ uses a neutral third party to render a decision.
     A.   Mediation
     B.   Peer review
     C.   The ombudsman
     D.   Arbitration

     ANSWER: D, 518

31. A person outside the normal chain of command who acts as a problem solver for management and employees is known as a(n)
     A.   ombudsman.
     B.   arbitrator.
     C.   mediator.
     D.   peer review panelist.

     ANSWER: A, 519

32. Which of the following is true about the Privacy Act of 1974, which includes provisions affecting HR record-keeping systems?
     A.   It protects employers who keep details of employees' off-the-job behavior.
     B.   It prevents employers from investigating the off-the-job behavior of employees.
     C.   It applies only to federal agencies and organizations supplying services to the federal government.
     D.   It requires employees to keep all personnel records confidential.

     ANSWER: C, 520

33. Which of the following is recommended regarding employee records?
     A.   Keep all medical, disciplinary, and performance reports together in a separate confidential file.
     B.   Release employee information only with employee's consent.
     C.   Permit an employee to review all records in his or her employment file.
     D.   To avoid law suits, keep only essential HR information on each employee.

     ANSWER: B, 522

34. Individuals who report real or perceived wrongs committed by their employers are called
     A   snitches.
     B.   public watchdogs.
     C.   Naderites.
     D.   whistle-blowers.

     ANSWER: D, 522

35. Federal constitutional rights, such as the right to protection from unreasonable search and seizure, protect
    A.   an individual only against the activities of the government.
    B.   employees from self-incrimination, such as providing urine samples.
    C.   all employees.
    D.   only those individuals employed in the private sector.

    ANSWER: A, 524

36. The U.S. Constitution protects _____ in the areas of due process, search and seizure, and privacy.
    A.   all employees
    B.   employees in the private sector
    C.   public-sector employees
    D.   only non-managerial employees

    ANSWER: C, 525

37. Which of the following statements is true about polygraph testing?
    A.   A certified professional must read and interpret polygraph test results before they can be admitted in court.
    B.   The Polygraph Protection Act prohibits the use of polygraphs for most pre-employment screening.
    C.   The American Psychological Association has certified the validity of polygraph tests.
    D.   Polygraph tests accurately measure changes in the heart rate when a person lies.

    ANSWER: B, 526

38. The Polygraph Protection Act
    A.   prohibits government contractors from using polygraphs for drug testing.
    B.   provides guidelines for the use and interpretation of polygraph tests.
    C.   permits government agencies to use polygraphs but only for new employees.
    D.   prohibits the use of polygraphs for judging a person's honesty while employed.

    ANSWER: D, 525

39. Which of the following statements is _false_ about paper-and-pencil honesty tests?
    A.   Because of their nature, they are unlikely to be prohibited under the Fifth Amendment (which protects persons from self-incrimination) in public-sector employment.
    B.   Their use has been challenged successfully in some court decisions.
    C.   Their use is not restricted by federal or state laws.
    D.   Because they are not restricted by the Polygraph Protection Act, they have become popular.

    ANSWER: A, 526

40. Which of the following actions can an employer take in response to an employee's off-the-job behavior?
    A.   Reassign a homosexual worker when other employees refuse to work with him.
    B.   Forbid employees from dating one another.
    C.   Take disciplinary action when there are clear job-related consequences.
    D.   Prohibit the private use of legal products (like tobacco and alcohol).

    ANSWER: C, 526

41. The Drug-Free Workplace Act of 1988 requires
    A.   tobacco and alcohol to be regulated as controlled substances.
    B.   government contractors to take steps to eliminate employee drug usage.
    C.   that employers cease testing for the off-the-job drug use of its workers.
    D.   that government contractors establish drug-awareness programs.

    ANSWER: B, 527

42. For U.S. government contractors, what is the major consequence of not providing employees with a drug free environment?
    A.   The contractor becomes liable for criminal law suits.
    B.   The contractor is liable for civil law suits by employees concerned about personal security.
    C.   State governments may require additional workers' compensation insurance.
    D.   The company may lose its government contracts.

    ANSWER: D, 527

43. Employee attitudes towards drug testing can be described as follows:
    A.   Drug testing appears to be most acceptable when employees see the procedures being used as fair.
    B.   There is more tolerance for drug use and drug users now than before.
    C.   Drug testing is still regarded as an unacceptable invasion of privacy, and as such is not acceptable to most employees.
    D.   To be accepted, all employees should be routinely tested.

    ANSWER: A, 528

44. Drug testing policies used by employers include each of the following, except:
    A.   random testing of everyone at periodic intervals.
    B.   testing only when there is probable cause.
    C.   testing before new, complicated equipment is installed.
    D.   testing after accidents.

    ANSWER: C, 528

45. Where there is a choice among actions, _____ act as general guidelines that focus organizational actions.
    A.   procedures
    B.   policies
    C.   practices
    D.   HR recommendations

    ANSWER: B, 529

46. _____ are general in nature, while _____ are specific to the situation.
    A.   Procedures and rules; policies
    B.   Procedures; rules and regulations
    C.   Rules; policies and procedures
    D.   Policies; procedures and rules

    ANSWER: D, 529

47. _____ are customary methods of handling activities.
    A.   Procedures
    B.   Practices
    C.   Rules
    D.   Policies

    ANSWER: A, 529

48. "Specific guidelines that regulate and restrict the behavior of individuals" is a definition of
    A.   policies.
    B.   procedures.
    C.   rules.
    D.   practices.

    ANSWER: C, 529

49. A(n) _____ is a formal method of obtaining employee input and upward communication.
    A.   employee handbook
    B.   suggestion system
    C.   TQM action
    D.   teleconference

    ANSWER: B, 532

50. Discipline is _____ that enforces organizational rules.
    A.   an outcome
    B.   negative reinforcement
    C.   punishment
    D.   a form of training

    ANSWER: D, 533

51. The disciplinary system can be viewed as an application of _____ for problem or unproductive employees.
    A.   behavior modification
    B.   punishment
    C.   negative rewards
    D.   a public rebuke

    ANSWER: A, 533

52.   The best discipline is clearly
       A.   administered in public.
       B.   administered off-the-job.
       C.   self discipline.
       D.   positive reinforcement.

       ANSWER: C, 533

53.   The _____ approach builds on the philosophy that violations are
       actions that usually can be constructively corrected without penalty.
       A.   behavior modification
       B.   positive discipline
       C.   progressive discipline
       D.   problem-solving

       ANSWER: B, 533

54.   What should be the goal of counseling as a part of the discipline process?
       A.   to use penalties to discourage undesirable behavior.
       B.   to reinforce organizational procedures and rules
       C.   to avoid law suits
       D.   to heighten employee awareness of organizational policies and rules.

       ANSWER: D, 533

55.   _____ incorporates a sequence of steps that are designed to change the
       employee's inappropriate behavior.
       A.   Progressive discipline
       B.   Step-wise punishment
       C.   Behavior modification
       D.   Employee counseling

       ANSWER: A, 534

56.   Progressive discipline procedures, from verbal caution through dismissal if
       necessary, are best applied for which of the following offenses?
       A.   intoxication at work.
       B.   possession of weapons.
       C.   absenteeism and tardiness.
       D.   falsifying employment application.

       ANSWER: C, 534

57.   When actions to modify behavior become more severe as the employee continues to
       show improper behavior, it is called
       A.   behavior conditioning.
       B.   progressive discipline.
       C.   operant conditioning.
       D.   counseling and discipline.

       ANSWER: B, 535

58. Managers may be reluctant to use discipline. Which of the following was <u>not</u> lists as a reason?
    A.   lack of support by higher management
    B.   guilt because they committed the same actions before they became managers
    C.   fear of lawsuits
    D.   discipline can harm performance

    ANSWER: D, 535

59. For discipline to be effective it must be
    A.   aimed at the behavior, not at the employee personally.
    B.   administered at a later date after tempers have cooled.
    C.   selectively applied.
    D.   publicly administered to "set an example."

    ANSWER: A, 536

60. The final stage in the discipline process is
    A.   arbitration.
    B.   counseling.
    C.   termination.
    D.   mediation.

    ANSWER: C, 536

True and False

61. Legal rights correspond to moral rights in that they belong to a person by nature or tradition.

    ANSWER: False, 510
    Legal rights may or may not correspond to moral rights. Legal rights belong to a person by law, moral rights by nature or tradition.

62. Rights and responsibilities are reciprocal in nature.

    ANSWER: True, 510

63. Courts are ruling that content of an employee handbook constitute a contract between an employer and its employee.

    ANSWER: True, 512-513

64. The employment-at-will doctrine provides workers with protection from arbitrary and capricious discharge through grievance procedures.

    ANSWER: False, 514
    EAW is a common-law doctrine stating that employers have the right to hire, fire, promote, or demote whomever they choose, unless there is a law or contract to the contrary.

65. In general, unionized workers cannot pursue employment-at-will actions as at-will employees, because they are covered by an alternative remedy: the grievance-arbitration process.

     ANSWER: True, 516

66. When an employee is dismissed for a well-documented breach of the organization's rules, it is a "just cause" termination.

     ANSWER: True, 516

67. If an employer deliberately makes conditions intolerable in an attempt to force an employee to resign, it is called a "wrongful termination."

     ANSWER: False, 517
     Constructive discharge occurs when an employer makes conditions so intolerable as to force a reasonable employee to resign.

68. The Privacy Act of 1974 applies only to federal agencies and organizations supplying services to the federal government.

     ANSWER: True, 520

69. Whistle-blowers are more likely to lose their jobs in public employment than in private employment, because most civil rights laws specifically exclude federal, state, and local governments from coverage.

     ANSWER: False, 522
     Most civil service systems have rules protecting whistle-blowers. There is no comprehensive whistle-blowing law that protects private-sector employees.

70. Federal constitutional rights, such as the right to protection from unreasonable search and seizure, protect employees from workplace monitoring.

     ANSWER: False, 524
     The constitutional protections refer to the actions of government. Private-sector employees can be monitored, observed, and searched at work by employer representatives.

71. The Polygraph Protection Act prohibits the use of polygraphs for most pre-employment screening and for judging a person's honesty while employed.

     ANSWER: True, 526

72. Federal law prohibits employers from firing workers for engaging in legal activities when away from the job.

     ANSWER: False, 526
     While many workers believe that their employers have no right to question employees' private lives, there is no federal legal protection.

73.   Drug testing by employers violates an employee's constitutional right to protection from unreasonable search and seizure.

ANSWER: False, 527-528
The Supreme Court has ruled that certain drug-testing plans do not violate the Constitution. The search and seizure provision of the Constitution applies to actions of government.

74.   The Drug-Free Workplace Act of 1988 permits federal officials to conduct random drug testing of federal government employees.

ANSWER: False, 527
The Act requires government contractors to take steps to eliminate employee drug use. This may involve drug testing by private-sector employers.

75.   Employers who conduct pre-employment drug tests have found that substance abusers do not even apply for employment.

ANSWER: True, 528

76.   To avoid costly law suits claiming that an implied contract was broken, employers should abandon all employee handbooks as a way of communicating HR policies to employees.

ANSWER: False, 530
Employee handbooks are a recommended reference source for company policies and rules. Not having a handbook can lead to costly litigation. The language in the handbook should be reviewed by legal counsel.

77.   It is recommended that employers use disclaimers in all employee handbooks.

ANSWER: True, 531

78.   Discipline is a form of training that enforces organizational rules.

ANSWER: True, 533

79.   Effective discipline should be aimed at the behavior, not at the employee personally.

ANSWER: True, 536

80.   In most cases, discipline has a negative effect on performance.

ANSWER: False, 536
The reason for discipline is to improve performance. Lack of discipline can cause problems for the work group.

Essay

81.   What is an employment contract? Discuss the provisions typically included in
       a formal employment contract.

       ANSWER: 511-512
       A formal employment contract outlines the details of an employment agreement.
       Typical provisions include terms and conditions of employment, general job
       duties and expectations, compensation and benefits, confidentiality and secrecy,
       non-piracy and non-compete agreements, non-solicitation of current employees
       upon departure, and termination/resignation.

82.   Explain the doctrine of employment-at-will. What is the relationship between
       this doctrine and the employment agreement?

       ANSWER: 514-516
       EAW is a common law doctrine stating that employers have the right to hire,
       fire, demote, or promote whomever they choose, unless there is a law or contract
       to the contrary. EAW defends employees' right to change jobs, as well as the
       employers' right to hire and fire. Wrongful discharge occurs when an employer
       terminates an individual for reasons that are illegal or improper

83.   Explain the growth in alternative means for resolving disputes. Describe three
       methods of alternative dispute resolution.

       ANSWER: 518-520
       A major reason for the growth of alternative dispute resolution is
       dissatisfaction with the expense and delays common in the court system. Methods
       include arbitration, peer review panels, and ombudsmen.

84.   Under what circumstances can an employer require drug testing? What tests are
       available? What are the legal consequences of drug testing?

       ANSWER: 526-529
       It is estimated that 70% of all uses of illegal drugs are employed. Private-
       sector employers can administer random drug tests at periodic intervals, test
       when there is probable cause, and/or test following an accident. In addition,
       job candidates can be tested as a condition of employment. The three types of
       drug tests are: urinalysis, radioimmunoassay of hair, and fitness-for-duty.
       These tests are generally accurate. The Drug-Free Workplace Act of 1988
       requires government contractors to take steps to eliminate employee drug use.
       Drug testing does not violate the Constitution. The Fifth Amendment does not
       apply to non-government testing.

85.   What is the purpose of employee discipline? Outline a typical disciplinary
       procedure. When discharge is appropriate, what actions can be taken to avoid
       a legal judgment?

       ANSWER: 533-537
       The purpose of discipline, a form of training that enforces organizational
       rules, is to improve individual, group, and organizational performance. A
       typical procedure progresses from verbal caution, written reprimand, suspension,
       to dismissal. Reasons for discharge should be documented and clearly stated.
       A witness should attend the termination meeting.

Chapter 17

Union-Management Relationship

Multiple Choice

1. A union is a formal association of workers that promotes the interests of its members through
   A. threats and strikes.
   B. collective action.
   C. negotiation.
   D. collective bargaining.

   ANSWER: B, 544

2. What is the primary reason why employees join unions?
   A. They want higher wages and believe that the union can pressure their employers to raise wages.
   B. They feel their benefits package is inadequate and want to bargain for an improved package.
   C. They fear losing their jobs to employees in foreign companies.
   D. They are dissatisfied with how they are treated by their employers and believe that unions can improve their work situations.

   ANSWER: D, 544

3. What is the primary determinant of whether employees unionize?
   A. management
   B. government
   C. co-workers
   D. union organizers

   ANSWER: A, 544

4. Unions in the United States typically have focused on
   A. achieving worker solidarity.
   B. increasing industrial democracy.
   C. economic issues.
   D. maintaining due process for all workers.

   ANSWER: C, 545

5. Which of the following is the HR unit's responsibility with unions in the typical division of responsibilities between the HR unit and operating managers.
   A.   Avoid unfair labor practices during organizing efforts.
   B.   Monitor the climate for unionization and union relationships.
   C.   Administer the labor agreement on a daily basis.
   D.   Resolve grievances and problems between management and employees.

   ANSWER: B, 546

6. The labor relations responsibilities of managers would include:
   A.   Dealing with union organizing attempts at the company level
   B.   Helping negotiate the labor agreements
   C.   Monitoring the climate for unionization and union relationships
   D.   Administering the labor agreement on a daily basis

   ANSWER: D, 546

7. A(n) _____ is one whose members do one type of work, often using specialized skills and training.
   A.   craft union
   B.   apprenticeship guild
   C.   industrial union
   D.   membership guild

   ANSWER: A, 546

8. Which type of union has many persons working in the same industry or company, regardless of job held.
   A.   company union
   B.   craft union
   C.   industrial union
   D.   federated union

   ANSWER: C, 546

9. The United Auto Workers is an example of
   A.   a craft union.
   B.   an industrial union.
   C.   a company union.
   D.   federated union.

   ANSWER: B, 546

10. A _____ is a group of autonomous national and international unions.
    A.   conciliation
    B.   union congress
    C.   union organization
    D.   federation

    ANSWER: D, 546

11. Who operates the union office, full time, and assist union members?
     A.   the business agent
     B.   the national union
     C.   the union steward
     D.   the chief negotiator

     ANSWER: A, 547

12. An employee of an organization who is elected to serve as the first-line
     representative of unionized workers is the
     A.   union organizer.
     B.   member rep.
     C.   union steward.
     D.   business agent.

     ANSWER: C, 547

13. Economists speculate that deregulation, foreign competition, and a larger number
     of people looking for jobs have
     A.   been caused by union militancy.
     B.   contributed to the decline of unions.
     C.   prompted increased government regulations of the union/management
           relationship.
     D.   been the catalyst for increases in union membership.

     ANSWER: B, 548

14. Unions have attempted to counteract the overall decline in membership by
     A.   reducing membership dues and initiation fees.
     B.   organizing manufacturing workers in third-world countries.
     C.   boycotting states with "employer-friendly" laws.
     D.   attempting to unionize contingent and part-time workers.

     ANSWER: D, 551

15. What the decision of a Philadelphia court when the shoemaker's union struck for
     higher wages in 1806?
     A.   Union members were guilty of engaging in a criminal conspiracy to raise
           wages.
     B.   No crimes had been committed.
     C.   Union leaders guilty of civil disobedience.
     D.   The employers were guilty of treason for importing cheap shoes at the
           expense of American jobs.

     ANSWER: A, 551

16. In 1886, the American Federation of Labor was formed to organize
     A.   workers from any industry.
     B.   workers from manufacturing industries.
     C.   skilled craft workers.
     D.   semiskilled and unskilled workers.

     ANSWER: C, 551

17.   The Congress of Industrial Unions was founded in 1938 to focus on
      A.   organizing workers in the public sector. ·
      B.   semiskilled and unskilled workers.
      C.   skilled craft workers.
      D.   establishing one large union embracing all workers.

      ANSWER: B, 551

18.   What was the purpose of the Railway Labor Act which was passed in 1926?
      A.   To prevent management from using the courts to interfere with union
             activities.
      B.   To limit workers in "essential industries" such as transportation from
             going on strike.
      C.   To establish the National Labor Relations Board to mediate labor
             disputes.
      D.   To give railroad employees the right to organize and bargain collectively
             through representatives of their own choosing.

      ANSWER: D, 552

19.   Passed in 1932, the _____ granted workers some rights to organize and
      freed union activity from court interference.
      A.   Norris-LaGuardia Act
      B.   Labor- Management Relations Act
      C.   Clayton Act
      D.   Wagner Act

      ANSWER: A, 552

20.   The Wagner Act, the Taft-Hartley Act, and the Landrum-Griffin Act are
      collectively known as
      A.   the *Magna Carta* of labor.
      B.   the Labor/Management Acts.
      C.   the National Labor Code.
      D.   the right-to-work code.

      ANSWER: C, 553

21.   Which act has been called the *Magna Carta* of labor in that it is pro-union?
      A.   Landrum-Griffin
      B.   Wagner
      C.   Railway Labor
      D.   Taft-Hartley

      ANSWER: B, 553

22.   Which act prohibited employers from undertaking certain unfair labor practices?
      A.   The Railway Labor Act
      B.   The Landrum-Griffin Act
      C.   The Taft-Hartley Act
      D.   The Wagner Act

      ANSWER: D, 553

23. Which agency, set up as an impartial umpire of the organizing process, enforces all of the provisions of the labor relations acts?
     A.   National Labor Relations Board
     B.   U.S. Department of Labor
     C.   Federal Labor-Management Conciliation Authority
     D.   Federal Workers Protection Board

     ANSWER: A, 554

24. Which act, passed in 1947, answered the concerns of many that unions had become too strong, and attempted to balance the collective bargaining equation?
     A.   The Norris-LaGuardia Act
     B.   The Landrum-Griffin Act
     C.   The Taft-Hartley Act
     D.   The Wagner Act

     ANSWER: C, 554

25. What is the purpose of right-to-work laws?
     A.   to encourage full employment
     B.   to prohibit both the closed chop and the union shop
     C.   to require that employers bargain in good faith with union representatives
     D.   to prohibit unions from organizing in a particular state

     ANSWER: B, 554

26. A firm that requires individuals to join a union before they can be hired is called
     A.   a limited-employment shop.
     B.   a union shop.
     C.   an agency shop.
     D.   a closed shop.

     ANSWER: D, 554

27. A union shop
     A.   requires that an employee join a union, usually 30 to 60 days after being hired.
     B.   requires employees who refuse to join a union to pay equivalent amounts equal to union dues and fees for the union's representative services.
     C.   requires individuals to join a union before they can be hired.
     D.   prohibits the employer from contracting out work to non-union firms.

     ANSWER: A, 555

28. A _____ requires employees who refuse to join a union to pay amounts equal to union dues in return for the union's representation services.
     A.   a limited-employment shop.
     B.   a union shop.
     C.   an agency shop.
     D.   a closed shop.

     ANSWER: C, 555

29. The Landrum-Griffin Act was aimed at
     A.   giving workers the right to engage in union activities.
     B.   protecting the rights of individual union members from union corruption.
     C.   defining unfair labor practices of both employers and union officials.
     D.   defining the behaviors expected during collective bargaining.

     ANSWER: B, 555

30. As a result of the Civil Service Reform Act of 1978,
     A.   federal contractors cannot hire replacement workers during a strike.
     B.   union pension funds are financially sound.
     C.   federal contractors are required to negotiate in good faith.
     D.   wages and benefits for federal government employees are not subject to
           bargaining

     ANSWER: D, 556

31. The process of unionization may begin in one of two ways, including
     A.   a request from individual workers expressing a desire to unionize.
     B.   a refusal by management to communicate with the union.
     C.   a change in state law regarding open shops.
     D.   an inquiry from the National Labor Relations Board.

     ANSWER: A, 556

32. _____ is the practice in which unions use paid organizers to apply for
     jobs at a targeted employer for the purpose of trying to organize other workers.
     A.   Espying
     B.   Penetrating
     C.   Salting
     D.   Intruding

     ANSWER: C, 557

33. If _____ of the employees in the targeted group sign authorization
     cards, the union can request that an election be held.
     A.   a majority
     B.   at least 30 percent
     C.   more than 20 percent
     D.   two-thirds

     ANSWER: B, 558

34. A _____ is composed of all employees eligible to select a single union
     to represent and bargain collectively for them.
     A.   contract unit
     B.   targeted unit
     C.   negotiating unit
     D.   bargaining unit

     ANSWER: D, 558

35. To win the election, the union must receive
     A.   the votes of the majority of those voting.
     B.   a majority of the votes of those who signed authorization cards.
     C.   two thirds of the votes cast.
     D.   the votes of the majority of the employees in the bargaining unit.

     ANSWER: A, 559

36. A number of legal tactics may be used by management representatives to try to
     defeat a unionization effort. These include:
     A.   threatening to close down or move the company if a union is voted in.
     B.   asking employees how they plan to vote or if they have signed
          authorization cards.
     C.   showing employees articles about unions and relating negative experiences
          others have had elsewhere.
     D.   urging employees to persuade others to vote against the union.

     ANSWER: C, 560

37. Which of the following activities by management would be considered an unfair
     labor practice during the unionization process?
     A.   Forbid distribution of union literature during work hours in work areas.
     B.   Promise employees pay increases if they vote against the union.
     C.   Tell employees the disadvantages of having a union.
     D.   Enforce disciplinary policies and rules in a consistent and fair manner.

     ANSWER: B, 560

38. Once certified, the union will
     A.   assess union dues.
     B.   collect the costs associated with the unionization process from the
          employer.
     C.   demand improved wages and benefits for the members of the bargaining unit.
     D.   attempt to negotiate a contract with the employer.

     ANSWER: D, 560

39. _____ is the process whereby a union is removed as the representative
     of a group of employees.
     A.   Decertification
     B.   Derepresentation
     C.   Deunionization
     D.   Union busting

     ANSWER: A, 560

40. The process whereby representatives of management and workers negotiate over
     wages, hours, and other terms and conditions of employment is called
     A.   arbitration.
     B.   power bargaining.
     C.   collective bargaining.
     D.   labor/management negotiations.

     ANSWER: C, 561

41. In order to reserve to the employer the right to manage, direct, and control its
     business, virtually all labor contracts include a _____ provision.
     A.   no challenge
     B.   management rights
     C.   shareholders' prerogative
     D.   flexibility

     ANSWER: B, 561

42. _____ refers to provisions to aid the union in obtaining and retaining
     members.
     A.   Union affiliation clauses
     B.   Union rights
     C.   Union-management collusion
     D.   Union security provisions

     ANSWER: D, 562

43. Which of the following has been identified as a mandatory subject for
     bargaining?
     A.   wages
     B.   dues checkoff
     C.   no-strike or lockout clause
     D.   benefits for retired employees

     ANSWER: A, 562

44. If both parties agree, bargaining over _____ issues is allowed.
     A.   optional
     B.   joint
     C.   permissive
     D.   acceptable

     ANSWER: C, 562

45. Which of the following bargaining issues would require either party to take
     illegal action?
     A.   requiring employees to take annual physical exams
     B.   giving preference to union members when hiring employees
     C.   management and unions negotiating before setting product prices
     D.   requiring management to deduct union dues from employee payroll checks

     ANSWER: B, 562

46. If the organization argues that it cannot afford to pay what the union is
     asking, the employer must
     A.   declare bankruptcy.
     B.   provide full financial disclosure information.
     C.   still negotiate in "good faith" until an agreement is reached.
     D.   provide necessary financial data if requested.

     ANSWER: D, 563

47. In _____, the parties agree to send negotiators who can bargain and make decisions, rather than people who do not have the authority to commit either group to a decision.
    A.   good-faith negotiations
    B.   labor/management negotiations
    C.   honest bargaining
    D.   collective bargaining

    ANSWER: A, 563

48. The process by which union members vote to accept the terms of a negotiated labor agreement is called
    A.   authorization.
    B.   certification.
    C.   ratification.
    D.   localization.

    ANSWER: C, 563

49. The process by which a third party attempts to keep the union and management negotiators talking so that they can reach a voluntary settlement, is known as
    A.   arbitration.
    B.   conciliation.
    C.   mediation.
    D.   resolution.

    ANSWER: B, 563

50. _____ is the process by which a third party assists negotiators in their discussions and also suggests settlement proposals.
    A.   arbitration.
    B.   conciliation.
    C.   resolution.
    D.   mediation

    ANSWER: D, 564

51. The process of _____ uses a neutral third party to make a decision.
    A.   arbitration.
    B.   conciliation.
    C.   mediation
    D.   resolution.

    ANSWER: A, 564

52. Union members refuse to work in order to put pressure on an employer during a
    A.   close-down.
    B.   lockout.
    C.   strike.
    D.   boycott.

    ANSWER: C, 564-565

53.   In a _____, management shuts down company operations to prevent union members from working.
    A.   strike
    B.   lockout
    C.   close-down
    D.   boycott

    ANSWER: B, 565

54.   What type of strikes occur when the parties fail to reach agreement during collective bargaining?
    A.   wildcat
    B.   jurisdictional
    C.   sympathy
    D.   economic

    ANSWER: D, 565

55.   _____ strikes occur during the life of the collective bargaining agreement without approval of union leadership and violate a no-strike clause in a labor contract.
    A.   Wildcat
    B.   Economic
    C.   Unfair labor practice
    D.   Jurisdictional

    ANSWER: A, 565

56.   Strikers can be discharged or disciplined for participating in a(n)
    A.   unfair labor practices strike.
    B.   economic strike.
    C.   wildcat strike.
    D.   jurisdictional strike.

    ANSWER: C, 565

57.   In a(n) _____, an employer is free to replace the striking workers; but in a(n) _____, workers who want their jobs back at the end of the strike must be reinstated.
    A.   unfair labor practices strike; jurisdictional strike
    B.   economic strike; unfair labor practices strike
    C.   jurisdictional strike; wildcat strike
    D.   economic strike; sympathy strike

    ANSWER: B, 565

58.   What is the difference between a complaint and a grievance?
    A.   They are different names for the same thing.
    B.   Grievances are more informal, and do not follow a set procedure.
    C.   Complaint relate to money issues; grievances to supervisory behavior.
    D.   A grievance is a complaint formally stated in writing.

    ANSWER: D, 567

59. _____ are formal communications channels designed to settle a grievance as soon as possible after the problem arises.
A.   Grievance procedures
B.   Contract procedures
C.   Legal processes
D.   Arbitration processes

ANSWER: A, 568

60. _____ is a means by which a third party settles disputes arising from different interpretations of a labor contract.
A.   Mediation
B.   Court-ordered negotiation
C.   Grievance arbitration
D.   The Department of Labor negotiating team

ANSWER: C, 569

True and False

61. Class consciousness and conflict between the working class and the management class is a primary cause of unionization attempts in the United States.

ANSWER: False, 545
U.S. unions have primarily focused on economic issues such as wages, benefits, job security, and working conditions.

62. The American Federation of Labor (AFL) was formed as a federation of independent unions that represented semiskilled and unskilled workers.

ANSWER: False, 551
The aim of the AFL was to organize skilled craft workers.

63. The Wagner Act declared, in effect, that the official policy of the U.S. government was to encourage collective bargaining.

ANSWER: True, 553

64. The National Labor Relations Board (NLRB) is an independent board, not influenced by politics in any way.

ANSWER: False, 554
Members of the NLRB are appointed by the President and confirmed by the Senate.

65. The Wagner Act allows the president of the United States to declare that a strike presents a national emergency.

ANSWER: False, 554
This is a provision of the Taft-Hartley Act.

66. The Taft-Hartley Act allowed states to pass laws that granted a person the right to work without having to join a union.

    ANSWER: True, 554

67. The Landrum-Griffin Act was passed to protect the rights of individual union members from corruption in the union, and to ensure the democratic rights of union members.

    ANSWER: True, 555-556

68. The process of unionization may begin with a union targeting an industry or a company.

    ANSWER: True, 556

69. Once the unionizing efforts begin, management activities must conform to the requirements established by the NLRB. Union leaders, however, are not similarly restricted.

    ANSWER: False, 556
    All activities of management **and** unions must conform to NLRB requirements.

70. The practice of "salting" involves unions hiring and paying people to apply for jobs at certain companies. When the people are hired, they begin union organizing efforts.

    ANSWER: True, 557

71. The Supreme Court has ruled that "salting" is an unfair labor practice of the unions.

    ANSWER: False, 557
    The Supreme Count has ruled that refusing to hire otherwise qualified applicants, even if they are also paid by the union, violates the Wagner Act.

72. During the unionization process, managers cannot urge employees to persuade others to vote against the union.

    ANSWER: True, 560

73. Unfair labor practices of management include forbidding the distribution of union literature during work hours in work areas.

    ANSWER: False, 560
    Managers may forbid distribution of union literature during work hours in work areas.

74. A majority of employees in the bargaining unit must vote for the union.

    ANSWER: False, 559
    A majority of those voting is required.

75. One union security provision involves requiring union membership of all employees, subject to right-to-work laws.

ANSWER: True, 562

76. The Wagner Act clearly expects management and the union to bargain over wages, hours, and other terms and conditions of employment.

ANSWER: True, 562

77. Such issues as giving preference to individuals who have been union members when hiring employees, are permissible issues that may be bargained over if both parties agree.

ANSWER: False, 562
This is an illegal issue.

78. The process of conciliation is a means of deciding a dispute in which negotiating parties submit the dispute to a third party to make a decision.

ANSWER: False, 563
Conciliation is the process by which a third party attempts to keep union and management negotiators talking so that they may reach a voluntary settlement.

79. During an unfair labor practices strike, workers who want their jobs back at the end of the strike must be reinstated.

ANSWER: True, 565

80. Grievance arbitration is a formal channel of communications used to resolve grievances.

ANSWER: False, 568
A grievance procedure is a formal channel of communication.

Essay

81. What is the current "state of labor unions" in the United States?

ANSWER: 547-551
Unions membership has fallen from over 30% of the workforce in 1960 to less than 14% today. Unlike most other countries, U.S. unions are primarily concerned with "bread and butter" issues of wages, benefits, job security, and working conditions. To some extent unions may be a victim of their own successes. Other causes of union decline include: deregulation, foreign competition, a larger number of people looking for jobs, and a general perception by firms that dealing with unions is expensive compared the nonunion alternative. The only increase in union membership appears to be among federal government employees.

82.   What is the "National Labor Code?" What has been its impact on labor/management relations?

ANSWER: 553-556
Three acts comprise the National Labor Code: The Wagner Act (1935), the Taft-Hartley Act (1947), and the Landrum-Griffin Act (1959). Together they give workers the right to organize, define unfair labor practices of management and unions, and protect the rights of union members from corrupt union officials. They also give workers the right not to participate in union activities.

83.   An employee at your factory has shown you a union leaflet she was given in the parking lot this morning. Discuss the possible significance of the leaflet and what you might expect to happen as a result of this leaflet.

ANSWER: 556-561
This leaflet is probably a request to sign an authorization cards If 30% of the factory employees sign a card, a representation election must be held. A simple majority of workers voting in the election will determine if the union is certified as the legal representative of the employees. The employer is then required to collectively bargain with the union.

84.   What is the role of collective bargaining in union/management relations? Describe a typical collective bargaining process.

ANSWER: 561-565
Collective bargaining is the process whereby representatives of management and workers negotiate over wages, hours, and other terms and conditions of employment. Management is required to collectively bargain once a union has been certified. The process begins with demands from the union and proposals from management. Negotiation continues in good faith. If an agreement is reached it is ratified by the employees. Alternatively, if a bargaining impasse occurs, disputes can be taken to conciliation, mediation, or arbitration. If a deadlock cannot be resolved, a strike or lockout may result.

85.   Why is grievance management essential in both union and nonunion organizations? Describe the steps in a typical grievance procedure.

ANSWER: 567-569
A grievance is a complaint that has been formally stated in writing. It is crucial for nonunion employers to have an effective grievance procedure. Failure to have one may result in employee dissatisfaction and union representation. For union organizations, the grievance procedure is spelled out in the contract. A typical procedure begins with the employee discussing the grievance with the union steward and the supervisor ... the steward discusses it with the supervisors manager ... union grievance committee with the plant manager or HR department ... national union with company's general manager ... impartial umpire or arbitrator.

Chapter 18

Globalization of HR Management

Multiple Choice

1. Firms such as Coca-Cola, Exxon, and Microsoft derive _____ of their total sales and profits outside the U.S.
    A.   almost 90 percent
    B.   half or more
    C.   about 40 percent of total sales and profits.
    D.   less than 20 percent of total sales and profits.

    ANSWER: B, 576

2. In addition to expanding trade opportunities among Canada, the United States, and Mexico, NAFTA also
    A.   required U.S. companies to pay U.S. wage rates in their Mexican plants.
    B.   banned the import of goods made in Mexican sweat shops.
    C.   limited trade with nations that did not sign the agreement.
    D.   placed restrictions on employers to ensure that HR practices in Mexico meet certain standards.

    ANSWER: D, 577

3. What is the purpose of the Commission of Labor Cooperation (CLC), which was established as part of NAFTA?
    A.   to review complaints regarding occupational safety and health, child labor, benefits, and labor-management relations
    B.   to facilitate free trade among the United States, Canada, and Mexico
    C.   to monitor labor union organizing efforts in cooperating nations
    D.   to maintain a comparable minimum wage for workers in the United States, Canada, and Mexico

    ANSWER: A, 577

4. What has been the impact of the labor standards adopted by individual European Union countries?
    A.   increased wage rates and benefits for employees of EU-based firms
    B.   the adoption of living-wage standards
    C.   greater similarity of HR practices in EU-based firms
    D.   restriction on goods manufactured by U.S. firms

    ANSWER: C, 577

5. The first phase of international interaction consists of
    A.   multinational enterprise.
    B.   importing and exporting.
    C.   multinational exploration.
    D.   global organization.

    ANSWER: B, 577

6. A(n) _____ operates in various countries with each foreign business
    unit operating separately.
    A.   foreign subsidiary
    B.   international enterprise
    C.   global organization
    D.   multinational enterprise

    ANSWER: D, 577

7. In a multinational enterprise, key management positions in the foreign
    operations are filled with
    A.   employees from the home country.
    B.   host-country nationals.
    C.   third-country nationals.
    D.   resident aliens.

    ANSWER: A, 578

8. A(n) _____ has corporate units in a number of countries that are
    integrated to operate as one organization worldwide.
    A.   international enterprise
    B.   multinational enterprise
    C.   global organization
    D.   importing and exporting organization

    ANSWER: C, 579

9. HR management in _____ moves people, especially key managers and
    professionals, throughout the world.
    A.   importing and exporting organizations
    B.   global organizations
    C.   multinational enterprises
    D.   international enterprises

    ANSWER: B, 579

10. U.S. firms are accustomed to a relatively _____ political system.
    A.   homogeneous
    B.   heterogeneous
    C.   turbulent
    D.   stable

    ANSWER: D, 579

11. The Foreign Corrupt Practices Act (FCPA)
    A.   prohibits U.S. firms from engaging in bribery in foreign countries.
    B.   controls the practices of foreign firms operating in the U.S.
    C.   is a U.N. sponsored pact regulating multinational organizations.
    D.   permits U.S. firms to offer bribes if that is an acceptable way of doing business.

    ANSWER: A, 580

12. In contrast with the United States, laws on labor unions and employment in Western European countries,
    A.   are consistently pro-business.
    B.   require relatively few employment-related benefits.
    C.   make it difficult to reduce the number of workers.
    D.   encourage firms to manufacture goods in EU countries.

    ANSWER: C, 581

13. What has been a consequence of the high costs imposed on employers in Western European countries?
    A.   Unemployment rates are low when compared with the U.S.
    B.   Many European firms are transferring jobs to lower-wage countries.
    C.   There has been a resurgence in economic nationalism.
    D.   Western European firms rarely lay off employees.

    ANSWER: B, 581

14. _____ is (are) composed of the societal forces affecting the values, beliefs, and actions of a distinct group of people.
    A.   Society
    B.   Norms
    C.   Globalization
    D.   Culture

    ANSWER: D, 581

15. In developing his classification of cultures, Geert Hofstede conducted research
    A.   on more than 100,000 IBM employees in 53 countries.
    B.   comparing the attitudes and style of the leaders of 67 nations.
    C.   into the religious and legal norms of each of the UN member nations.
    D.   assuming that all men are created equal and develop differences through socialization.

    ANSWER: A, 581

16. The dimension of _____ refers to the inequality among the people of a nation.
    A.   status difference
    B.   gentry
    C.   power distance
    D.   elitism

    ANSWER: C, 582

17. In which of the following countries is there the largest power distance?
     A.   the Netherlands
     B.   Mexico
     C.   the United States
     D.   Israel

     ANSWER: B, 582

18. More collective action and less individual competition is likely in those
     countries that de-emphasize
     A.   collectivism.
     B.   free enterprise.
     C.   socialism.
     D.   individualism.

     ANSWER: D, 583

19. _____ values identified by Hofstede were assertiveness, performance-
     orientation, success, and competitiveness.
     A.   Masculine
     B.   Feminine
     C.   Individualism
     D.   Integrative

     ANSWER: A, 583

20. Which of the following are feminine values identified by Hofstede?
     A.   assertiveness, success
     B.   justice, equity
     C.   quality of life, close personal relationships
     D.   traditional family relationships, conflict avoidance

     ANSWER: C, 583

21. Which of the following countries had the highest femininity-oriented values?
     A.   the United States
     B.   the Netherlands
     C.   Japan
     D.   Mexico

     ANSWER: B, 583

22. Hofstede's dimension of _____ refers to the preference of people in
     a country for structured rather than unstructured situations.
     A.   structure orientation
     B.   formalization
     C.   bureaucracy
     D.   uncertainty avoidance

     ANSWER: D, 583

23. Nations high on the uncertainty-avoidance dimension tend to be
     A.   more resistant to change and more rigid.
     B.   more intriguing and challenging.
     C.   more acceptable for women.
     D.   more flexible and to have more "business energy."

     ANSWER: A, 583

24. We can expect to find greater entrepreneurship and risk taking in cultures that
     are more
     A.   masculine.
     B.   feminine.
     C.   flexible.
     D.   rigid.

     ANSWER: C, 583

25. Long-term values, according to Hofstede, include
     A.   a respect for traditions.
     B.   thrift and persistence.
     C.   resistance to change.
     D.   strategic optimism.

     ANSWER: B, 583

26. _____ values include respecting tradition and fulfilling social
     obligations.
     A.   Rigid
     B.   Flexible
     C.   Long-term
     D.   Short-term

     ANSWER: D, 583

27. In which of the following countries did the people score highest on long-term
     orientation?
     A.   Japan
     B.   the United States
     C.   Canada
     D.   France

     ANSWER: A, 583

28. Employees working in an operation, who are not citizens of the country in which
     the operation is located, but are citizens of the country of the headquartered
     organization are
     A.   resident aliens.
     B.   host-country nationals.
     C.   expatriates.
     D.   third-country nationals.

     ANSWER: C, 585

29.   Why do many multinational enterprises use expatriates?
      A.   to ensure that the values and culture of the home country are maintained
            in the foreign operation
      B.   to ensure that foreign operations are linked effectively with the parent
            organization
      C.   it is less expensive in terms of salary and benefits
      D.   to establish clearly that it is making a commitment to the host country

      ANSWER: B, 585

30.   A(n) _____ is an employee working for a firm in an operation who is
      a citizen of the country where the operation is located, but where the
      headquarters for the firm are in another country.
      A.   expatriate
      B.   third-country national
      C.   resident alien
      D.   host-country national

      ANSWER: D, 585

31.   Using host-country nationals is important if the organization wants to
      A.   establish clearly that it is making a commitment to the host country.
      B.   emphasize that a global approach is being taken.
      C.   ensure that foreign operations are linked effectively with the parent
            organization.
      D.   indicate that it is setting up a foreign operation.

      ANSWER: A, 585-586

32.   Organizations often hire _____ because they know the culture,
      politics, laws, and business customs better than an outsider would.
      A.   second-country nationals
      B.   expatriates
      C.   host-country nationals
      D.   third-country nationals

      ANSWER: C, 586

33.   An employee who is a citizen of one country, working in a second country, and
      employed by an organization headquartered in a third country is called a(n)
      A.   expatriate.
      B.   third-country national.
      C.   second-country national.
      D.   host-country national.

      ANSWER: B, 586

34.   Organizations will use third-country nationals as a way to
      A.   it is less expensive in terms of salary and benefits.
      B.   indicate that it is setting up a foreign operation.
      C.   establish clearly that it is making a commitment to the host country.
      D.   emphasize that a global approach is being taken.

      ANSWER: D, 586

35. For _____ assignments, individuals are sent to broaden their understanding of global operations.
    A. developmental assignments
    B. functional assignments
    C. strategic assignments
    D. technical assignments

    ANSWER: A, 586

36. Which of the following types of global assignments is intercultural understanding and skills critical to success?
    A. developmental assignments
    B. functional assignments
    C. · strategic assignments
    D. technical assignments

    ANSWER: C, 586-587

37. The selection process for international assignments should
    A. test language skills.
    B. provide a realistic picture of the life, work, and culture to which the employee may be sent.
    C. examine the employee's willingness to be separated from family and friends.
    D. be guided by the fact that a good employee in the domestic operation will usually make a good expatriate.

    ANSWER: B, 587

38. The most common reason(s) for turning down international assignments is(are)
    A. pre-assignment visits by the employee to the host country.
    B. a fear for the personal safety of family members.
    C. a lack of understanding of the business culture and legal environment of the host country.
    D. family considerations and spouses' careers.

    ANSWER: D, 590

39. The Civil Rights Act of 1991 states that, with respect to U.S. citizens working internationally for U.S.-controlled companies,
    A   all EEO laws and regulations apply, except when they conflict with the laws of the foreign country.
    B. all EEO laws and regulations apply, except when they conflict with the customs, culture, or laws of the foreign country.
    C. all EEO laws and regulations apply in all circumstances.
    D. the EEO regulations of Title VII do not apply internationally.

    ANSWER: A, 591

40. Why have many U.S. firms been reluctant to consider women for international assignments?
    A   Most husbands were unwilling to accompany their wives on international assignments.
    B.   It is generally more expensive to relocate female employees.
    C.   Concerns about the acceptance of women in certain foreign cultures.
    D.   Women generally do not function effectively in foreign countries.

    ANSWER: C, 591

41. Which of the following is true about foreign-owned firms operating in the U.S.?
    A.   All EEO laws and regulations apply, no exceptions.
    B.   Most EEO laws and regulations apply.
    C.   Only the EEO laws relating to national origin apply.
    D.   Foreign-owned firms are exempted from all EEO laws and regulations.

    ANSWER: B, 591

42. During the _____ phase, the organization prepares and sends global employees to their foreign assignments.
    A.   repatriation.
    B.   naturalization.
    C.   orientation
    D.   expatriation

    ANSWER: D, 592

43. The process of bringing expatriates home is called
    A.   repatriation.
    B.   naturalization.
    C.   reentry.
    D.   expatriation

    ANSWER: A, 592

44. Which of the following was not given as a type of training activity for international assignments?
    A.   pre-departure orientation for employees and their families
    B.   continuing employee support and development
    C.   on-the-job training upon arrival in the host country
    D.   repatriation planning and training

    ANSWER: C, 592

45. A foreign organization, operating in the U.S., which plans to appoint an expatriate manager to a U.S. position must first
    A.   obtain clearance from the Equal Employment Opportunity Commission.
    B.   train the U.S. workers to ensure acceptance of the foreign boss.
    C.   prove to the Immigration and Naturalization Service that no American is qualified for the position.
    D.   demonstrate that the expatriate is fluent in English.

    ANSWER: B, 593

46. The _____ approach provides international employees with a compensation package that equalizes cost differences between the international assignment and the same assignment in the home country of the individual or the corporation.
    A. equalization
    B. global market
    C. home-country reference
    D. balance-sheet

    ANSWER: D, 596

47. One basic premise of the balance-sheet approach is that
    A. expatriate employees generally will have international assignments lasting two to three years.
    B. international employees should be compensated for the hardships encountered overseas.
    C. international assignments are usually long term.
    D. expatriate employees will receive a significant salary increase on their return to the U.S.

    ANSWER: A, 596-597

48. The major focus of the balance-sheet approach to compensating international expatriate employees is to
    A. provide a compensation package that avoids U.S. tax liability.
    B. compensate international employees for the hardships encountered overseas.
    C. keep the expatriates "whole" for a few years until they can be reintegrated into the home country compensation program.
    D. recognize that most overseas assignments provide the employee with invaluable psychological rewards.

    ANSWER: C, 597

49. Which of the following assumptions applies to the balance-sheet approach to compensating expatriate employees?
    A. The international assignment will be long term.
    B. The international employee will retire in the home country.
    C. Benefits should be consistent across the organization.
    D. Many employee benefits will be provided by the host-country government.

    ANSWER: B, 597

50. The _____ to compensation views international assignment as continual, not just temporary.
    A. equalization plan approach
    B. home country reference approach
    C. balance-sheet approach
    D. global market approach

    ANSWER: D, 597

51.   Under a tax equalization plan,
A.   expatriates are protected from negative tax consequences.
B.   the IRS gives special consideration to U.S. citizens working overseas.
C.   expatriates are still expected to pay their fair share of income taxes.
D.   expatriates are protected from negative tax consequences.

ANSWER: A, 598

52.   The _____ helps ensure that expatriates will not pay any more or less taxes than if they had stayed in the United States.
A.   Internal Revenue Service
B.   International Tax Treaty
C.   tax equalization plan
D.   tax mitigation scheme

ANSWER: C, 598

53.   In _____ labor unions either do not exist or are relatively weak.
A.   Australia
B.   China
C.   Italy
D.   Germany

ANSWER: B, 598

54.   Which of the following countries has the largest union membership as a percentage of the workforce?
A.   France
B.   Japan
C.   United Kingdom
D.   Norway

ANSWER: D, 599

55.   A practice whereby union or worker representatives are given positions on a company's board of directors is called
A.   co-determination.
B.   collective bargaining.
C.   worker councils.
D.   participative management.

ANSWER: A, 599

56.   In _____, local unions bargain with individual employers to set wages and working conditions.
A.   Scandinavia
B.   Australia
C.   the United States
D.   Germany

ANSWER: C, 599

57. In _____, unions argue their cases for wages and working conditions before arbitration tribunals.
    A.   Scandinavia
    B.   Australia
    C.   the United States
    D.   Germany

    ANSWER: B, 599

58. What is the purpose of the International Labour Organization?
    A.   to represent workers in disputes with global organizations.
    B.   to lobby for union or worker representation on boards of directors
    C.   to ensure standardized union-management relationships across national boundaries
    D.   to serve as a forum for labor unions worldwide to coordinate their efforts

    ANSWER: D, 599

59. Global firms often contract with such organizations as International SOS, Global Assistance Network, or U.S. Assist to
    A.   provide emergency medical services for expatriates.
    B.   provide bodyguard protection for expatriates.
    C.   maintain security devices for employees' families.
    D.   ensure labor union free operations in the host country.

    ANSWER: A, 600

60. U.S. expatriates are warned that kidnapping, murder, home invasion, robberies, and carjackings happen relatively frequently in
    A.   New York
    B.   Tokyo
    C.   Mexico City
    D.   Paris

    ANSWER: C, 601

True and False

61. While promoting free trade, NAFTA also requires U.S. organizations operating in Mexico to pay U.S. level wages.

    ANSWER: False [page 4/7]
    While NAFTA didn't specifically address wage rates, it did place restrictions on employers to ensure that their HR practices in Mexico met certain standards.

62. The Commission on Labor Cooperation was established as part of NAFTA to review complaints filed in the United States, Canada, or Mexico regarding occupational safety and health, child labor, benefits, and labor-management relations.

    ANSWER: True, 577

63.   Many MNEs use host-country nationals to ensure that foreign operations are linked effectively with the parent organization.

ANSWER: False, 578
Home-country employees are used to ensure that foreign operations are linked effectively with the parent corporations.

64.   HR policies and activities for global organizations need to be established and standardized throughout the organization to ensure fairness and equity.

ANSWER: False, 579
Global HR policies and activities are developed, but decentralized is necessary in order for country-specific adjustments to be made.

65.   Flexible labor laws in Western Europe make it easier to lay off workers and close plants than is possible in the United States.

ANSWER: False, 581
Laws on labor unions and employment make it difficult to reduce the number of workers because required payments to ex-employees can be very high.

66.   In some countries, because of religious or ethical differences, employment discrimination may be an accepted practice.

ANSWER: True, 581

67.   The high costs imposed on employers in Western European countries such as Germany and France have led many European-headquartered organizations to transfer jobs to lower-wage countries such as Romania and Thailand.

ANSWER: True, 581

68.   Cultural differences not only exist between nations, but within countries also.

ANSWER: True, 583-584

69.   Host-country nationals are important in indicating a commitment to the host country.

ANSWER: True, 585-586

70.   The use of third-country nationals is a way to emphasize that a global approach is being taken.

ANSWER: True, 586

71.   A successful global employee makes a special effort to maintain an American distinctiveness, and does not try to be molded by the host-country culture.

ANSWER: False, 588
Crucial to global success for individuals is how they adjust to the culture differences in their foreign assignments.

72.   Financial concerns (salaries, relocation expenses, and loss of benefits) is one
      of the most common reasons why executives turn down foreign assignments.

      ANSWER: False, 590
      The most common reasons are family considerations and spouses' careers.

73.   The Civil Rights Act of 1991 extended coverage of EEO laws and regulations to
      U.S. citizens working internationally for U.S.-controlled companies.

      ANSWER: True, 591

74.   The Civil Rights Act if 1991 extended coverage of EEO laws and regulations to
      all employees of U.S.-controlled companies working anywhere in the world.

      ANSWER: False, 591
      Coverage is limited to U.S. citizens working internationally for U.S.-controlled
      companies.

75.   The U.S.-based subsidiary of a Japanese-owned firm would be exempt from EEO laws
      and regulations if Japanese culture prescribes alternate practices.

      ANSWER: False, 591
      In most cases EEO regulations and laws do apply to foreign-owned firms.

76.   One of the greatest deterrents to accepting foreign assignments is employees'
      anxiety about continued career progression.

      ANSWER: True, 594

77.   The balance-sheet approach to international employees attempts to equalize
      salary differences between expatriates and host-country employees.

      ANSWER: False, 596
      The approach attempts to equalize cost differences between the international
      assignment and the same assignment in the home country of the individual or the
      corporation.

78.   A basic premise of the balance-sheet approach is that expatriate employees
      generally will have international assignments lasting two to three years.

      ANSWER: True, 596-597

79.   Unlike the balance-sheet approach to compensation, a global market approach
      views international assignments as continual, not just temporary.

      ANSWER: True, 597

80.   Under a tax equalization plan, the corporation attempt to ensure that all
      international employees pay taxes at the same rate.

      ANSWER: False, 598
      The intent of the tax equalization plan is to ensure that expatriates will not
      pay any more or less in taxes than if they had stayed in the United States

Essay

81.   Identify and discuss some of the legal, political, economic, and cultural issues affecting global HR management.

ANSWER: 579-584
Legal and political issues - NAFTA, EEO, Foreign Corrupt Practices Act, in addition to the laws and regulations of the host country. Economic issues - different economic systems, economic conditions including cost of living, wages, benefits, levels of unemployment. Cultural factors - differing values, beliefs, actions within and between different countries.

82.   What are the advantages and disadvantages of using host-country nationals rather than expatriate employees?

ANSWER: 584-586
Host-country nationals indicate a commitment to the host country. They know the culture, politics, laws, and business customs better than an outsider would. They can better tap into the power networks. Also less expensive in terms of compensation, benefits, and training.

83.   A manufacturing firm is considering the possibility of moving its production facilities from the U.S. to a less-developed country. What are some of the ethical questions management should discuss before making the final decision?

ANSWER: 590-592
Foreign Corrupt Practices Act - what is the distinction between legal agent fees and bribery? Conflict between EEO laws and host-country laws and customs, and the role of women in the host country.

84.   What are some of the actions HR professionals should take to prepare a manager for an international assignment?

ANSWER: 587-596
Careful selection. Pre-departure orientation and training for the employee and family members - including language, culture, history, and living conditions of the host country.

85.   Discuss the unique challenges involved in international compensation. Describe some of the approaches available for international compensation.

ANSWER: 596-598
Consider living costs, tax policies, fluctuations in the value of the U.S. dollar, costs of housing, schooling of children, and yearly transportation home. Options include the balance-sheet approach and the global market approach. The tax equalization plan attempts to minimize negative tax consequences.